Knowledge for the new age...

Management Skills & Leadership Development Course

"How to be a Great Manager & Strong Leader in 10 Lessons"

A practical and theoretical training course in Management, Leadership, and Business Basics

William L Evans

MasterClassManagement.com Books

Copyright© 2009 by William L Evans
MasterClassManagement.com - All rights reserved.

This book can be used in conjunction with the MasterClassManagement.com "Online Management Training - Business Management & Leadership Program - Management Skills & Leadership Development Course." A "Professional Certificate of Completion" will be awarded to those who complete and pass the course.

Contents

MASTER CLASS MANAGEMENT SKILLS & LEADERSHIP DEVELOPMENT TRAINING

Course Introduction

Great managers understand their role in a business and know about organizational structure and strong leadership. The fact that you are reading this shows you not only have the interest and desire to succeed in management, but to truly be a great manager and a strong leader.

There are many factors that separate average managers from great managers. In most cases, a person becomes a manager due to working their way up the company ladder, however, being a great manager is more than just being knowledgeable of your company's products or services offered. You will need the essential management and leadership skills and knowledge to become a great manager.

Business will always need effective managers and effective management practices. If management is marginal, services and products will suffer. If management is exceptional, services and products will flourish.

This 10-lesson management and leadership training course will give you the management skills needed to *direct* your employees, and the leadership skills needed to *inspire* your employees. You will also learn the basics in business, similar to those taught in an MBA course. This crash course approach to business management will give you a better understanding on how a business functions, and an overview of each of the major departments that help run a business.

By combining practical management and leadership skills, with theoretical business school studies, you will be able to handle the realistic everyday scenarios with the utmost confidence. This course will give you the insightful knowledge you need to become an all around great manager.

Points to keep in mind when reading this course material:

o This course is written as if the course instructor is speaking directly to you, no matter what the subject.

o Whenever the pronoun's antecedent could refer to either gender, we will be using the third-person plural pronoun *they* instead of he or she. The same can be said for using *them* instead of him or her. Here's an example: "If the employee wants a copy of *their* performance appraisal, *they* should go to the Human Resources department. It's up to *them* to get the information from HR."

o There will be a few instances when the same point is made a few times throughout the course as it pertains to the particular subject being taught in that lesson.

This book can be used in conjunction with the MasterClassManagement.com "Online Management Training - Business Management & Leadership Program - Management Skills & Leadership Development Course." A "Professional Certificate of Completion" will be awarded to those who complete and pass the course.

LESSON 1 – HOW TO BE A GREAT MANAGER THROUGH STRONG LEADERSHIP

Introduction: Those who succeed in Management are Great Leaders

Whereas management skills pertain to the needed planning and coordination to meet the goals, leadership skills pertain to the inspiration, motivation, and building of trust needed to believe in the goals. These skills, although different, need to work together and intertwine in harmony.

The management skill of meeting goals is related to the leadership skill of sharing a vision. You as a leader must have a vision for a better future and motivate a group of people toward that vision while following the plans, procedures, and tasks you as a manager created.

As a leader you need to be proactive and creative. As a manager you need to be directive, action-oriented and responsive. You as a leader must get your organization to believe that the work and goals are worthwhile. As a manager, you need to make sure each individual has the skills necessary to achieve those goals. Quite simply, it takes a strong leader to get the *group* to see the big picture, and a great manager to get the *individual* to be a part of the big picture. They are different roles, but combined they create an incredible overall management style.

The more confident you are with the learned management skills taught in this course, the more effective you can establish yourself as a leader. The best leaders recognize that what they know pales in comparison to what they still need to learn. They are always open to ideas and insights that can lead to better ways to accomplishing goals. By constant dialogue with their employees, co-managers, and upper-management, it makes them more proficient in pursuing and achieving the objectives.

Effective leaders are virtually idolized by the people they lead. Part of it is because of their unique personal skills, however, the leaders who are willing to take the heat, accept risks, and make decisions under fire makes people want to follow them. Their courage, intelligence, and decisiveness impress people and inspire confidence.

In this lesson, leadership skills, which are essential to great management, will be discussed through some invaluable tips, tricks and secrets to success.

Five key points to Strong Leadership (thus a Great Manager)

Being known as a strong leader is easy to obtain when you know in your heart you are doing the right thing for the "good of all." Here are five key points, which are the pillars to being a successful leader, that you should absorb into your psyche:

1. **Develop trust and credibility**. When people trust you, they will be more inclined to follow you. If they follow you, and you have all the pieces of the puzzle in place as described throughout this course, you will succeed. A leader builds trust by considering the "good of all" when making decisions. Leaders do not abuse their power, but build trust by using it properly. Trust fosters collaboration, which contributes to openly sharing information, which then creates a solid team who supports each other. Trust is based on the respect and expectations of a leader who cares and acts with compassion in a most positive way. With trust there is:

   - Honesty
   - Integrity
   - Compassion
   - Fairness
   - Good relationships

   Incorporating these five traits will help guide you on the right path to strong leadership.

2. **Share the vision with absolute clarity**. Leaders need to share the vision of what they want their department to achieve. For example, a leader might share a vision like, "We will be a world class customer service organization that provides the benchmark for customer satisfaction." To get others to see and understand your vision, you need to motivate and inspire with the same enthusiasm and positivity you have inside you.

   It is vital, however, that your team understands the vision, and is 100% clear on the objectives. You are striving for a better and secure future, while eliminating the common work related fears. People with a shared vision are more productive and have a greater sense of achievement. Inspire them to follow the processes and procedures you will put in place to achieve the vision.

   You also need to listen to what they are saying. Doing all the talking does not let them participate in the vision quest with their ideas.

   A way to see the dream come true is by charting successes, as well as failures. If the employees always know where they stand, they will know what part they played in achieving the vision.

3. **Be there to help them succeed - Coaching, mentoring, communicating, and listening**. Great interpersonal skills are vital for a successful leader. You don't lead by hiding behind your desk. Be out there and find the strengths and talents of your employees, and place them where they can shine. They need to know how their strengths serve the objectives. Show them the respect they deserve, and you have their interests at heart.

   The bottom line is that they need to know that you will be there to help them succeed. You can do this by:

   - *Coaching.* Try and help them improve their skills to do their job better. Give them feedback on their performance with

- observations and give good advice. Use specific statements rather than general comments, whether good or bad.
- *Mentoring.* Help them understand what you are all about, guide them for a better chance of promotion, and have them learn about other aspects and functions of the business.
- *Communicating.* Clearly share your visions and goals, encourage individuals and groups, praise when praise is due, and take the time for one-on-one meetings.
- *Listening.* Let them share ideas, concerns, and know you are approachable and caring.

The most important aspect here is that you are always looking at ways to help develop your employees' unique skills, both individually and as a group, for a better future including possible growth in the company. This is a win for the company as well. The company will gain more productive employees, not to mention you will look good in upper managements eyes.

4. **Make the decisions and be held accountable**. With the skills developed throughout this course, you will mostly make the right decisions and guide your department into the right direction. You need to:

   - Sift the data for facts and relevance.
   - Look closely at the issue at hand while never losing sight of the big picture
   - Talk to subject experts if needed.
   - Don't make a decision too quickly unless necessary.
   - Think about the cost-benefit for both short-term and long-term.
   - Once a decision is made, do not be wishy-washy or unsure about yourself. You will be seen as a person who can be easily persuaded with little confidence.

You as a leader are expected to take some chances and you might make some risky decisions. In saying that, as people expect to be held accountable in their job performance, they also expect you to be held accountable as their leader. If you fail or deny any wrong doing on your part, or place blame on someone else, you will lose credibility and not be seen as an effective leader.

You also need to know when it is better to follow, rather than lead, by trusting your employees' suggestions. Leaders realize they can't know all the answers, and earn respect when they seek advice of others when needed.

If you make a decision that is obviously seen as showing favoritism, or just a lack of judgment, by promoting someone who has bad work ethics, no respect, or below average performance, you will not only lose respect, but also hurt team morale.

Being held accountable is also a positive thing, as you want to be known for the good things that you do. The same goes for your employees as it makes them feel important and appreciated. You do, however, need to allow people to sometimes fail or make mistakes during the process of achieving difficult goals. You do, however, also need to confront them. By using your management and leadership skills, people will admit their mistakes and accept accountability. Your skills as leader will also help and coach them to improve. If you do not already have the nerve and confidence to confront people, you will eventually, as the contents of this course should lift your confidence and ego immensely.

Make sure your decisions are always ethically sound. Do not ask or expect your team to get the results unethically or use a "no matter what it takes" approach.

5. **Keep it all under control and headed in the right direction**. The objective of every leader should come with the mindset of striving for "mission accomplished." You, as leader and manager, need to focus on what's most important related to the vision and goals of the organization. You need to eliminate chaos and be known as a person with authority who can make the right decisions. You might have 5 projects going on at once, but focusing more on the least important when the most important is in need of help will destroy your vision and miss your goals. Make sure you get your team to focus on the most important and critical tasks to achieve the goals related to your vision. By delegating tasks to the right people, fulfillment of the vision will become more likely.

   Everyone needs to have the same focus and direction you have. A sense of community within the team, with a common goal, is key. If you waver and change your mind and direction continually, you will lose trust. Consistency is key to maintaining control and keep things going in the right direction.

These "five key points" are the core competencies to strong leadership. We will continue on this path later in this lesson with 101 tips, tricks and secrets to success in Leadership and Management.

Great Leaders are never 100% satisfied and know how to find the balance

One of the key elements in effective leadership is to never become complacent with the business model, no matter how sound and well crafted. Even if the department seems to be running well enough on autopilot, the fact is nothing is ever truly fixed, finished, or completed because every aspect of business is a work in progress. The most successful leaders continually look to improve their department's performance. They continue to learn and find self-improvement, do things better, keep spreading information throughout their organization, and improving the skills and abilities of their employees.

One of the most dangerous traps a new manager faces is once they made an immediate improvement; they think they've basically fixed the problem. They are satisfied with their immediate contribution. The short-term fix looks good in everyone's eyes, however, without continuous nurturing, the cracks will start to appear. Minor flaws in the processes and procedures start appearing, and employees start to become negatively anxious. The clear vision you shared with your team in the beginning starts to become hazy.

A common misperception at this point is to think that in order to make sure the cracks do not appear, you need to seek personal perfection. This usually leads to having more of a dictatorship approach to leadership, which will inevitably fail. You need to collaborate, not dictate. Abandon the idea that you have to know it all right now, as there will always be more to learn. Shift your focus from individual perfection to organizational excellence.

The good news is that as long as you plan, coach, and facilitate team contribution and performance, you will build an excellent organization. By encouraging ideas, suggestions, criticisms, and feedback, you and your employees will have a much better chance at fixing the cracks. Better yet, if you start your management approach with this mindset, the cracks will never appear in the first place.

You need to balance the skills and capabilities of your employees. Give people the freedom to make mistakes, but make sure they learn, regroup, and try again. Don't ignore the mistakes; just don't bring out the sword.

Effective leadership demands a delicate balance between sensitivity and authority. Most managers fail to establish a sufficient balance to make the equation work. When they give too much free rein towards employee empowerment, the plane tilts too far. The manager will sooner or later end up having to counter balance with exceeded authority, which then tilts too far in the opposite direction. People need to operate within a framework of boundaries and ground rules. These boundaries and ground rules need to be made aware of right from the beginning. Leaders do have to lead and be authority figures, but have the wisdom of relating to people less as a boss, and more as a mentor and collaborator. Finding that happy medium is the true sign of an inspired and effective leader.

Great leaders embrace the process of discovery by never giving up the quest for information. They control their destiny so that no one else controls it for them. They are never 100% satisfied as there is always room for improvement. Keeping a sharp focus, all the time, and never drifting from the big picture, is key to great leadership. Another key is to embrace and manage critical opposites in every facet of business whether it is balancing the focus towards shareholders vs. employees, authoritarian rule vs. ungoverned freedom, or employee expectations vs. employee capabilities.

101 Tips, Tricks & Secrets to Success in Leadership and Management

In the following sections, we will discuss 101 insightful secrets and key principles that will help get you started right away to a successful management career. These valuable management and leadership skills are part of the everyday life of a successful manager. They are not in any particular order of importance, as they are all extremely valuable. Some of these tips will be mentioned again in other pertaining lessons within the course.

These 101 "management through leadership tips" are broken up into four parts:

Part 1 - Employee Interaction, which deals with communication skills.
Part 2 - Professional Advice, which gives some tips on running a department.
Part 3 - Personal Advice, which is focused on inner-self qualities.
Part 4 - Words of Wisdom, which contains some gems to incorporate into your leadership style.

Always try to keep these important tips, tricks and secrets to success in mind throughout your management career. These tips will help you on your road to success.

Part 1 - Employee Interaction

1. **Get them excited about a better future.** As a leader, you need to rally the troops as a whole to find at least one common goal for all, and then focus a shared vision around that commonality. There might be a lot of ways to inspire, but in the same token, different people have different opinions on a better future. Where some might be inspired, some will miss the point. Find the one goal in which they can all rally behind, and they will truly be able to share in the same vision as yours. They will see you as an inspiring leader, which will make them even closer to you. The common goal might be a key metric for company growth, or satisfaction results that shows they are providing world-class customer service, etc. By keeping them all focused and inspired on at least one common key metric, you will have a more unified and better performing team to obtain that goal. You want your employees to have faith in the future by eliminating the possible fears we all have in common. By making them feel secure about the company, providing a clear and shared hope for the future, keeping everything under control, being someone they can count on, and someone they respect who respects them back, you will be seen as an effective leader.

2. **Make sure your employees listen to you**. If they are not listening, they will not follow. If they are not following, then you are not leading. You need to establish the fact that when you talk, you expect their full-undivided attention. If you are losing their attention, stop what you are doing or saying, and let them know you need them to focus on what is being said or shown. It doesn't have to be awkward, just say it as a matter of fact, in a normal tone of voice, and get back to business. Once it has been established that you will not tolerate being ignored, it will stop happening.

3. **You define, and then let your employees conquer, the goals and expectations.** It is more important to define the outcome you desire, rather than the steps on how to get there. If you hired and/or trained your staff right, then they should be able to accomplish this through teamwork and pride. Let them know that they are smart and bright, and that you have the confidence that they can achieve the expectations and goals. They just need to utilize the skills they already possess. Also make sure the goals are truly attainable and reachable with a realistic timeline. If you ask for the near impossible in an unrealistic timeframe, you will not only miss the goal, but lose the respect from your team.

4. **Make it a point to personally meet with everyone in your department.** If possible, take a person to lunch each day until you have gone through your whole department. At least meet with them one-on-one for 15 minutes or so. If your department or company is just too big (i.e. over 100 employees), then you might want to have a couple of small, but still very personal group meetings or lunches. Also make it a point to meet with your fellow managers. Get their ideas and feedback which will not only break the ice, it will make them feel good about themselves. This in turn will make them like you more. You might learn some valuable information as well.

5. **Motivating a group differs from that of motivating an individual.** Part of being a great leader is to know your employees' strengths and weaknesses. What inspires one person differs from another. Once you know what makes each person tick, you can capitalize on it by inspiring in a way that finds the positive, which will make them feel good about themselves. At the same time, you are earning respect and more credibility in their eyes. We will discuss more about motivating in lesson 3.

6. **When motivating, focus on the employee's strengths and accomplishments.** You can use past examples of achieved goals, customer compliments, etc. Leave the weakness out, and only bring it up at a later time if there is a disciplinary action. Also, again find out what makes each employee tick. Some are more motivated by the way you present a challenge. Some are more motivated by recognition either publicly or privately. Some are more motivated at different times of the day, week or month such as month-end sales. Some are more motivated by needing constant reassurance, yet some are more motivated by just letting them work independently. You need to know your employees to get the most out of motivation. One thing to keep in mind, you should never try to motivate by using threats. It might get short-term results, but you will pay for it in the long run, and most likely lose some good employees.

7. **Find the strong points and unlock the employee's potential.** When your developing an employee, point them in the right direction that will truly help their career in what they would like to do. For example, promoting a great employee to customer service supervisor, when their strengths are more technical engineering related, might not be the best idea for both of you. Let them shine, and make sure they know that you are spreading the good word about them. That you are sharing their ideas, contributions, successes, and customer compliments with upper management. Never steal their glory or thunder. You will already look good because you have a great employee that you manage and are mentoring. That is enough of an award in itself. It will also show your fellow managers and upper management that you truly are a team player who wants everyone to succeed, and not one to hold all the cards...

8. **Keep your employees close, but your best employees even closer**. Of course, as a leader, you want to make sure your employees are close to you. But lets face it, there are always a few people in your department that truly make a difference that you want even closer. You might have someone whose skills and talents are beyond all others and are just supreme, or you

might have someone who is just so customer focused that you know you can always trust that person to provide the greatest customer service, etc. These key individuals can make a big difference to the overall big picture. It shouldn't be that way, but that is just the way it is. You do not want to lose these key players, unless, it is for possible promotion outside of your department but still within the company. These individuals should get extra good personal treatment such as praise and raises. Just watch the fine line of showing favoritism.

9. **Be personable, and show you care about your employees as a person.** One of the most effective ways to have people want to follow you as a leader is to make them feel like you truly care about them. Ask about their interests and genuinely be curious about their lives. Many employees who feel you are uncaring or unfair are more willing to cheat on their expected workload and think they can get away with it. They will feel like they are just a number, so what does it matter what they do? If they feel they are being managed by someone who is trustworthy and acts with integrity, and at the same time cares about people as well as the business, they will feel like they are a true part of the company. They will see you as a leader to follow and will perform better.

10. **Open communication and honesty with the team.** Be yourself while always maintaining a professional persona. People deal with situations, good or bad, when they feel you are being honest in a professional yet personable way. This will also create a good union-company relationship if applicable. Encourage input and opinions. Be open for debate. Also, always suggest that an employee, or group of employees, talk to you first with any grievances before going to HR or upper management. Most of the time the issue will be worked out right then and there. Human Resources will love you for it as well.

11. **Continually communicate.** Always keep the communication line open whether in person, chat, phone call, or e-mail. There will be times when you are so busy that you will forget to talk to your staff. Don't be so involved in your own projects that you end up ignoring the hard work performed by your staff. If you do not talk to your employees, you might be looked at as not trying or caring. We will discuss more about communication skills in lesson 7.

12. **Sometimes make them find the answer.** Giving your team the responsibility to find the answers, even if they have to struggle a bit, challenges and shows trust in the team. You might be able to do it quickly, but what about the next time a situation pops up? Don't get caught in the trap of doing everything yourself. It's stressful for both you and your team. Instead of finding the answer for them right away, you should instead ask questions like, "What would you do?" They will learn by committing mistakes, and that should be the time you coach them. They will learn and build confidence over time. You should always be there to look after them, but not do it for them. This also goes for tasks you delegate, but somehow comes back to you. Try not to let this happen.

13. **Make your employees believe that you are in awe of their skills and that their work is challenging**. The more self-assured a person is, the

better they will perform. You are making them feel good about themselves by letting them know that you recognize the difficulty in their tasks. Show them you recognize their strengths, and then even challenge them more. You get more productivity, and they do not feel like their job is meaningless.

14. **Praise when praise is due**. Everyone likes to be complimented and receive a good pat on the back. When goals have been exceeded, exceptional work has been done, or employees went beyond the call of duty to ensure customer satisfaction, be sure to praise your employees. There is a difference between *praise* and saying *thank you*. You thank your employees for the hard work they have done, but you praise when exceptional work has been done. Praising the team for a true accomplishment goes a lot farther than praising for every completed task. It shows you have the leadership trait to recognize meaningful projects. We will discuss more about praising and recognizing in lesson 3.

15. **Do not be scared of your employees' success.** You want to see your employees shine with confidence and build their skills, even if you start feeling like they are surpassing you. You want to continually build up their self-assurance to utilize their strengths. The more they grow, the more you grow. It is a compliment to you when praise is given to your group or one of your team members. A successful employee usually means the manager must be doing something right, and upper management recognizes that fact The only way you can be surpassed is if you lose the individual and teams respect by holding them down. Loss of respect turns into a lack of confidence in you as a leader. The last thing you want is a *"coup d'état"* type of mentality amongst your team.

16. **Get the most out of recognition**. The saying, "Different strokes for different folks," comes into play here. Some people prefer public recognition, so you can praise them in front of their peers, whereas others are more inclined to private recognition and praise. Also, giving recognition to an employee's true strength and passion goes much further than praise for something they are not passionate about. For example, one person might be more technically inclined who will get more out of technically related praise, whereas another might be more focused on providing excellent customer service who will get more out of praise due to a customer compliment, yet they are both in the same group. You need to find the right buttons to push to get the most out of recognition and praise. Again, this goes back to knowing what makes them tick. Something else to keep in mind, do not praise an individual in public when it was a team effort. It can destroy team morale.

17. **Learn what makes them learn.** Part of sharing the vision as a leader, and making sure everyone performs their job functions correctly as a manager, requires that they understand just what it is you are trying to relate. You can't assume that a blanket statement or process will be fully understood by all. Each person learns a little differently than others. Some people get more by looking at visual examples, while others like watching others do it. Some like a hands on approach, while others like to analyze the data. *As a leader*, you need to make sure the whole team understands what you are trying to share. *As a manager*, you would want to know how each individual learns best. *A leader* would visually show ideas and visions in charts or slide

presentations, have the team participate with ideas based on your vision, and document for those who want to dig a little deeper into your vision. *A manager* might want to take a hands on approach with those who are better at doing it rather than reading about it, give documentation to those who are more comfortable by analyzing and applying the information to the project themselves, use a visual step-by-step approach to those who get more out of visual learning, or just have them watch others do it. You need to use whatever method works best, both from a leaders and managers point of view, even if it is in a few different formats. This will ensure that the goals of the overall vision will be achieved. In short, you might need to adapt your style and figure out how to work well with the competencies of your team members, rather than always expecting that they adapt to you.

18. **Always keep an "open door" policy.** Your employees need to know that they can talk to you at any time. You need to have this open door policy no matter the person or issue. Whenever an employee approaches you, you always have to be ready to feel sympathetic and show you care. Show them you are willing to help. It might be about money, a conflict with another employee, or a personal issue. No matter the situation, make sure they know you are listening. You don't necessarily need to come up with any magic solution at the time, but make sure you get back with them as soon as possible. Even if it is not what they want to hear, they will know you tried and took their concerns seriously. Most of the time it is just an opportunity to let them vent, however, you come out looking good. This is because you did not shrug it off or made them feel stupid for talking to you in the first place. Look them in the eyes while they are talking, and do not work on e-mail or answer a call unless absolutely necessary. If you need to interrupt them, make sure you let them know the urgency of the immediate situation. You would politely ask them to either wait a few minutes, or come back in around 15 minutes. The main point is not making them feel you do not care. If, however, this person is a constant bother to you, you will at one point need to let them know that these continuous problems need to stop. You will have to draw the line. You might suggest a meeting with human resources, which might scare them off in presenting future complaints. No one wants to be known as a complainer.

19. **Always be open, flexible and approachable**. Being laid back and approachable, while at the same time showing you have a desired commitment to achieving results, is truly a successful combination. Do not come across like an unreasonable, mean, or sarcastic person. Intimidation might seem like it gives you more power, but it backfires most of the time. You will lose respect. People will pretend to like you, but secretly hate you. They will leave the first chance they can get. Humble yourself with honor, and you will get the best out of your staff. This only makes your job easier. Always keep in mind this old saying, "You catch more fly's with honey than vinegar." Be nice, open to new ideas, and show flexibility. Even the smallest gesture will look big in your employees' eyes. Be open to everything, even if you know within the first few seconds that it will never work.

20. **Do not rule by intimidation, but don't be intimidated either...** Leaders need to have a certain dominance about them and be assertive in both their thinking and ability to deal with others. However, dominance and

intimidation are two separate entities. Only short-term gain is usually achieved through intimidation and a higher rate of attrition usually occurs. It is good for a little healthy fear associated with the natural approach to hierarchy and respect for the position, but that is as far as it should go. If, however, you start to feel intimidated by someone else or with particular events, remember this: You are reading this paragraph right now for a reason, you desire to excel at your management and leadership skills. That desire, and what is taught throughout this course, should instill confidence in you to never be, nor show that you are, intimidated by anyone. Maturity in your management style by empowering, rather than ruling, will show you do not intimidate nor are intimidated.

21. **Develop a collaborative approach.** When your employees are engaged in the vision and goals of the department, they will feel a sense of pride. Creativity, loyalty, and motivation will grow. Absenteeism and employee turnover will decrease, while problem solving and productivity will increase.

22. **You have to deal with conflict with confidence**. You will most likely have, at one point in your managerial career, an argumentative troublemaker with a bad attitude. You will also have employees with poor performance. You need to react immediately and know when it is time to fire the individual, unless of course you can remedy the situation. We will discuss more about conflict and firing in lesson 5.

23. **Have effective meetings**. Communicating with upper management and to your staff, as described throughout this course, is extremely important in creating clear-cut direction to achieve the well-defined goals and objectives. Meeting with staff is of vital importance, however, you need the meetings to follow an agenda and stick to the point to truly be effective. We will discuss more about holding great meetings in lesson 7.

24. **Stand behind your team**. If you feel justified, and it is within reason, you should always go to battle for your team. If your team feels passionately about something, you need to show them that you have their best interests at heart. If someone has a complaint about someone in your department, make sure you deal with the issue and not let another manager or supervisor bypass your authority. You need to always show that you are an advocate for your team.

25. **Empower your employees.** Give them bigger projects to handle rather than just the simple hour-to-hour assignments. Once they have tackled a few of the bigger types of projects, both you and your employees will have more confidence in the projects yet to come.

26. **Get the most out of your employees**. In order to do this, you need to give the most of yourself to them. Continuously ask if there is anything you can do for them. Be there for them and always let them know you have their back. Always keep their best interests at heart. The more you do for them, the more they will follow your lead.

27. **Help people grow their skills and develop their careers.** You do this through training, providing opportunities, and spreading the word through upper management. This will make you the person people want to work for.

When employees feel they are learning and growing, they work harder and more efficiently. Don't let them become board and stagnant or else they will become sluggish, both personally and professionally. Challenge and empower your employees with tasks, projects, and assignments. You will both win, they are improving and you are getting more work done. Coaching and mentoring your employees, by focusing on the needed strengths for them to learn and grow, is one of the best things you can do as manager and leader. Build their confidence when they are unsure about themselves, bring them out of their shell when they are shy, and help with reporting and process skills when they are not documentation experts. By helping your employees learn and grow, you will have more people in which you can delegate tasks. This in turn gives you more time to focus on other aspects of improving your department, which is another win/win situation.

Part 2 - Professional Advice

28. **Make sure your employees are 100% clear on the objectives.** If you are not absolutely clear and provide the clarity needed for all to understand, you will have a confused team. They will not truly understand the mission, vision, and goals. Confusion turns into anxiety, which then turns into fear. Your team clearly needs to know what is expected of them, the value of their strengths, and the actions you will take to achieve the objective. With the information you will learn throughout this course, you will be able to confidently implement the necessary actions for the team to achieve the objectives and goals.

29. **Analyze the problem; map out all possible answers, and then implement**. In most cases when faced with a problem, there is not just one clear-cut answer. Making the right decisions when solving problems is one of the most important aspects of management and leadership. When you start to see the cracks, you need to fix them as soon as possible, just don't use a Band-Aid fix on a major fracture. Truly identify the problem, look at all of the possible reasons and needed resolutions, and implement the best idea to fix the problem. Utilize your team to help look at all of the possible scenarios and ideas, even the illogical and unpractical ideas might turn out to be a solid solution to short-term or long-term problems. One very important thing to keep in mind; focus on fixing the problem rather than on finding the blame. Finger pointing will get you nowhere. We will discuss more about problem solving and decision making in lesson 6.

30. **If possible, take your time on making the right decision.** Unless you need to make an on the spot decision, you should always take your time and reflect on all of the possible ramifications. Just let your boss, upper management, or whomever is waiting on the decision know that you will think about it and get back to them as soon as possible, or at least by the deadline. You are most likely to make the best major decisions outside of work. It can be before you go to bed, in the shower, on the train, on the plane, etc. When you're away from the hustle and bustle of the office, you can calmly think everything through. This also pertains to ideas and improvements. Jot down your notes and bring them into work. You can

even e-mail yourself so you have them ready to read when you are back in the office.

31. **You need to be able to delegate.** It might seem hard to let go of certain tasks because you feel it might not get done right, but as a leader, it is one of the best things you can do for your employees. Besides, if you do not give up most of the daily tasks, you will feel bogged down and stressed. It will also free up some time for you to take on more pressing issues. Do not feel embarrassed, shy, or like you are passing the buck when it comes to delegating. It is expected of you as manager. It is vital that you let your staff take on most of the tasks and projects. This also gives them a chance to show what they can do. It breaks up the monotony of the day and gives some excitement. You also want them to get the credit on the delegated task to build their self-esteem. It is a compliment to you when they are complimented, and besides, your self-esteem should already be high since you are the manager. The most important thing is to know whom to delegate to and when. Make sure you know exactly what needs to be accomplished before you give the task to someone else. You need to confidently tell your employee on what needs to be done, and show you have the confidence in them to do it. Some tasks will need more monitoring than others, and some are more important. Set up a timeframe on when you expect the job to be completed, and have them report back to you with the progress. It is up to you to determine who can get the job done quickly. However, don't always pick the same person. Spread the tasks around to those who show interest. Make sure you have a commitment from the employee, and give them the authority needed to get the job done. If you have your eye on someone to promote, delegating to that person is a win/win solution. Just be careful that you do not show favoritism as you could run into Human Resource issues. We will discuss more about delegating in lesson 6.

32. **Know how to multitask and prioritize**. A good leadership skill is being able to handle more than one project at a time, and knowing which is the most important. You will find yourself creating a procedure, checking e-mail, answering your phone, a person will come into your office, and on top of all that, getting ready for a meeting. This is inevitable, and is a part of being a manager and leader. Don't stress, make the decision on what is the most important and put the most energy into that task. For example, if the employee who walked into your office looks or is acting distressed, that should take priority. You can ask the person to sit down, quickly reply to the e-mails and phone calls stating you will get back to them as soon as possible, and put your process document to the side. If you are running late for a meeting, you need to make the decision on whether you should continue to talk to your employee, or schedule a time to further discuss the matter. If you cannot make the meeting, make sure to inform the meeting leader that you are taking care of a personal issue. It should be noted that your employees should always come first. We will discuss more about multitasking and prioritizing in lesson 6.

33. **Always be ready to react, embrace, and manage change**. Always show that you are ready for any challenge that comes your way. The saying, "The only constant is change," particularly holds true to business management. One of the key strengths of a great leader and manager is the ability to

accept change and orders that come down from above with enthusiasm and confidence. You would then translate the directive with the same enthusiasm to your team. This is how you impress your boss, and your bosses' boss, and build confidence within the team that you have everything under control. The leader is the rock, and gives stability to the group. You will most likely get some worrisome and sarcastic remarks from a few of the team members, but that's natural and you should not worry about it. Don't get angry about complaints, even though you may be angry about the change yourself. They might just need to blow off some steam, and the best thing you can do is show that you do care and understand their frustrations. You might want to share some of your own frustrations as well; as long as the main take away point is optimism for the future. Your main concern is to make sure the change or transition goes smoothly, and that everyone knows the new objective. Don't wait for someone else to tell you what you should do. Take the steps to prevent unwanted surprises, continually meet with your boss and staff to keep them updated, and don't make or implement major changes until you have consulted with your staff. If you show you are embracing the changes with optimism and leading by example, your staff will most likely follow. We will discuss more about communicating change in lesson 7.

34. **Strong teams do not need to be micromanaged**. If you manage people too closely, you are subjecting them to constant scrutiny. If a team works well together and has a sense of unity, purpose, and pride, including being knowledgeable, you should not have to closely monitor them and continually be on their back. This in turn gives them more freedom knowing the boss is not breathing down their neck all of the time. This sense of independence can also be a great motivator. If you have a team where you feel like you have to make all of the decisions, and expect them to follow your orders like a robot, then you will most likely have a high rate of attrition as it creates an uncomfortable atmosphere. If you have a brand new team of somewhat inexperienced employees, then you do need to manage with more direction, all the while taking full responsibility. However, once everyone understands the goals and functions expected of them, you need to back off and let them act as a true team. Basically, provide more direction and develop the inexperienced group to become a strong team, and let the experienced well functioning group act as the strong team that is already created. It is up to you to determine the skill set and what you have to work with regarding experience and knowledge. Just make sure you make the right decisions on your approach, and do not feel like just because you are the manager, you are expected to re-invent the wheel. Pride sometimes gets in the way because of the management title. You will be more respected if you do not try to fix something that is not broke. Be there in time of need, instead of micromanaging when it is unnecessary. It's a win/win situation when you have a strong independent team working closely together that does not need to be closely supervised. This frees up time for you to work on other projects that can enhance your department. Don't feel like you have to hold all of the cards for job security. Sometimes managers feel they are no longer needed if the team is working like a well-oiled machine. That is not the case at all. In fact, you will be recognized for the team you created and most likely given more responsibilities, thus strengthening your position. It may even lead to promotion. Just remember, micromanagement won't work when teamwork is, and should be, a priority.

35. **Know as much as possible of what your staff does daily**. For example, know how to take a customer call and document it in the ticketing system, or know how to do the basic troubleshooting for repairs. It is human nature for leaders to devote most of their time and energy on the functions they know and perform best. This can be a trap, and it is just a matter of time before you find yourself in a situation where you should have been able to perform the simple task. Keep a list of all of your weaknesses pertaining to what you need to know, and address each issue one-by-one. You should always seek and strive for constant improvement.

36. **Have a clear cut organizational chart.** Org charts give a clear reporting structure for all employees to follow. For example, supervisor A and B report to you, the manager. Supervisor A is in charge of Tier 1, and supervisor B is in charge of Tier 2. It should also show your direct report. There is an example of an org chart in lesson 2 that you can use as a guideline.

37. **Remember to think in terms of cost and results.** You always have to balance the two together. You have to look for ways to reach the goal with minimal cost.

38. **Chart it out.** Make sure you have a white board for mapping projects, prioritizing tasks, sharing ideas, modifying schedules, making seating arrangements, etc. This will be a constant visual reminder for you and applicable staff to see.

39. **Hire, then lead, then monitor, then reward, and finally retain the right people**. You will need to get the right people, know their strengths and weaknesses, know what motivates them, know how to set clear expectations, evaluate the persons performance, and when applicable, reward for a job well done. If you understand how to apply this information, your department will succeed and you will have a better chance at keeping the good people. All of these topics will be discussed in greater detail throughout this course.

40. **Brainstorm with key members of your department or fellow managers.** There is no reason you should feel you need to come up with all of the answers, on the contrary, the more help you can get the better. By brainstorming with key staff members or fellow managers, new and positive ideas that benefit all are usually the outcome. Hear the suggestions, discuss the possible solutions, work on a plan that makes sense, see if you have the necessary resources, think how you will implement the plan, then write it and distribute it to all with clear-cut communication. Lessons 2 and 6 go into more detail on planning and problem solving.

41. **Create an effective work environment**. Ask your employees what they need to perform to their optimum. It can be a process modification, better tools to get the job done, and even to make their surroundings esthetically pleasing. The goal is to create a positive workplace with as much positive energy as possible.

42. **Follow the same process you expect your team to follow**. For example, if you expect detailed documentation to be entered into the

company database, then you should not cut any corners if you are the one entering the information.

43. **Keep upper management and financial issues that are considered confidential to yourself**. You might think you are showing off by telling some company secrets, but you can get in trouble, not to mention the person you told will always expect future information. This is especially important when it is bad news.

44. **Always be prepared for meetings**. Arrive a little early, and have all of the documentation and notes you need for the meeting. Make copies of the pertinent documentation for everyone at the meeting if applicable. You can refer to your notes if you get asked any questions you are not immediately able to answer. Practice and refine your speech if you are expected to present. Practice saying some quips that pertains to certain situations, telling clear and concise short stories, and have a good joke or two to tell when the timing is right. Know when to shorten or stop a speech, and most of all, be clear and precise. A few choice statements will go much further than a lot of mumbo jumbo. Your ability to quickly communicate and have answers to questions from your staff and upper management shows great leadership skills. We will discuss more about meeting management in lesson 7.

45. **Post important information on the wall using large-scale wall charts in clear view for all to see**. You and your team should take pride in achieving the goals set. There should be constant reminders around the office on what you are aiming for as far as goals and objectives are concerned. There can also be large boards for the most important customer issues, work schedules, tips of the day, etc. These charts and boards can also be in an electronic format such as a monitor and reader board.

46. **Fully understand the goals of the company**. Especially the financial goals. You will get this information from management meetings or from CEO announcements. You need to know the key short-term and long-term objectives. You should be able to answer questions from your staff that relate to these matters.

47. **Fully understand what upper management wants from you**. You need to be 100% clear and fully focused on what is expected from you so you can lead your team to achieve these objectives. We will discuss more about company expectations in lesson 2.

48. **Under promise and over deliver**. It is better to be honest and state how long a project might take, or if you're not sure you can do the project at all. Don't just tell your boss or upper management what they want to hear. You do not want to say you can have something done by the end of the week, when you know darn well it would be near impossible to complete. You do not want to turn in poor work to meet a deadline. By setting a realistic timeframe upfront, and if possible completed a head of schedule - thus over deliver, not only will it make you look good, but will also reduce some stress. Just be careful not to push the requested project too far out in the future. For example, if you are requested to complete a project in the next week, but you come back saying it will take one month; you will look bad and not a

team player. You should be more compromising and suggest two weeks if you feel it can be done in that timeframe. The optimum scenario is to be able to adhere to the requested project deadline, but that is not always the case. The point here is that it is better to give a realistic timeframe and hopefully be ahead of schedule, than to agree on a given timeframe and fail.

49. **Make and meet your deadlines**. As previously stated, meeting a deadline makes you look good as a manager who plans to get the work done, and leader who inspires to get the work done. Never miss a deadline. Be known as the person who always gets the job done right and on time. Map out the project if needed by using a program like "Microsoft Project". You can also just map it out by creating a timeframe for each phase. Make sure you prioritize the most important tasks. You would enter these phases on the calendar by putting the project complete date first, and then work backwards. This will help you determine the true start date to be able to hit the project complete date. Make sure to give yourself some leeway and extra time for possible unseen or unplanned complications. If you feel there is a chance you might miss the deadline, you would have to either modify the phases, or let your boss know you will not be able to make the deadline, which would be the absolute worse case scenario. Lessons 2 and 9 go into more detail on basic project planning and project tools.

50. **Have a good understanding of the basics of a business.** You should know the functions of each department and how they interact. You should especially know the basics in finance, marketing and sales. You want to be able to understand just what is being said in management meetings. You do not want to feel like you are blinded with science and have no clue on what is being discussed. Lessons 8, 9 and 10 are dedicated to business basics.

51. **Be able to report the statistics that matter.** A good leader understands the value of statistics, and a good manager understands the data that matters. You can be sure your boss or upper management will expect you to give reports on your department's performance. You should add data you feel is important, and eliminate the data that is redundant or not important. These statistical reports are your report card, and you always want to strive for an "A." You need to make sure the data is 100% accurate, whether the results are good or bad. If the results are good, you help justify your job as manager and will get a good pat on the back. If the results are bad, you have the data to back up what you need to be able to improve. For example, if you have long hold times in your customer service department, and you have absolutely structured your department to its optimum, you can justify hiring more staff. The stats don't lie and you absolutely need to master all departmental reports. Although lesson 2 gives reporting examples you can use as a guideline, it is highly suggested you become extremely proficient working with spreadsheets.

52. **Hold a meeting with all of your staff on the first day**. If you are new to the company or department, you want to establish yourself from day one. Introduce yourself and give them a brief history of your previous work experience, tell them what upper management expects you to do, go over the vision you have for the department, and what it is you expect from them. Let them ask questions, and take notes with immediate follow up to any questions you could not answer upfront. Give a quick summary on all

that was discussed. Thank them and close the meeting in a professional manner. Make sure they leave the meeting with the feeling that the future looks good. This will instill confidence and break the ice so you can get started on making your mark.

53. **The first few months on the job...** Make sure you meet with key people within your department, ask a lot of questions, and take notes of their suggestions. Take these suggestions and incorporate into new policies and procedures if applicable. It builds rapport and your staff will start feeling like you are going to make some positive changes. This works great if you are following a manager who has not done such a great job. Be careful with this approach if you are following a manager who was loved and respected. Also, turn on your radar to find the complainers who will try and drag you down, as well as the good people who will work hard. Make sure you tell the good people how much you appreciate all of their hard work. Don't ignore the complainers, however, at least make some small talk. They just might have some insightful information that can help improve processes. Last of all, make sure you nail your first assignments and meet the deadlines given by your boss, no matter how many hours you have to work. You should always meet your deadlines, but it is imperative you do so in the first few months on the job.

Part 3 - Personal Advice

54. **Have a positive attitude**. Don't be negative. Your actions can create a positive morale amongst the team. This will be contagious and you will get more out of your team. Try to make your staff believe things are better than they seem, even when the pressure is on. The worst thing you can do is to badmouth any person or department within the company. You can kind of joke about company related issues, but in a lighthearted way. Sometimes a good laugh or feeling of solidarity can work to your benefit, just don't be malicious or slanderous. It could also come back to haunt you. You would be surprised at the loss of respect you would receive if you acted unprofessionally in this manner. Remember this old adage, "It takes years to build respect, and only seconds to lose it..."

55. **Be passionate about the objectives and organization.** When you become passionate about a task, project, or departmental goal, your team will also become passionate. Channel your passion to be the best into your employees. Passion is the key ingredient between being good and being great. You want your department to be exceptional, not just good enough. Be passionate about becoming a world-class organization and your team is sure to follow.

56. **Be enthusiastic and optimistic.** Striving for a better future with an energetic drive is contagious. Your team will pick up on the same vibe. They want a better future just as much as you do. Your job is to make them want to be the best and take pride in their work. The more enthusiastic and optimistic you are, the more they can identify with working in a success driven department.

57. **Be self-assured yet humble with strong character traits**. A modest and honest person with charisma, integrity, accountability, drive and aggression, is easy to follow and respect. You should still be self-confident, just not conceited. Self-confidence and resiliency are key elements of a strong leader. Confidence with a touch of humility is a great mixture and people will be more drawn to you.

58. **Have a high standard of excellence.** You should always have an internal desire to do your best. Have a sense of duty and take pride in your work. Pay attention to every detail, and never stop striving to be the best.

59. **Be ethically sound**. Always practice good business ethics and you will not get caught up in any troubles. Sounds simple, but this is extremely important. Basically, do not lie to your staff, ignore your customers, steal from the company, ship faulty goods, misuse company property, etc. We will discuss more about business ethics in lesson 8.

60. **Be friendly, but not their best friend**. This is how rumors of favoritism start. It is impossible to say that you can no longer be friends if you have been recently promoted, however, you should keep the friendship very quiet. One of the toughest things about being a great leader is finding the balance between being friendly, and being too friendly, with your employees. A great leader is someone who holds a great deal of respect. You will start losing respect if you become too involved in personal friendships with your employees. It's just natural. Your mystique as a leader will start to evaporate. You have to find the line between being friendly, and being their best friend. If you do have a best friend who works for you, be very careful about showing too much favoritism, and keep your friendship outside of work. You can be friendly to each other at work, just not as best friends do away from work. Also, dating one of your employees should be out of the question, unless you are ready for some major turmoil. It rarely works out when you are in a managerial position, unless they move to another department altogether.

61. **Be thick-skinned and ready to take risks**. Although it is nice to fly below the radar and keep a sense of status quo, there are times when you need to be aggressive and responsive to the needs of your team. This is expected of you as manager, and a good leader knows when the time is right. Even though you do not want to be known as the person shouting, "The sky is falling!" you do need to sound the alarm when you start seeing the cracks. You will need to make the right decisions and take the necessary risks to change the situation. Also, if you feel it's time to take your department to the next level, and you have done the cost-benefit analysis, then you should take the risk. Be thick-skinned and stand firm behind your decision. If you never take risks, you will never grow.

62. **Have a mental toughness**. You need to be able to deal with disappointments and adversity. Be cool under pressure, and don't waste time worrying about what could have been. Learn from it and move on to the next project.

63. **Be able to take criticism.** Your actions when being criticized tell a lot about your strength in management. Whatever you do, do not be defensive. Your first reaction will be to take it personally, however, try to hold on to your emotions and stay cool. Really listen to what they have to say and don't brush it off. If they are good points, be sure to acknowledge and address them in a professional, and even thankful, manner. If they are bad points, calmly state your objections, but ensure you will take the points into consideration. Do this without sounding sarcastic.

64. **Be empathetic.** When dealing with any crisis from your employees, try to put yourself in the other person's shoes. Looking at issues from their point of view will give you more insight on how to deal with emotional type of issues that come your way.

65. **Keep a cool head.** Employees and customers might be irrational, show no common sense, uncooperative, mean and disrespectful. When in a difficult situation, always keep a cool head, use a calm tone, and make sure you present yourself with an understanding attitude. Let them know that you do care and will do all that you can to resolve the issue. Always treat the other person with respect no matter how absurd they may be. Say please, sir, madam, thank you, or whatever sign of respect that is proper for the moment. Do this without using a condescending tone. If this problem truly goes beyond your control or reason, then you will have to take necessary steps with the employee, or pass the customer on to upper management to try and save the account. Be sure you have full documentation on everything that has led up to this point. Just remember, grace under pressure is absolutely needed in the world of management.

66. **Don't lose your temper.** When you lose your temper you lose respect. You can show that you are serious about something by being a bit more stern and direct, but never blow your top. Have an indicator of sorts to use as a reminder the moment you are ready to explode. It can be an image or object, such as a wedding ring, that is meaningful to you. That will be your reminder to stop and think about what you're going to say next. It will be your "negative reaction" alert. Also, try to stay away from using foul language. You rarely see a truly respected leader cussing.

67. **Dress the part.** You will build subconscious respect as a leader amongst your team when you look and dress in a professional manner. If you are uncomfortable dressing professionally, or feel embarrassed because everyone knows you as a "jean" type of person, you need to change your attitude and dress the part. You never know when there might be an upper management meeting, surprise visit by the CEO, or a visit from an important customer. You need to always be ready to represent your department, both in appearance and knowledge. You should own at least one professional business looking suit with nice shoes. Men should always wear a tie when wearing a suit. This would also be a good time to change the department's dress code if needed, especially if your employees deal with the customer in person. People tend to work more professionally when they dress more professionally. You will most likely have to work with Human Resources regarding any dress code modifications.

68. **Be on time to work and any appointments.** If you show up late, then you will slowly start seeing your supervisors and staff showing up late. This is a contagious habit that you do not want others to pick up. Build respect as a leader by being on time, or better yet, a few minutes early to work and appointments.

69. **Try not to leave early**. It brings down morale when the boss leaves early regularly. A few times here and there is actually all right, as it gives both you and the staff some relief, but you should not be known as the manager who cuts out early most of the time.

70. **Try not to call out sick**. Have the reputation that you never call out sick unless you are truly ill. If you call out sick frequently, your staff will as well. Being known as the manager that always comes to work, even when they are under the weather, is a strong leadership trait.

71. **When there is manual work to be done, help out**. Moving a couple of chairs or boxes every now and then shows that you are a team player and do not consider yourself too good for the task.

72. **Try not to gossip, be too goofy, or joke around too much.** You might gain some attention or get a laugh in the short-term, but in the long-term you will start losing respect and credibility. Some joking around is all right; just don't be the manager who acts like a clown. You don't want people joking about you behind your back. You should also try to squash employee gossip or mean comments being said about each other. Also, if rumors get out of control, set the record straight as soon as possible. *However*, don't come across too serious and unfriendly. Just because you are a manager does not mean you no longer have a personality. Pick the right times to let your guard down and tell funny stories or a joke or two. Also laugh at stories and jokes told to you. People trust a person who has both a serious, yet funny side to them. Quickly try to tap into your memory of any stories, trivial tidbits, or quick one-liners that are relevant to the conversation at hand. Don't be shy, as part of being a manager and an effective leader is being a people person. Humor can help relieve tension and keep things into perspective. Just be careful not to come across as too sarcastic or say anything that can offend or be considered unethical.

73. **Be controlled and precise in your social interactions**. Protect your integrity and reputation by having the foresight regarding the ramifications on what you say and do. Be careful when making decisions or determining specific actions that might have a negative social impact.

74. **Act professional, even at parties.** There will be times when you attend an office party or event where drinking is involved. Keep the after work drinking to a minimum. A couple times a year is fun and exciting for all, however, a regular habit usually turns into things being said that should be confidential. A sign of a good leader is to know when to walk away with your integrity still in tack.

75. **Take a break when needed.** When you start feeling stressed or overwhelmed, you should take a break and walk around the building or get a glass of water. Clear your mind while getting some exercise. You do not

want to take your stress out on someone else, especially when unjustified. We will discuss more about how to deal with stress in lesson 6.

76. **Do what you say you are going to do as soon as possible**. You start establishing yourself as a leader when you show interest in making positive or necessary changes. When you do what you said you were going to do right away, you earn immediate respect. If, however, you do not follow up on your promise, you will start losing credibility as a leader. If you cannot do it, make sure you provide a solid reason why and let them know immediately. They will at least know you tried and did not just brush it off.

77. **Be emotionally stable.** Frustration and stress are challenges every leader and manager must face. Take your psychological maturity to the next level by having a leadership mentality embedded in your mind. You always need to be prepared and able to deal with stressful situations that come your way.

78. **Don't be defensive**. The respect you have earned, or are trying to earn, will evaporate in just moments. This is not to say that you should not debate a point or have an opinion. You should not take a suggestion you do not like, or a performance related comment, too personally. Calmly reply, without excuses, that you will look into their suggestions or performance related improvements, and will get back to them as soon as possible.

79. **Never talk negatively about customers or other departments.** It is so easy to complain and criticize. People are always finding faults with customers or other departments. For example, customer service will complain that the sales department makes promises they cannot keep. Even when the complaint is justified, you do not want to add fuel to the fire. You might have a lighthearted thing to say like, "Sales sure seems to pass the buck." Just make sure to follow it up with something like, "We need sales to sell or else they will not bring income into the company." Then follow up with letting them know that if it gets too out of hand, you will meet with the sales persons manager. You should truly have a brief discussion with this person's manager if it gets to that point. You also have to make sure to remind your staff that without your customers, there might not be a company.

80. **Never backstab anyone, ever**. It will always come back to haunt you. A person who is known as a backstabber is not known as a solid leader.

81. **Try being a leader outside of the work place**. Leading people may not be the most natural aspect of your personality, but you can use the skills taught in this course through volunteer work, such as being a coach, or other venture. The more you practice outside of work, the better you will be inside of work.

Part 4 - Words of Wisdom

82. **Have confidence in yourself.** Always believe in your abilities to be a great manager and leader. Tackle all situations and dilemmas that come your way with enthusiasm and gusto. The fact that you are reading this shows you have the desire and talent that exists within you. Show you have the confidence and believe in yourself, and others will believe in you as well. In time you will develop a sort of "instinct" when something needs attention, and a "presence" that people will find ensuring. You will come across like a leader without even having to say a word.

83. **Act the way you want others to act, walk the walk you talk, lead by example, practice what you preach, etc**. These are old clichés but some of the most important tips to build respect within your organization. If your team sees you working hard, they will work hard. If they think your slacking, they will start slacking off. If you tell them what to do, but you do it differently, they will not see you as an honest leader. If you want an optimistic and positive team, then you need to always be optimistic and positive. When your employees see that you act in the same manner you expect from them, a true sense of respect will begin to build. These are just a few of some obvious, but extremely important, leadership skills.

84. **Honesty and integrity is key**. People do not necessarily expect managers to always have a quick fix to solve the issues, but do expect fundamental leadership principles of honesty and goodness. In due time you will earn credibility, which is a major leadership trait. With the high level of integrity they will see in you as a leader, comes the trust that you are not the cause of the issues. They will automatically know that you, as a manager, will truly do all you can to solve the issues.

85. **Emulate a person who you truly respect as a leader.** There must be someone you know whose leadership skills you thought were admirable. It could be, or could have been, a boss, a teacher, a friend, or a relative who you admired as a person with respectable leadership characteristics. Someone who inspired you to want to work hard, to not only try to impress, but to show you cared about the mission at hand. Study how they made the right and effective decisions using certain facts, opinions, and ideas. Look for the leadership qualities you would like to incorporate into your leadership style. By remembering what it was about them that inspired you, you can emulate that style when your leadership skills are called upon.

86. **Listen more than talk**. You will earn a great deal of respect and credibility by actively listening, rather than just blowing your own hot air. Let them share their passion, and when the time is right, you can interject with passion of your own about the subject at hand.

87. **Take chances and do not limit yourself**. Part of becoming a strong leader and great manager is creating something new, and not be intimidated by failure.

88. **Make great impressions from day one.** Build relationships and make as many good first impressions on the first day if you are starting in a new company or have been recently promoted. You want people talking about you in a positive manner from day one. You will start earning credibility and respect right away.

89. **Say less and you will get more.** By not doing all the talking, especially if it is redundant or meaningless to the meeting or conversation, you will develop a professional persona and a sense of quiet intelligence, dignity and wisdom. When you do talk, make it count. You will be taken seriously with true interest.

90. **Make sure the team sees you as a knowledgeable and dependable leader.** They will have comfort knowing that you know what you are doing. If you come across as unknowledgeable or unsupportive, you will lose respect as a leader. Be exceptionally hard working and dedicated to the mission you advocated. Even if you have been recently promoted within your department and everyone knows you as, lets say, a customer support representative, now is your time to step up to the plate and learn the fundamentals of leadership.

91. **Work smarter, not harder.** Another cliché, but you should eliminate redundancy whenever possible. A morale breaker is when employees have to make repeated entries or tasks for each case or product. For example, when a representative has to enter information into one database, and then enter the same information into another database. Find ways to tie things together, and determine what is not needed. Not only is this a management responsibility, but will also help you gain respect as a leader to eliminate future redundancy within the department.

92. **Always follow the Golden Rule.** Treat others, as you would like to be treated. If people like and respect you, they will work harder for you. This might sound like an obvious and general statement, however, it is so important and true. It needs to be said just to make sure you understand that the most basic rule of great management is to have a team who wants to work hard, feels happy, respects you, and is totally secure in their leadership. You also need to practice this golden rule with your fellow managers and upper Management.

93. **Follow it to the end.** Always see your projects through to completion with no loose ends. Mediocre performance shows a mediocre manager and leader.

94. **Think like it's a perfect world.** Don't automatically assume you cannot achieve certain goals, or be hindered by certain limitations. Always try to see the possibilities come true in every idea and dream you have. For example, you might come up with the idea of having a system everyone in the company can share. You would look at it like "in a perfect world, we would have an easy to use unified database in which all can use," and then do all you can to make that happen. Don't be pessimistic and say it can't, or won't, happen.

95. **Never let them see you sweat**. This might remind you of an old TV commercial, but still holds true in the world of management. Always keep your cool and create an impression that you always know exactly what is going on. For example, when you are in an upper management meeting and you do not know what they are talking about, do not continually ask the simple questions. A somewhat vague question or two is acceptable, but if you still do not understand the subject matter, stay focused but do not have the "deer in the headlights" look about you. Wait until that particular subject is over before you participate any further. You can look up the subject matter or ask a close colleague after the meeting is over. Another example could be; if your company has experienced an outage, you would stay cool and focused to resolve the issue, and not panic in any way.

96. **Be straightforward and always look them straight in the eyes**. People like an honest answer from someone they trust, even when you do not know the answer. This not only goes for your employees, but with upper management as well.

97. **Show you have the courage it takes**. Show confidence in the decisions you make, and do not put your tail between your legs if confronted about any problems related to your decisions or processes. It is all right if someone disagrees with you and you have a healthy debate, but don't back down when you know it's right. This does not mean that you should be stubborn and stick to your guns no matter what. You are not perfect and there will always be some areas where you can improve. You should, however, confidently be able to say that you are not opposed to make changes if it is for the greater good. Upper management will notice the way you handle these types of situations with the courage in standing by your decisions, and the courage to know when to make a change.

98. **Always bite your tongue.** Before you make a heated statement, stop yourself before you say, do, or send something you might regret. All of the respect you have gained can be lost in a single word or action. Actions like certain hand gestures, crossing your arms in a defiant way, confused facial expressions, demoralized posture, too much eye contact, sounds and grunts of discontent, can have a huge negative impact. This also holds true when sending or answering heated e-mails. Before you hit the send button when creating or replying to an aggravated type of e-mail, take at least a 5-minute break before hitting send. There might be times when you should take an hour or even day before hitting the send button. When you come back, re-read both the original e-mail and your response. Chances are you will re-write your response in a much more controlled and professional manner. You will get your point across more effectively if you keep it professional at all times.

99. **Learn from your mistakes, but don't be affected by them**. Your going to make mistakes, and yes, you will learn from them. But you will also have to be able to let the mistake go, and not dwell on it enough to affect your psyche. A confident leader moves on, always remember that.

100. **Giving up or not trying is the only failure**. You fail only when you give up or there is a lack of effort. If something went wrong, find out what it was and correct it. After all, part of being a leader is taking chances, and with

chances comes the risks of unforeseen problems. Don't hang your head low, show your team, upper management, and especially yourself that you have the determination to resolve the problem and not give up. This can also pertain to an individual employee performance issue. If they are failing, contribute it to a lack of effort, rather than lack of talent, to eliminate any self-doubt. If the effort is there, provide the training to sharpen the needed skills. You can also set up a buddy system so that the employee will not only learn, but also absorb the needed talent for the job. If the effort and skills are there, but the talent is still missing, manage around the weakness and find another strength in which to utilize. While you are doing this, make sure they are not feeling any self-doubt. You might need to assign different responsibilities so that the weaknesses are no longer applicable. The point here is to never give up on yourself, or your employees. Again, giving up or not trying is the only failure.

101. **Don't ignore your intuitiveness**. Sometimes reason and logic are outweighed by the instinct to follow your "guts" when making tough decisions. By absorbing all of the information in this course, you can have the confidence that you are a strong leader and manager, and use this strength when making the "gut" type of decisions.

A short story about Leadership

John Smith was once a field technician who was recognized as having great technical skills and a good personality. He was known as a nice person and received many compliments from both customers and fellow employees.

The company he worked for was expanding and a managerial position was available. He was offered and accepted the position, even though he had no management experience and never really led anyone. He stated this to upper management, but they had the confidence he would pick it up due to his aptitude and attitude.

John knew that he would be faced with leadership challenges, and quickly found out that his decisions mattered. He focused too much on the small things, which needed to be addressed, but missed the big picture. He did not prioritize like he should have and tried to do everything himself so that he would not bother his staff. No one really knew the goals or objectives, or where the department was headed. He did all of the talking because he thought that is what a leader and manager is supposed to do. He thought the only way to get things done was to intimidate, and he would lose his temper when things did not go right. If anyone criticized him, he would become immediately defensive. He did not even think about motivating his staff, he thought they should just do the work they were getting paid for.

Although his staff respected his technical capabilities and liked him, they did not look at him as a leader. Once he talked to a couple of his closest staff members, he realized that he needed to take a good look at how he could improve. He thought about people he respected as leaders, and realized that they never seemed to get upset and were usually calm. He found that he needed to build trust and make sure everyone saw the same vision for the future. He started meeting more with his staff and asking for their opinions and suggestions. He knew not to let any criticism affect him personally, as everyone wants to succeed and enjoy their job at the same time. He realized the importance of proper multitasking and prioritization. He made the decisions he was confident about, and asked key employees for help or confirmation whenever he was not 100% sure. He also started freeing up the responsibilities he held tight by delegating out tasks. His stress levels were decreasing, and he started to act the part of a leader by being more calm and self-assured.

Even though he made some mistakes, and quite often would seek advice, he was earning trust from his team. This was due to always keeping them informed truthfully, and never giving up until the issues were resolved. They felt he truly had things under control. He had their best interests at heart, and tried to motivate by mentoring, coaching and helping them grow. He listened to what they had to say, and remained quiet until he had something useful or powerful to say. With this new humbled confidence, his leadership abilities improved to a point to where he was promoted to director, and soon after, vice-president.

Epilogue: This field tech, with no management or leadership experience, was able to grow once he realized the skills needed in order to succeed. By incorporating the information taught in this lesson into your daily routine as manager, you will earn respect and be known as a solid leader. There will be much more in-depth information regarding managerial skills with the mindset of a great leader in the following lessons. John's story will continue as well as it relates to each lesson.

Quick Lesson Summary

- To be a great manager, you need to be a strong leader. Management skills pertain to finding ways to achieve the goals that the leader inspired the team to obtain.

- Leadership is about sharing a vision in which people will want to follow to reach the goal.

- One of the key elements in effective leadership is to never become complacent with the business model, no matter how sound and well crafted. Effective leadership demands a delicate balance between sensitivity and authority. They are never 100% satisfied as there is always room for improvement.

- Five key points to strong leadership are when your employees:

   o   Trust you and know that you are looking out for the good of all.
   o   Share in your vision and want to achieve the same goals
   o   Know that you will do your all to help them succeed
   o   Are confident in your decisions
   o   Know that you have everything under control and that the future looks bright.

- Lead by example in every way. The way you act, how you talk, the way you dress, your optimistic view, your positive approach, what you say about others, and how well you control yourself, all pertain to how you are viewed as a leader.

- When in doubt, utilize key members of your staff to come up with the right solution. Many times, listening more than talking will get you further and you will also be seen as a leader with quiet confidence.

LESSON 2 – HOW TO MANAGE AND ORGANIZE YOUR DEPARTMENT TO MEET THE GOALS

Introduction: Managers need to plan and guide the work for their employees

In order to accomplish the goals desired, you will need to have a good strategic and tactical plan. You will need a basic roadmap on where you are now, and where you are going. You would also need to determine the best way on how to get from point A to point B. Finally, you would need to make sure you have the means to get to your final destination.

For example, if providing excellent customer service were your main objective, you would need to come up with a strategy to make sure the customers are satisfied in every way. This is where managing and organizing your department comes into play.

You might need to organize the department differently to achieve the goal such as setting up a Tier 1 group to handle the simple and quick calls, and a Tier 2 group to handle the difficult longer lasting calls. You would need to determine who would go into each group and where they would sit. You would have to have the calls routed differently. You will need to direct the staff to follow the process and monitor the performance to make sure all functions are running smoothly and in a coordinated fashion.   You also at the same time need to take into consideration the costs associated in structuring your department while staying within budget. These are the kinds of the decisions that come with structured planning and organizing. How you deal with these kinds of decisions are a big part of being a successful manager.

In this lesson we will look at a model that can help you fully understand and improve your organization, and ways to set up your department to its optimum performance to be able to meet any goals or objectives that may come your way.

Also in this lesson, and throughout the course, we will be using management examples of a Customer Service/Technical Support Manager. Customer service is so important and just about every manager has some sort of customer service expectations related to their goals and duties. This makes these examples exemplary. We will use an example company that provides telephone and Internet service called Sample Corp. The fictitious product being used is called a Widget, which is an Internet service related product. The manager's name that is being used in the short stories in lessons 1 through 7 is John Smith. Be sure to keep in mind that the basic premise and logic of these examples can be translated into just about every managerial scenario and function.

The 7-S Model and how it can help improve your organization

The 7-S model is a useful way to look at the many interrelated aspects of a complex organization and it's a great way to help you understand your organization and leverage it to maximum efficiency and profitability. It was developed by Tom Peters and Robert Waterman while working at McKinsey & Company.

The basic premise of the model is that there are seven internal aspects of an organization that need to be aligned if it is to be successful. It is the seven key elements of an organization that are critical to understand its effectiveness. These seven elements are: Strategy, Structure, Systems, Shared Values, Style, Staff, and Skills. The beauty of the 7-S model is that it can be used in a wide variety of situations such as:

- A diagnostic tool for an ineffective organization.
- Improve the performance of a company.
- Guides organizational changes.
- Align departments and processes during a merger or acquisition.
- Determine how best to implement a proposed strategy.
- Combines rational and hard elements with emotional and soft elements.

Managers must act on all S's in parallel as all S's are interrelated. All elements must align equally:

The seven elements are distinguished in so called hard S's and soft S's. The hard elements (consisting with Strategy, Structure, and Systems) are feasible and easy to identify. They are easier to change than the others. They can be found in strategy statements, corporate plans, organizational charts and other documentations.

The four soft S's (consisting of Skills, Staff, Style, and Shared Values) are not as feasible. They are harder to change directly, and typically take longer to do so. They are harder to describe since capabilities, values and elements of corporate culture are continuously developing and changing. They are highly determined by the people at work in the organization. Effective companies, however, tend to pay as much attention to these factors as to the hard S's.

Essentially, you'll want to run through each of the seven points and analyze how they fit in with your business. The concepts remain fairly similar, with some minor changes:

1. **Strategy:** Refers to the plan or route-map to maintain competitive advantage. What is your plan for the future? How do you intend to achieve the objectives? When was the last time you looked at your business plan? What were the actions you took after looking at it? When was the last time you updated your business plan? How do you deal with competitive pressure? What are the sources of sustainable competitive advantage such as cost, quality, service and technical leadership? What are the key strategic priorities such as improved customer service? How are changes in customer demand dealt with? How do you deliver greater value to customers?

2. **Structure:** Refers to the framework in which the activities of the organization's members are coordinated. A key function of structure is to focus employees' attention on what needs to get done by defining the work they do and whom they should be working with. How is the organizational structure designed right now? How is the team divided? How do the various departments coordinate activities? How do the team members organize and align themselves? Is decision making and controlling centralized or decentralized? Is this as it should be, given what you're doing? Where are the lines of communication? If you had to suddenly hire another 6 employees tomorrow, what would it look like? What changes would you have to make? If your customer has a complaint, or if there is some kind of emergency, how are problems escalated? Is there a stated hierarchy and an "in-practice" hierarchy?

3. **Systems:** Refers to the day-to-day processes and procedures. Having effective systems helps reduce redundancy and streamlines process. How do you gather business intelligence? Do you have a unified database? Does the organization have the systems it needs to run your department such as monitoring for customer satisfaction? If you have to put together a report on something, could you do it quickly? What happens if one of your staff leaves; will they take with them a key part of your business intelligence? What are the main systems that run the organization? Where are the controls and how are they monitored and evaluated? What internal rules and processes does the team use to keep on track?

4. **Shared Values:** (also known as Superordinate goals): Refers to the guiding principles of the organization. These are the core values of the company and your department. What are your core and stated values? What do you measure and reward? Are they the same thing? How can you make minor changes to bring them in line with each other? What are your stated values supposed to contribute to your business? Do they contribute what you want them to contribute? Does your employees have a shared understanding of why the company exists? Do they share the same company and departmental vision? How do they described the ways in which the company is distinctive? Is the focus on quality, emphasis on people, etc?

5. **Style:** Refers to the leadership approach and the organizations overall operating approach. How would you describe your department? How would your employees describe your department? How would your competitors

describe your department? How would your customers describe your department? How would your vendors describe your department? If all five would say the same thing then you're on the right track; if they say different things then it could indicate a potential problem. Is this same style and culture going to carry you through the next few years? What will have to change for you to grow? How participative is your management and leadership style? How effective is your leadership? How good are you at making decisions? Where do you focus most of your time and attention? Do your employees tend to be competitive or cooperative? Are there real teams functioning within the organization, or are they just nominal groups?

6. **Staff:** Refers to the staff levels and how people are hired, developed, trained, socialized, integrated, and ultimately how their careers are managed. Are you staffed to serve customers adequately? Will the addition or deletion of one or two staff members change anything? How do you train and mentor employees? Is your training methods effective? Are your staff members trained to do their jobs? Can you give them any other skills or resources to do their job better? What's holding them back from helping you grow your business? Are they "bought in" to seeing your business develop? What positions or specializations are represented within the team? What positions need to be filled? Are there gaps in required competencies?

7. **Skills:** Refers to the distinctive competencies of people within the organization. What skills have you been hiring for? What skills do you need? What skills will you need in 1 or 2 years from now? Does someone in your organization have those skills and are you grooming them for an important role in the next 1 or 2 years? What skills will you need to possess in two years that are different than the skills you possess today? What are the strongest skills represented within the team? Are there any skills gaps? What is the team known for doing well? Do the current employees have the ability to do the job? How are skills monitored and assessed?

An example of the 7-S model in action, for an improvement opportunity, would be if the department was misaligned resulting in poor performance.

We will act on some of the questions just described from the 7-S model in the next section of this lesson "Manage your Department to its Optimum in 10 steps."

Manage your Department to its Optimum in 10 steps

Managing a department that is successful in meeting its goals is the goal of every manager. You want a solid organization that knows the goals and runs like a well-oiled machine. Everyone should be on the same wavelength with the same unified vision and shared core values. By following the right steps, you can be sure you have covered every angle to achieve success in meeting the department's goals and objectives.

To begin with, you need to fully understand what is expected of you as manager. You need to know what products and/or services you are supporting, what the goals and objectives are of the company, and what the goals and objectives are of your department. Once all of that has been determined, you can start on creating a well organized, planned out, fully trained and controlled department.

Here are the 10 steps to plan and build your department to its optimum to meet the goals:

Step 1 - Determine your part in the company's goals and objectives
Step 2 - Absolutely know what's expected of you as manager
Step 3 - Fully know the company's products, services, and the systems used to support them
Step 4 - Establish goals and objectives for your department
Step 5 - Strategize, plan and structure to meet the objective
Step 6 - Get the right people you need to meet the objective
Step 7 - Get the right materials to get the job done right
Step 8 - Get your staff all of the training it needs
Step 9 - Organize it all to put the plan into effect
Step 10 - Monitor and control it all to keep it running smoothly

Each one of these 10 steps will be discussed in the following segments. There will also be examples used from the point of view of a customer service/technical support manager.

Step 1 – Determine your part in the company's goals and objectives.

A company needs to always think strategically and be focused on the future in order to succeed. Goals and objectives could be a new product or service the company wants to produce or provide, targeting the markets through research analysis that best suit the company's product line, raising capital based on financial projections through potential sales and earnings, or increase customer satisfaction through its operational strategies.

Once the plan is fully in place, the pieces of the puzzle need to be put together. Anytime a plan has been established, the information to the entire company usually flows something like this:

1. The company's goals and objectives will be filtered down to all department managers, most likely while in meetings with upper management.

2. Department managers will take their part of the plan and fully understand the goals and objectives.

3. A timeline to achieve these goals would need to be put into place.

4. The department manager will create the projects and tasks associated with the plan and clearly state the goals and objectives to their employees. Training is given and processes are created.

5. The project is monitored to ensure quality and maintain focus.

6. The manager reacts to any problem with the process as soon as possible.

7. Status reports and updates are given to upper management.

Sounds simple, but without careful planning it can get muddled, confusing, and unorganized. The most important aspect of the plan is to be able to clearly translate it throughout the company.

Once your managerial responsibilities of the plan have been determined, you must clearly translate the goals and objectives to your staff along with a timeframe. You need to tell them why the goals are important and what they mean to the company. There should never be a reason why your staff does not know the reasons and goals of each project that comes their way.

You need to develop processes and procedures that are easy to follow and make sure everyone is trained. It is up to you to direct them toward objectives, monitor their progress and react when necessary. You need to be able to show upper management the progress being made by reporting stats, survey results, and any other relevant data.

Remember, when dealing with upper management, "It is better to under promise, and over deliver." Most managers do the opposite. Always remember this simple phrase whenever you feel a project that comes your way is bigger than what it first appears to be.

Step 2 – Absolutely know what's expected of you as manager

You need to know exactly what it is upper management expects from you. If you have any doubt, chances are they are expecting something you might not be able to deliver. This is why the information flow as stated in step 1 is so important. What you should expect from yourself is to always think big. You are either in management, or inspiring to be in management, because deep down you know you can do the job.

One thing that is for certain, you are expected to create a strong team, inspire the team to perform well, clearly state the goals expected of the team, achieve those goals with proof from statistical data, and recognize and reward a job well done.

In order to achieve and even surpass expectations, you will always need a good solid plan that is well understood by all. You will need to figure out how to best develop, communicate, and train the processes and procedures associated with the plan. You need to make sure that there is no doubt from your staff regarding the goals at hand. These goals can vary from call center metrics such as customer satisfaction survey results, to a production line such as how many units need to be made per hour.

How you structure your department can determine whether or not you hit your goals. You need to make sure the setup and flow of the department works in efficiency and harmony. In order for the department to flow in harmony, you first need to make sure you and your team fully understands the company's systems, products and/or services.

Step 3 – Fully know the company's products, services, and the systems used to support them

You have to know the company's products. When you and your staff don't have a good grasp on the products or services your company provides, more mistakes, less confidence and wasted energy is inevitable. How can you expect your team to support a new product release or service offering when they are not even certain about the existing products and services that are being offered?

This not only pertains to the products and services, but the company's systems and tools used to track, troubleshoot, and enter pertinent data. Your job is to make sure everyone is 100% comfortable with the tools and systems they use as well as the products and services they are supporting. Make it a point to demystify everything that is involved within your department. You should also make it a point to personally know how to use or work on the products, tools, and systems as that of your staff. This way you will be able to better relate to any comments or suggestions they may have as well as give you more confidence.

When we talk about a product, we are talking about a tangible item that can be physically touched. When talking about a service, we are talking about an intangible action performed by someone or a service provided. For example, if you buy a car battery, you're buying a product. If you elect to have someone install the battery, that person is providing a service. There are many times when the product and service are combined from the customer's point of view. For example, the steak from a restaurant is considered a product, whereas the cook who cooks the steak and the waitress who then brings the steak to the customer is considered a service. Managers in these types of companies have both product and service to worry about.

There are important quality distinctions that must be made regarding products and services:

- A good *product* is an entity that meets all quality standards. Products that are flawed are considered of low quality. This is a problem for both the customer and the company employees who have to support the product.

- A good *service* is complete satisfaction from the customer's point of view with the quality of the company's help and action taken. Service that is bad is considered of low quality customer interaction. Bad service can also be related to numerous outages from service providing entities such as your electric or Internet service.

By fully knowing the company's systems, products and/or services, and how the quality can alter the customer's perception and the employees' morale, are detrimental to the success or failure of a manager.

Your staff also needs to be aware of the reason why the products they produce, or services they provide, goes beyond the marketplace so their customers will continue to be loyal.

Step 4 – Establish goals and objectives for your department

As manager, you need to determine how the goals and objectives for your department are set. These goals might be established through your boss, upper management, or might even be determined by you. In any case, the goals are most likely based on industry standards, or using the competition as a benchmark. No matter how the goals are set; you need to fully understand their meaning. You also have to be able to clearly communicate these goals with your staff.

Your employees need to firmly know what is expected of them. They should be able to quote these goals when asked, and have the meaning of these goals engrained into their memory. This way they will always have a unified focus on where they are now, and where they need to be headed. Goal setting encourages employees to put in substantial effort; because they know exactly what is expected of them. There is little room left for a lack of effort going unnoticed. Goal setting also provides direction and a sense of purpose. Goals are the motivating force to work harder. To make the goals worthwhile, there needs to be a reward of some sort, once the goal is achieved. We will discuss more about compensation and rewards in Lesson 3.

You should set up both long-term and short-term goals. The long-term goals capture the main objective. The short-term goals provide guidance on a day-to-day basis to meet that objective. An example of a long-term goal would be to improve customer satisfaction ratings from 80% to 95%. The short-term goals towards that increased customer satisfaction would be to address issues such as service outages, provide more technical training, focus on personal skills, or to develop a more standard format to increase efficiency. The short-term goals should always be related to the greater good of the long-term goal. If the long-term goal is measured in months, then the short-term goals should be achieved in just a few days, or a couple of weeks. Determining the timeframe of long-term and short-term goals can vary depending on the size or severity of the project.

Dealing with numbers is a necessary part of being a manager, and is the nature of business. Managers have to deal with schedules, production costs, service statistics, quality measures, and satisfaction results, just to name a few. Numbers should be an important part of the guiding principles in running your department, however, not the only driving force. You need to set targets and goals, but if you live by the numbers alone, you might lose the personal touch. Your employees will be more worried about their personal stats, rather than providing a pleasant customer experience. For example, if a company prides themselves on providing an exceptional customer experience, yet the employees are being judged with the amount of orders they took, not by the extra personal customer touch they gave, you are in for a conflict of interest. Besides, once they hit their quota, they may not be inspired to do any extra work.

It is a fine art to balance the metrics with a personal touch. For example, you need your customer service representatives to quickly answer the calls, provide the information, and get to the next call as soon as possible so that you do not have too many customers on hold (which is a measured metric). You might hit your numbers, but the customer felt rushed and did not have a pleasant customer experience. If, however, you gave too much attention to every call, then you would have longer hold times, thus aggravated customers who just wanted a quick and easy answer, thus poor customer satisfaction ratings because of long hold times. This is a typical catch-22 scenario that most managers have to face.

Structuring your department to its optimum plays a key role in these types of situations. The skills taught in this lesson and throughout this course will help you face these types of scenarios.

Here is a list of some typical goals and objectives that are common within a business that you might have to face as a manager:

- Improve customer satisfaction
- Reduce churn rate (customers who no longer use your service, product, etc)
- Prepare for a new product launch
- Improve project management
- Reduce attrition rate (employees leaving the company)
- Reduce product defects
- Reduce service outages
- Reduce hold times
- Reduce costs, and increase profits
- Coordinate efforts on acquiring another company
- Outsource specific projects
- Expand operations
- Improve product delivery time
- Improve order delivery time
- Implement new (or upgrade) your company's information systems such as an inventory database, trouble ticket database, testing software, or order processing system.

Step 5 – Strategize, plan and structure to meet the objective

A great plan comes from absolute attention to detail, which is key to setting up and structuring for success. Not only do you want to meet the general goal, but set up a specific standard. A *general* goal might be to answer calls quickly. A *specific* goal would be to answer all calls in an average of 30 seconds.

Before you start planning, you need to know the general and specific goals, the expectations, the type of products and/or services, what is coming down the pipeline, or the anticipated projects in the near future. Each situation calls for a different plan. Some plans are smaller and not as important, whereas some are major projects with utmost priority. You need to know which projects to start planning on first and be prepared for any surprises that may come your way. You will normally find out during your management meetings with your boss or upper management what is to be expected (which was covered in step 1).

Once determined, you start planning on how to accomplish the task at hand. You should first share this information with your key staff members like your supervisors, leads, and your subject matter experts (SME). You will most likely use a whiteboard to chart all the requirements. If there is any confidential information, use initials or codes that only you and key members of your staff understand. There may be just one big project that requires your full attention, or many smaller projects working concurrently. In most cases it is both. It is important that you prioritize the most crucial projects. You need to be able to make the right call.

You also need to create and stick to a realistic timeline. It needs to be challenging yet attainable. Map out the plan from start to finish with a description of each task and projected completed dates. Again, think about the saying, "Under promise and over deliver." What might look amazing to upper management at first could come back to haunt you when you miss your target date. Depending on the type of business, a simple spreadsheet will normally do. If it is a large and intense project, Microsoft Project Manager is a great tool to use.

Example – Simple timeline

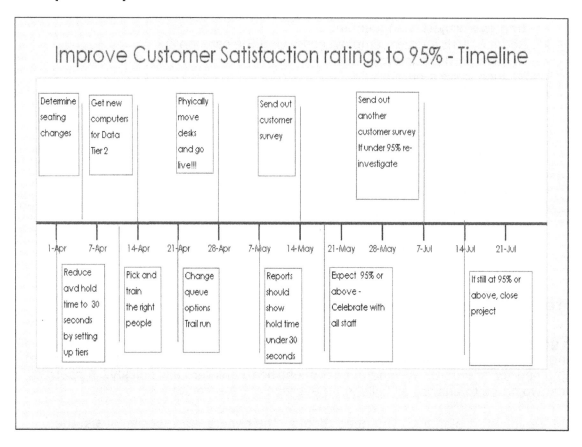

Whether you inherited the department by being promoted from within, or from another department or another company, the best time to plan and make major structural changes is within the first couple of months of becoming manager. However, be careful if you are following a manager who was very respected. Major changes might look like a slap in the face and your staff might resent you for it. It is much easier to make major changes when you follow a manager who was inefficient, even though it's harder to clean up the mess that was left behind.

Upper management is usually more lenient about certain expenses and disruption while you are making your mark in your first few months as manager. For example, you may want to re-organize the seating arrangement, request new computers, buy software upgrades, buy extra monitors, get better tools for the trade, get new uniforms, invest in advanced training, move to a new location, or even change the overall direction of the department. Once you are settled and things are running smoothly, it is harder to get the finances to make major improvements, even if it is within your budget.

Lets look at a scenario from a customer service/technical support point of view in a company that provides telephone and Internet service. Lets say you are a new manager who has taken over a department with poor customer satisfaction ratings due to long hold times that is also losing customers (known as "Churn") because of repeat issues and the time it takes to repair the problem. When you were hired by upper management, they let you know that your main objective was to improve customer satisfaction ratings and reduce churn. After discussing with upper management and comparing industry standards, your goal as manager is to obtain the following metrics:

- Calls are answered in an average of 30 seconds
- Abandon rate needs to be under 3%
- Repeat cases needs to be under 5%
- MTTR (Mean Time To Repair – which is the average time it took to open, troubleshoot and close the case) needs to be under 90 minutes
- Customer Satisfaction surveys of all customers polled within your department needs to be 95% or greater

To obtain these numbers you first need to look at the way your department is setup. You would need to figure out problems such as the number of staff needed, how long each call should last, find out the skills sets of your employees, find the right balance between quality and quantity, etc. You would also need to look at methods on how to make an effective and streamlined process to reduce call handle time.

The way the department is set up at the moment is one big group that takes on all calls, no matter the skill set or the nature of the reported problem. These calls can vary from regular telephone service repair calls to Internet access repair calls. These incoming calls can also vary from easy to fix repairs to intense troubleshooting repairs. Some people's strengths were more related to voice repair while others were more related to Internet data repair. Unfortunately for the customer, when they called into repair, they were getting bounced around quite a bit.

After careful analysis, the best plan might just be to restructure the department. To make the department run more efficiently, it makes more sense to split the group into two teams, one that deals with voice repair issues and another that deals with data repair issues. The next step would be to split those groups in two to have one team that answers the easy questions with short call handle times, and one that works on the harder and longer duration repairs. A supervisor would be appointed to each team as well as a lead technician or a SME (Subject Matter Expert, pronounced "Smee"). With a couple of programming changes to redirect the incoming call flow and some seating changes, the restructured plan would be complete.

Depending on the type of business you are in, many times it does helps to divide the department into a tiered structure. You can create a team within each tier and modify the goals of each tier to fit the overall goal of the department. You will need to determine both the *physical setup* (i.e. where your employees should sit and be grouped, etc) and the *logical setup* (i.e. the incoming call flow, etc).

Sometimes if you are lucky, one big group or an "all for one, one for all" strategy works, however, what usually happens is your better "A & B" employees spend half of their time with the simple issues or easy orders, while the "C" employees spend half of their time on difficult issues or the bigger/harder orders. You're A & B employees have a higher skill set and are your top performing employees.

Another incentive to create a tiered structure is to pay the more qualified people more money. This gives incentive for the Tier 1 people to want to learn more in order to be promoted into the Tier 2 group. This is a good idea as long as you have the money to do so in your budget.

Going back to the customer service example, what tends to happen is a call will be in queue (on hold in the order received), which tends to make the abandon rate increase (people do not like to be on hold...). This also increases the time it takes to repair a problem and also results in more repeat cases because the less qualified employees are potentially working on the hard issues. The end result would then be a dissatisfied customer who would give poor marks on their satisfaction survey. By breaking the department into a tiered structure, you would be able to set up the department like this:

1. Tier 1 answers all incoming calls. They have an easy to follow flow chart and would only answer questions that are easy in nature and do not take up too much time to explain. Even though they have a flow chart to follow the troubleshooting steps, you should make sure they have adequate training to have the confidence to troubleshoot the basics on their own. They have an average of 5 minutes per call to resolve the issue. If they cannot resolve the issue, they would pass the call to Tier 2.

2. Tier 2 takes over the call. All of the troubleshooting done by the Tier 1 technician will be noted in the trouble case. The Tier 2 technician would pick up from that point on, which will mean the customers would not have to repeat themselves. Tier 2 has an average of 1 hour per case, as the problem will most likely take some time to troubleshoot.

What would happen with this simple yet effective set up would help reduce time in queue, which would lower the abandon rate, which would also reduce MTTR along with a reduction of repeat cases, which would leave the customer more satisfied, which would result in fewer customers leaving the company. Higher customer satisfaction is achieved and the churn rate is reduced. All of the objectives and goals would be achieved with this restructuring move.

The goals for each tier would be different. You would not want to have a generic goal for both groups. The goals for Tier 1 would be based more on quantity, whereas the goals for Tier 2 would be based more on quality. That is not to say that Tier 1 shouldn't do quality work. It just means that Tier 1's main goal is to answer calls quickly and if they do not know the answer, pass the call to Tier 2. Tier 2 would also be expected to perform a certain quantity, but their main concern is more on reducing repeated issues and chronic type of problems. Something to keep in mind, you can always have one group help the other in times of need.

As part of the restructuring in this example, a knowledgebase could also be built so that Tier 2 can document the troubleshooting steps for certain problems. By utilizing the knowledgebase, technicians can cut down their troubleshooting time, thus reducing MTTR. Some of these troubleshooting steps can also be placed on a FAQ page on the company's website. Customers might be able to fix the problem themselves, thus reducing the amount of calls into Tier 1, thus reducing hold time even further, thus reducing abandon calls. This would reduce having to hire more staff to hit the goals, thus saving the company money, which makes upper management very happy.

Even though this example was based on a particular customer service scenario, the same logic could apply to any planning and structuring situations you might face.

Step 6 – Get the right people you need to meet the objective

It's pretty obvious that you need to have good people to do a good job. The tricky part is to have the right person for the right job. If you have been out on the floor getting to know your employees, knowing their strengths and weaknesses, trusting in your supervision staff on your top performers, and knowing who has the right attitude and aptitude, you should be able to find the right people for the job. If you have done your job correctly, you will have an inspired staff, full of knowledge, just waiting to show you their talents and strengths. You will also need to start off with hiring, and keeping, the right people, as well as keeping the good people you already have.

This section alone is a lesson or two within itself. We have dedicated much more information to this subject in lesson 3 regarding ideas on how to create, motivate, recognize, evaluate, and compensate your people, and Lesson 4, which is dedicated to hiring and retaining the right people.

Step 6 is probably the most important step in this lesson. It really is all about the people within your organization who truly make a difference. Your job as manager is so much easier when you're surrounded by nothing but the best people.

Step 7 – Get the right materials to get the job done right

You need to make sure your staff has all the tools it needs to get the job done right such as efficient equipment, materials, and supplies. Do things like making sure your staff has good working computers with plenty of disk space and memory. Nothing is worse than having a slow computer, especially while on the phone with a customer. Continually communicating with your staff is the key to finding out what they need to make things run more efficiently. Many managers assume everyone has what they need because they do not ask for anything. They might think it is too trivial or that they do not want to waste your time with small requests. Don't let this happen to you. Encourage your staff to look for any improvements that can make their lives a little easier.

Hopefully you have enough in your budget to adhere to the requests. Many times, items such as computers are part of Capex (capital expenditures) and should not necessarily come out of your budget (basic finance and creating a budget will be discussed in more detail in lesson 8). Insist from upper management that you need this equipment in order to achieve your objectives and goals. The software you choose is also of vital importance. Clumsy and hard to use programs like old DOS type of software is hard to use and takes extra time to find and enter information. You should also be able to show how the benefits outweigh the costs. Lesson 9 goes into detail regarding how to determine the cost-benefit analysis. Getting fast computers with easy to use software programs makes for easier training and efficiency improvements.

Step 8 – Get your staff all of the training it needs

Before anyone can do anything, they need to know how to do it. When surveying employees for what they would like and need, training is the most requested item, besides of course, more money. Everyone wants to be trained whether they are new and just starting, or are a seasoned pro who wants to get even better. Proper training and support for all levels of work produce better and more productive employees. You will find that the cost of training is met quickly with lower turnover and higher productivity. You should periodically ask each employee, while you make your rounds, on what training they would like to receive.

You want training done by experts who understands, and can clearly explain, the subject matter. This could be someone in your department or an outside resource. The point is to truly make the training count. It is a total waste of time if you train just for trainings sake. No one will get anything from it. It might not even apply to the real training need. Training needs to relate to what your employees do on the job.

Here are 20 training ideas that could pertain to your department:

1. Work with one of your most knowledgeable employees to develop a training process and procedure manual. You would want to document everything from beginning to end. Using customer service as an example, it would start off with how to answer a call and exactly what to say, how and what information should be documented into the order or ticketing system, how to look up all pricing and billing info, etc. This should be printed and put into a binder. You should also meet with your staff and go through the manual to make sure everyone fully understands the process, flow charts, etc. Whenever there are any major updates, make sure you modify the process. If it starts to become outdated, no one will use it when new products are released or procedures are modified.

2. Set up weekly training sessions for the supervisor or lead to go over training issues that popped up during the week with their staff. For example, people might be using the wrong codes, there is not enough documentation in the trouble case, orders are incorrect, etc.

3. Find online training programs such as technical schools that your staff can take. Put aside some time during the day or even pay overtime for after hours study at home.

4. Have a "Lunch and Learn." Provide lunch for the staff in a training or conference room, and train while they are eating. It's a win/win situation as the employee gets a free lunch and you get the opportunity to go over some training issues that does not interfere with their normal work schedule. This is also motivational and helps in team building. Make sure to clear this with HR to make sure there are no labor laws violated.

5. Find a webinar or workshop that specializes in the subject matter. It can be viewed either in house or at a yearly retreat type of event.

6. You might find someone who can benefit from some one-on-one mentoring. A gesture like this goes a long way not to mention builds morale and shows leadership.

7. Take the time to get with your staff to discuss the optimal training they would like to receive. What might look good to you is not really what they need or want to learn. Take a poll by having them list the top 5 training needs in a secret ballot due to some individuals might be too embarrassed to publicly state the training they need. Gather the information and find the main trend. If the majority requests the same training need, you can start setting up the training process right away. If there are a few different ideas, you can either set up a few different training sessions, or gather your staff together to discuss all possible options.

8. If it is within the budget, offer a company paid tuition to a local college. This is a huge motivational and retaining tool to use.

9. Try to relate the training to something they already know and are confident doing. It is easier to learn something new when you can relate it to what you already know.

10. Training should be as visual as possible with true hands on participation. They need to actually perform the tasks they are being taught.

11. Make sure your boss or upper management shows their excitement towards this training amongst your employees. This will generate more enthusiasm and determination.

12. Make sure they are motivated and want to learn. They should feel a sense of excitement about enhancing their career by becoming more knowledgeable. The more motivated they are, the more they will want to learn.

13. Keep the training area away from any office or factory related noise and commotion. They need to be 100% focused with no distractions. This also includes turning off cell phones and not checking e-mail from their laptops.

14. Make sure you take a quick break after each main subject. Each subject should be no more than 1 to 2 hours. Too much information all at once is too much to take in.

15. It is ok to do repetitive training if it is needed. The more your employees see, hear and do something, the better they will be able to remember it.

16. If anyone cannot make the training, ask one of the employees who took the training to train other employees with the information learned. This could be thought of as "train the trainer."

17. During the training seminar, make sure to discuss how the material being taught applies to real life scenarios. If there are good examples to use, this would be a great time to discuss.

18. If you cannot set up a training course or provide online training, you can always purchase business books for the employees. Ask them to read it during slow times at work or at home. You might even want to start up a book club to meet once a week so that the employees can discuss facts with one another.

19. Set up a buddy system. Pair up a seasoned knowledgeable employee with a less experienced employee. This would improve skills and build confidence. This also builds a strong work ethic, morale, and loyalty within the team. Just make sure the knowledgeable employee adheres to these rules:

    - Puts the less experienced employee at ease by not showing off and is humble with stories about when they first started out.

    - Asks what the person knows or does not know about the training subject. Nothing should be assumed, as the person might be afraid to ask any questions. Don't blind the person with science by using acronyms or terms they do not understand.

    - Covers the main objectives and goals including how their job relates to the big picture.

    - Motivates and creates excitement. This is a time for positive interaction, not negative opinion.

    - Clearly goes over the workflow both visually and in theory. Have the less experienced person repeat it back until fully understood.

    - Makes sure the less experienced person performs the tasks. The main goal is to fully understand the processes, procedures and expectations. Total quality is always imperative and is absolutely key to the persons and company's success.

    - Sets up a post meeting, and if necessary another training session, to make sure all is good.

20. Training is an ongoing commitment you need to make to your team. You need to always keep on top of any training needs. Always remember, "The more you train, the more they retain."

Step 9 – Organize it all to put the plan into effect

Now that you know your part in the company, know what is expected of you, know the products and/or services that pertain to your department, know the goals and objectives expected of your department, developed a plan to achieve those goals and objectives, picked the right people for the job, have the materials needed for optimal efficiency, and made sure they have been fully trained, it's time to organize it all and put the plan into effect. This is the time to make the physical moves, get the project underway, start the task, etc. It is imperative that everyone involved is fully aware of these moves, projects, and tasks and are fully prepared to make it happen.

It is a good idea to utilize programs such as Visio or spreadsheets to make visual representations of your structuring plan such as organizational charts, schedules, and seating assignments. Enterprise iPBX's are very beneficial for a call center phone system with incorporated reporting tools.

Using the same customer service example, it was decided that in order to achieve the goals, we first split the customer service technical support team into two sections: Voice Repair for telephone service, and Data Repair for Internet service. It was determined that you needed supervisors for each group and lead technicians to provide support for the technical support representatives. This was based on measuring call volume, time on the call, time it took to fix the problem, trending future call volume based on POS (point of sale, pronounced "paws") reports, determining the need for 24/7 coverage, and customer satisfaction results. Here are some visual examples of the restructuring plan:

Example - Org chart (short for organization chart) with a visually simple hierarchy. Microsoft Visio is great for creating an org chart and any type of flow chart. PowerPoint also has an org chart template you can use. This chart was made using an excel spreadsheet.

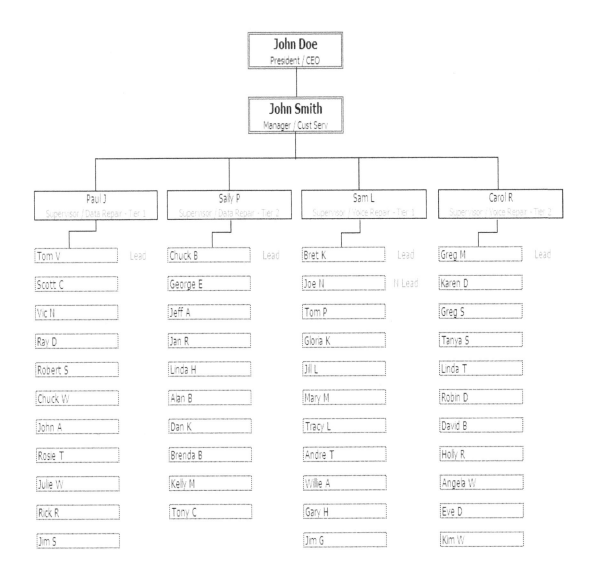

Total Headcount: Data Repair: 23 - Voice Repair: 24 - Manager: 1 - Total: 48

Example - Seating Chart with desk number, color code by group, first and last name, and phone extension. It was determined that by laying out the department in this fashion, a better group dynamic and teamwork would happen. Your staff can bounce ideas off of each other, and discuss unusual or difficult customer situations.

Legend					Manager's Office				
Manager									
Supervisor									
Lead									
Voice Tier II									
Voice Tier I									
Data Tier II									
Data Tier I									
Desk # 1	2	**3**	4	5		6	7	8	9	10
Printer	Fax	First Last Ext. 124	Training LAB	Training LAB		Training LAB	Training LAB	Vacant	Vacant	Printer
11 First Last Ext. 125	12 First Last Ext. 126	13 First Last Ext. 127	14 First Last Ext. 128	15 First Last Ext. 129		16 First Last Ext. 300	17 First Last Ext. 301	18 First Last Ext. 302	19 First Last Ext. 303	20 First Last Ext. 304
21 First Last Ext. 130	22 First Last Ext. 131	23 First Last Ext. 132	24 First Last Ext. 133	25 First Last Ext. 134		26 First Last Ext. 305	27 First Last Ext. 306	28 First Last Ext. 307	29 First Last Ext. 308	30 First Last Ext. 309
31 First Last Ext. 204	32 First Last Ext. 205	33 First Last Ext. 206	34 First Last Ext. 207	35 First Last Ext. 208		36 First Last Ext. 310	37 First Last Ext. 311	38 First Last Ext. 312	39 First Last Ext. 313	40 First Last Ext. 314
41 First Last Ext. 209	42 First Last Ext. 214	43 First Last Ext. 215	44 First Last Ext. 216	45 First Last Ext. 217		46 First Last Ext 400	47 First Last Ext 401	48 First Last Ext 402	49 First Last Ext 403	50 First Last Ext 404
51 Printer	52 Fax	53 First Last Ext. 218	54 First Last Ext. 219	55 First Last Ext. 220		56 First Last Ext 405	57 First Last Ext 406	58 First Last Ext 407	59 First Last Ext 408	60 First Last Ext 409

Example - Voice and Data Repair Schedules – These schedules are based on providing 24/7 service, however, with minimal after hours coverage. There are a couple of 4-10 hour shifts as well. The scheduling and break times were based on call volume throughout a 24-hour period. It is split into two repair sections, Voice Repair and Data Repair. There are great software tools you can use to create and modify scheduling and even import into you outlook calendar. This schedule was done on a simple spreadsheet.

Sample Corp Customer Service- Voice Repair	Days	Time	1st Brk	Lunch	2nd Brk
Sam L (Tier I Supervisor)	Mon-Fri	8:00-17:00		13:00	
Carol R (Tier II Supervisor)	Wed-Sun	7:00-16:00		12:00	
Tier I	**Days**	**Time**	**1st Brk**	**Lunch**	**2nd Brk**
Bret K (Lead)	Mon-Fri	7:00-16:00	9:00	11:00	14:00
Joe N (Night Lead)	Mon-Fri	1600-0030	6:00	8:00	10:00
Tom P	Sat-Wed	8:00-16:30	8:30	11:00	12:45
Gloria k	Mon-Fri	8:00-16:30	9:15	11:15	13:15
Jill L	Mon-Fri	8:00-16:30	10:45	13:00	15:00
Mary M	Mon-Fri	8:00-16:30	9:45	12:15	14:30
Tracy L	Mon-Fri	8:00-16:30	10:15	11:45	14:15
Andre T	Mon-Fri	10:30-19:00	12:00	14:00	15:45
Willie A	Mon-Fri	10:30-19:00	12:15	14:15	16:00
Gary H	Tue-Sat	21:30-6:00	23:15	1:30	3:30
Jim G	Sun-Thur	21:30-6:00	23:30	1:45	3:45
Tier II	**Days**	**Time**	**1st Brk**	**Lunch**	**2nd Brk**
Greg M (Tier II Lead)	Mon-Fri	8:00-17:00	10:00	13:00	15:30
Karen D	Wed-Sat	19:00-6:00	21:30	0:00	3:00
Greg S	Sat-Wed	6:00-14:30	8:00	11:00	13:00
Tanya S	Mon-Fri	8:00-16:30	10:00	12:30	14:30
Linda T	Sat-Wed	13:00-21:30	15:30	17:00	19:00
Robin D	Mon-Fri	6:00-14:30	8:15	11:30	13:15
David B	Sun-Tues	21:00-6:00	21:30	0:00	3:00
	Wed	21:00-6:00	21:15	1:00	3:15
Holly R	Tues-Fri	8:00-19:00	11:00	14:00	16:30
Angela W	Mon-Fri	20:00-04:30	22:00	0:30	2:30
Eve D	Mon-Fri	8:00-16:30	10:00	13:00	15:15
Kim W	Mon-Fri	8:00-16:30	10:15	12:30	15:00

Sample Corp Customer Service- Data Repair	Days	Time	1st Brk	Lunch	2nd Brk
Paul J (Tier I Supervisor)	Mon-Fri	8:00-17:00		13:00	
Sally P (Tier II Supervisor)	Wed-Sun	10:00-19:00		15:00	
Tier I	**Days**	**Time**	**1st Brk**	**Lunch**	**2nd Brk**
Tom V (Tier I Lead)	Mon-Fri	9:00-18:00	10:30	14:00	16:15
	Sat & Sun	8:30-17:00	10:00	12:00	14:00
Scott C	Tue & Thu-Fri	6:00-14:30	8:15	9:30	12:00
Vic N	Mon-Fri	8:00-16:30	9:45	11:45	14:45
Ray D	Sat-Wed	8:00-16:30	10:00	12:00	14:15
Robert S	Mon-Fri	7:00-15:30	8:45	10:30	13:15
Chuck W	Mon-Fri	8:00-16:30	10:15	12:30	14:15
John A	Mon-Fri	8:30-17:00	10:45	12:45	14:30
Rosie T	Mon-Fri	6:00-14:30	8:15	11:00	13:00
Julie W	Mon-Fri	8:30-17:00	10:30	13:00	15:00
Rick R (Swing Shift)	Tues-Fri	13:30-24:00	15:15	17:00	21:00
Jim S (Swing Shift)	Fri-Mon	13:00-24:00	15:00	16:30	21:15
Tier II	**Days**	**Time**	**1st Brk**	**Lunch**	**2nd Brk**
Chuck B (Tier II Lead)	Mon-Fri	8:00-17:00	10:15	13:00	15:45
George E (Graveyard)	Sun-Thu	23:00-08:00	10:30	13:00	15:45
Jeff A	Fri-Tue	9:00-18:00	10:45	14:00	16:00
Jan R	Mon-Fri	7:00-16:00	9:00	11:00	14:00
Linda H	Mon-Fri	8:00-17:00	10:00	12:00	15:00
Alan B	Mon-Fri	11:00-20:00	13:00	15:00	17:00
Dan K	Mon-Fri	7:00-16:00	9:30	11:00	14:15
Brenda B	Mon-Fri	7:00-16:00	8:45	10:30	13:45
Kelly M	Mon-Fri	9:00-18:00	11:00	13:00	16:00
Tony C (Graveyard)	Sat-Tue	0:00-11:00	2:30	6:00	8:15

Example - Full 24/7 coverage at a glance PST. A coverage chart is made to see how many techs are on the floor throughout the 24/7 period at any given time. The swing and graveyard techs are cross-trained in both Voice and Data. This will also help for holiday scheduling when staffing needs to be minimal but still covered.

	Monday	Tuesday	Wednesda	Thursday	Friday	Saturday	Sunday
6:00	4	5	5	4	4	4	4
6:30	4	5	5	4	4	4	4
7:00	8	10	10	9	9	5	4
7:30	8	10	10	9	9	5	4
8:00	22	25	25	22	22	8	7
8:30	24	28	27	25	25	9	8
9:00	27	31	29	27	28	10	9
9:30	27	31	29	27	28	10	9
10:00	27	32	30	28	29	10	9
10:30	28	33	31	29	30	10	9
11:00	29	34	33	31	32	11	10
11:30	29	34	33	31	32	11	10
12:00	29	34	33	31	32	11	10
12:30	29	34	33	31	32	11	10
13:00	29	34	33	31	32	11	10
13:30	29	34	33	31	32	11	10
14:00	29	34	33	31	32	11	10
14:30	26	30	30	29	30	8	7
15:00	25	29	28	27	28	7	6
15:30	24	27	26	25	26	6	6
16:00	23	25	24	23	25	7	7
16:30	12	13	12	13	15	4	4
17:00	7	7	7	7	9	3	3
17:30	7	7	7	7	9	3	3
18:00	4	4	5	5	6	2	2
18:30	4	4	5	5	6	2	2
19:00	4	3	4	3	4	2	3
19:30	3	2	3	2	3	2	3
20:00	4	3	4	3	4	2	3
20:30	4	3	4	3	4	2	3
21:00	5	4	5	4	4	2	4
21:30	5	5	6	5	5	3	5
22:00	6	6	7	6	6	3	5
22:30	6	7	7	6	5	3	5
23:00	5	6	6	5	4	3	5
23:30	4	5	5	5	4	3	4
0:00	4	5	4	4	3	2	3
4:30	3	4	3	3	2	2	3

Processes and Procedures are extremely important to develop to make sure everyone fully understands what is expected of them, and that everyone knows exactly the correct steps to follow. This also helps keep uniformity.

Example – Simple step-by-step order process

EXAMPLE WIDGET ORDER PROCESS

(Points to keep in mind with this example: Define a logical sequence of steps that are short and cover the important points. Write it as if you are talking to the individual who is going to use the procedure. Think of the reader's ability to ensure that all directions will be easily understood. Be sure to define unfamiliar terms and acronyms. Use hints and analogies whenever needed. Insert pictures, flowcharts, or illustrations if desired.)

This section covers the internal order process for a Widget from a Distributor:

1. Distributor calls Customer Care to order a Widget.

2. Customer Care will verify the account number and password.

3. Customer Care will enter the number of Widgets ordered into the company's database and give the Distributor a confirmation number. The order information must include:

   - Widget model number
   - Number of Widgets ordered

   *If an account hold has been placed (due to the Distributor is not in good standing), Care will inform that at this time they cannot place the order and that the company Controller will contact the Distributor to work out the details ASAP.

4. Once verified and confirmed eligible, Customer Care will process the order and change the queue in the database to Shipping.

5. Shipping will ship the Widget(s) to the Distributor. Once shipped, Shipping will update the database and change the dispatch action to Accounting.

6. Information is pulled from the database into the accounting books. Accounting will send an invoice to the Distributor.

7. Once payment has received, Accounting will close the order. *If payment has not been made within 30 days, Accounting will notify the Controller to contact the Distributor. ---End---

By deciding and planning correctly, your staff will understand what is expected of them and their place within the organization. Putting your head in the sand and hoping for the best will inevitably catch up to you. Always plan ahead. Here are some planning pointers to follow:

- Utilize your resources to their optimal performance. If you have a great plan and do not have the resources, then you need to back up that plan with documented reasoning on why you need more staff, equipment, seating area, etc. to upper management.

- Look at all the possible scenarios and make sure there are clear benefits to each decision.

- When in doubt map it out. That is what the white board is for and you should use it whenever possible. Visually looking at possible structure changes makes things so much easier.

- Hold daily meetings with your supervisors to make sure the plan will work as good in real life as it looks on paper. They will be the ones who will be in direct contact with the employees on a daily, if not hourly basis, and you want to make sure they are happy with the plan.

- Make sure you get your employees suggestions, as they are the ones in the trenches who really know which processes work and which don't.

Again, even though we are using customer service as an example of a department to manage, the same principles apply to most any management scenario.

Point to keep in mind: You always want to keep your boss informed before making any changes or implementing any plans. By giving well-documented processes, procedures, and laid out plans, you will look good as well as make your boss look good. Upper management expects this type of detail to achieve success from you, the manager.

Step 10 – Monitor and control it all to keep it running smoothly

Now that you have the department in order, everyone is trained and happy, and you have all of your processes and procedures in place, the best way to determine how things are going is through reports and feedback.

Continuous employee feedback and communication, statistical reporting, customer based surveys, feedback from suppliers, feedback from other departments that are closely involved with yours, sales performance, financial analysis, inventory control, monitoring order accuracy, and employee evaluations are just a few of the necessary tools to monitor how your department is performing.

There might be problems and unforeseen bumps in the road ahead such as a new product line or taking on additional responsibilities, however, with all of the planning and organization you have put into place, you will just need to do some slight modifications to keep it all running smoothly.

The following charts are just a few examples of the types of statistical reporting you can use as a guide for tracking goals and looking for trends. The screenshots that follow were pulled from spreadsheets. For simplicity, we are focusing on Data Repair from the customer service example (you would want to keep Voice Repair separate anyways as they have different metrics to report).

Example – Data Repair Dashboard. This is a snapshot of the current month, previous month, and 6-month trend covering all of the major area that need to be measured within Data Repair. This is the kind of quick status report you would bring to an upper management meeting. You want to easily be able to show whether you are hitting your goals, or if there are any noticeable trends. From this example you can see that the goals are being obtained by comparing not only the this months worth of data, but by also comparing it to last months and trending over the past 6 months. The top problem reported, which we are just generically calling Problem 1, represents 30% of all cases opened. This could be a serious problem and should be investigated. The data on this report is pulled from data within other areas on the same spreadsheet:

Sample Corp - Customer Service Technical Support - Data Repair

Tech Support call/e-mail Statistics	This month	Last month	Past 6 month's average	Daily average
Total Calls Received	4,682	4,890	5,380	256
Total support e-mails	636	597	644	31
Average time in Tier 1 queue (goal avg 30 seconds)	26	27	33	
Average time in Tier 2 queue (goal avg 5 minutes)	2:13	2:14	3:25	
Abandon call % Tier 1 queue (goal under 5%)	3%	4%	5%	
Abandon call % Tier 2 queue (goal under 5%)	4%	4%	5%	
Average Tier 1 call handle time (goal under 7 minutes)	6:22	5:16	5:59	
Average Tier 2 call handle time (goal under 20 minutes)	14:24	13:11	14:50	
MTTR (goal under 90 minutes - this example is one agent's EOM data)	49	68	54	
Ratio total contacts per widgets sold - current month	0.33	0.34	0.39	
Ratio total contacts per widgets sold - lifetime	0.02	0.02	0.03	
Top 10 Problems (this example is just one agent's EOM data)	%			
Problem 1	30%			
Problem 2	15%			
Problem 4	10%			
Problem 6	10%			
Problem 10	10%			
Problem 3	5%			
Problem 5	5%			
Problem 7	5%			
Problem 8	5%			
Problem 9	5%			

Example – Data Repair Stats. This screenshot comes from the same spreadsheet as described in the previous example. It shows the past 6 months worth of total calls, e-mails, ratio of total contacts per widget sold each month and lifetime, MTTR, abandon call %, average time in queue, and average call handle time in both the Tier 1 and Tier 2 queue's. The charts that follow are pulled from this data to quickly spot any trends:

Sample Corp - Data Repair Stats - 6 Month Trend

Month	Total # of calls	Total # of e-mails	Total # of contacts	Running monthly total of all contacts from Widget release date	Total Widgets sold this month	Ratio of contacts per Widgets sold - current month	Total Widgets sold from release date	Ratio of contacts per Widgets sold - lifetime	MTTR (Mean Time to Repair) goal under 90 minutes	Abandon % Tier 1 queue (goal under 5%)	Abandon % Tier 2 queue (goal under 5%)	Average time in Tier 1 Queue (goal avg 30 seconds)	Average time in Tier 2 Queue (goal avg 5 minutes)	Average Tier 1 team call handle time (goal under 7:00 minutes)	Average Tier 2 team call handle time (goal under 20:00 minutes)
1-Oct	6011	705	6716	74731	14934	0.45	165234	0.04	76	7%	6%	45	5:37	5:57	15:01
1-Nov	5687	698	6385	81116	15393	0.41	180627	0.04	35	6%	6%	38	5:35	6:16	15:10
1-Dec	5706	640	6346	87462	15497	0.41	196124	0.03	41	6%	5%	32	2:15	5:57	16:18
1-Jan	5306	585	5891	93353	15684	0.38	211808	0.03	57	5%	5%	30	2:41	6:08	14:58
1-Feb	4890	597	5487	98840	16135	0.34	227943	0.02	68	4%	4%	27	2:14	5:16	13:11
1-Mar	4682	636	5318	104158	16195	0.33	244138	0.02	49	3%	4%	26	2:13	6:22	14:24

Example line chart - calls and e-mails received. You can see from the chart below that trend line is showing that both calls and e-mails to Data Repair are decreasing. This can suggest a few things such as less repeat calls, better product stability, and customers troubleshooting more themselves through the posted FAQ's. This trend can help you determine whether total contacts in the past 6 months are increasing or decreasing. If you have your department structured to its optimum and yet calls are increasing, you might need to hire more technicians. This is the kind of data that would support that decision:

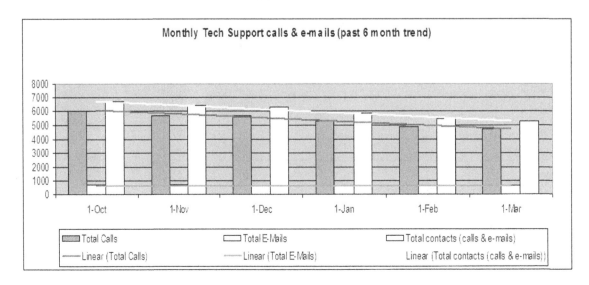

Example line chart – Ratio of contacts per Widgets sold – current month.
You can trend problems with the product based on the amount of calls and e-mails received versus the amount of sales. From this example, the amount of contacts per widget sold each month is trending downward, which is a good sign. This can also tell us that there might be less repeat calls, which would show that your support team is doing a good job on First Call Resolution's (you could determine if this was true by pulling repeated customer problem reports):

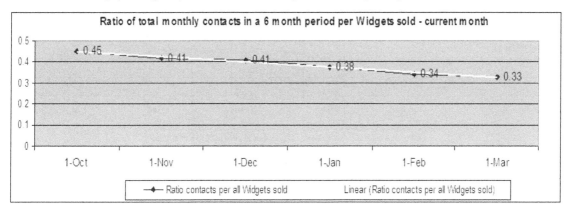

Example line chart – Ratio of contacts per Widgets sold - lifetime. This report follows the same format as the example just described, however, this is tracking data based on *all* of the Widgets sold lifetime:

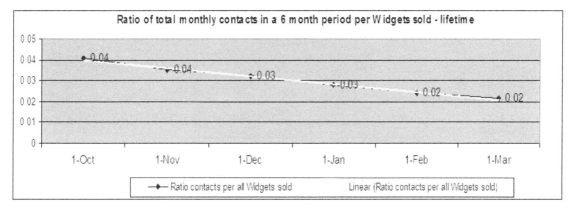

Example line chart – MTTR (Mean Time To Repair) – one agent. This chart shows the average time it takes to open and close a case. This particular example is based on the cases worked on the last day of the month by just one technician. You can trend agent performance in this type of format:

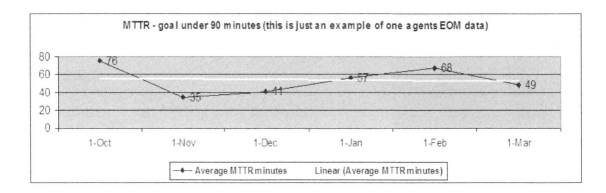

Example line chart – Abandon rate in the Data Repair Tier 1 queue. Part of increasing customer satisfaction is to reduce time in queue. When people hang up before an agent picks up the phone, satisfaction levels go down. In this case you can see that the goals have been met for the past 3 months, and that trending is showing the abandon call % is continually going down, which is a great thing:

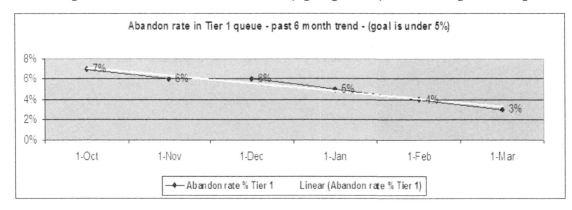

Example line chart – Average time in the Data Repair Tier 1 queue. This chart shows the average time in queue. Again, part of increasing customer satisfaction is to reduce time in queue. When people are on hold for a long time before an agent picks up the phone, satisfaction levels go down. In this case, you can see that the goals have been met for the past 3 months and that trending is showing the average time in queue is going down. Trending here also correlates to the previous example and proves that lower queue times results in lower abandon %'s:

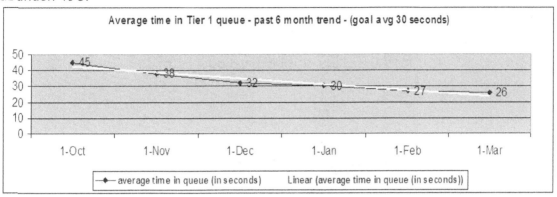

Example line chart – Average time spent on each call - Tier 1. Through analysis, it was determined that an average of 7 minutes per call was determined in order to keep the hold time at a sufficient level. In this case you can see that the goals have been met and that trending is showing the average time spent on calls is steady and looks good. One thing to keep in mind, never sacrifice a positive customer experience with trying to limit the time spent on calls. This is an average, and there will be some calls that will last 15 to 20 minutes, and some that are only 30 seconds long. This is a crucial fine balance:

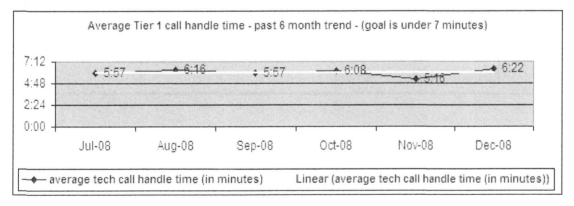

Example pie chart – Trending the most common problems found. This is an useful tool to find a common problem based on the proper use of codes in the ticketing system. With detailed analysis like this, you can investigate as to why and what is causing the problem. This kind of data helps engineers to find a root cause. Poor data would be stating, "It doesn't work." Good data would state something like, "Widget reboots when latest code is loaded." In this example, the generically named "Problem 1" contributes to 30% of all cases opened. That is one you would want to investigate as soon as possible:

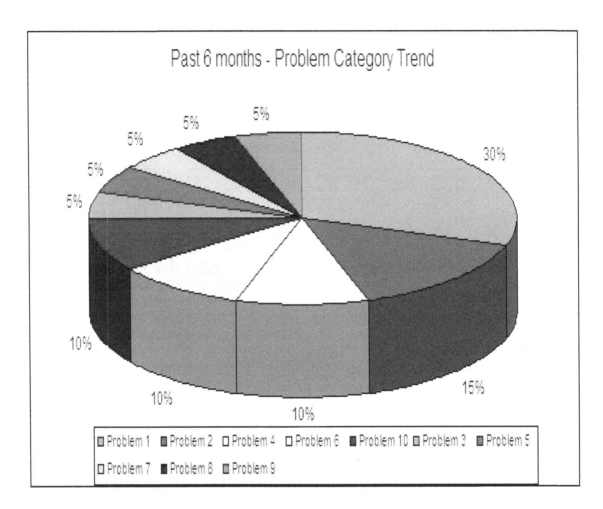

Example – Average hourly call volume in the past 6 months. This line chart shows the average amount of calls received hourly in a 24-hour period for the past 6 months. It starts at 12:00am and is used to track the busiest hours of the day in order to best determine when to staff and to strategically manage lunch and break times:

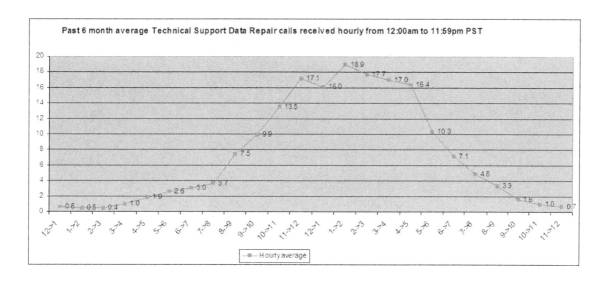

Example – Average hourly call volume <u>in each</u> of the past 6 months. This data is based on the previous chart but shows individual monthly detail on each of the past six months. With this data you can see if there are any particular monthly trends such as common peaks and drops:

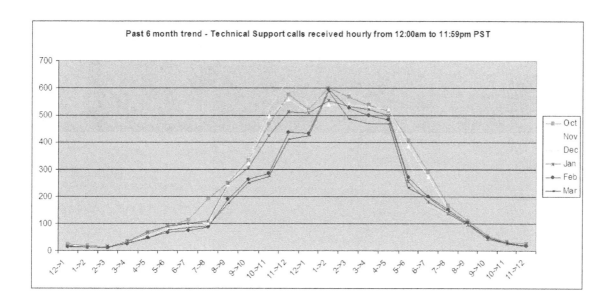

Example – Data Repair Customer Satisfaction Survey summary. Though customer surveys, you can determine the satisfaction levels and areas where you can improve. The goal of 95% or greater was achieved due to the planning and structural changes made by developing a tiered system. The screenshot below is from one of the last pages of the PowerPoint presentation:

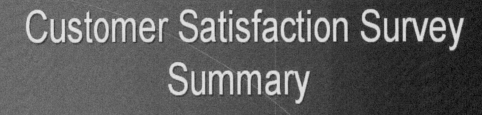

You need to have the right tools to measure productivity and process effectiveness. At a minimum, you need to know how to read, create and manipulate a spreadsheet, know how to create and present a PowerPoint presentation, and work with a Word Processing doc. Other great tools are Visio for creating flow charts, and Microsoft Project for large task related projects.

Being able to analyze the data not only helps you find trends, it also keeps upper management informed. They can either see the progress you are making or the problems you are having. Either way, they will appreciate the fact that they are not being kept in the dark.

If any problems arise when monitoring productivity, make sure you have created a systematic approach in finding the root cause and correct resolution. In order to do this, you need to have accurate data as previously presented. You would then set up a meeting with key players in your department, and if necessary, key players from other departments. The key point here is to make sure you have the accurate data to back up the issues at hand.

For example, if your team is getting inundated with calls due to a faulty product complaint, you need to have a system in place that tracks by problem report code, category, and resolution along with accurate documentation. This is needed to help spot the trend. With accurate data you can report something like "an 18% increase in customer complaints due to a power failure." This is much better than making a generic statement like, "Customers are complaining that the product doesn't work."

With this type of information, you can present the data with confidence to the other areas within the company. With this accurate data, they should be able to find the source of the issue. You need to be exact, precise, timely, and confident with the data you provide. Don't come off like you don't know what you are doing. You will not be taken seriously, the customers will continue to be upset, future sales will go down, and the department morale will decline due to the increase in work and complaints. All of this because of insufficient data.

Do not be afraid or intimidated to bring issues up to other department heads. This is expected of you. As the manager of your department it is your job to make sure everything is running smoothly, including issues that might be out of your control. At the same time you need to be careful that you do not look like you're on a witch-hunt to find the culprits. It's all about finding the perfect balance between being easy going and aggressive. You need to make sure that you, and the other departments involved, understand that this is for the greater good of the company's success. Your part is just to make sure it is clear you are doing everything you can to achieve the company's goals.

Utilizing all that has been taught in this lesson will help build your value and effectiveness as a manager. A department that is structured to achieve its goals is key to being a successful manager. Following through on your well thought out plans will show off your management and leadership skills, it will also earn you a great deal of respect.

A short story about structuring a department

John Smith is the manager of a customer service department that he had recently inherited. He provides support for Internet and telephone services. He has a staff of 50 employees who have different skill levels and technical expertise. His department seemed to be doing fine, however, customers were complaining of bad service. John made sure everyone was trained but the customers still kept on complaining. He thought he had his department in order but there were no true goals or objectives set, nor was there a good way to capture the data.

John realized that he needed to come up with a plan to improve customer service. He decided to dig deeper through departmental reports to see what was going on. Unfortunately the reports did not show much as the data was too generic and meaningless.

John met with key members of his staff to address the issues and map out a timeline to investigate and resolve the problems. John also made customer satisfaction a prime objective and made sure his staff fully understood the targeted goal of high satisfaction percentages. He delegated certain tasks such as updating and adding codes to the ticketing system. This was done to track the root cause of the problems. A customer satisfaction survey was also created and was sent out to each customer who recently dealt with customer service. John also tracked how long the calls were on hold, how long each call took, etc. Once the data was analyzed, he started finding trends.

What he found was that technicians who were more inclined to work a case quickly, had more repeats due to not fixing it right the first time. He also found that the technicians who took their time on a case, had less repeats, but longer customer hold times. He found that certain technicians had better skills at Internet related issues than telephone related issues. He found certain times of the day were much busier than others. Customer survey results showed the main complaints were long hold times and repeated trouble. He also found that more cases were opened in a certain area of the country than any other city. This was due to network issues that were captured through his new coding system.

Through all of this analysis, John was able to determine how to structure his department. He utilized his staff more efficiently by transferring them to the area that best suited their skills. He organized a tiered system so that Tier 1 addressed the quick and easy issues, and Tier 2 addressed the long and more difficult issues. He applied this system to both the Internet and telephone sides of the department. He made seating arrangements that put them into smaller groups associated with the tiers. He scheduled his techs accordingly to cover the busiest times of the day. He also worked with engineering to investigate network related problems. Engineering was able to find the problem due to the accurate data they received.

All of these changes directly improved hold times and repeated issues. Customer satisfaction results went way up due to hold times and repeated problems going way down. This also improved employee morale. John made sure from this point on to always look for trends and structure his department based on a plan, not just because it seemed right.

Epilogue: A solid plan to obtain the goals and objectives is mandatory. You can then decide how to set your department based on the results of that plan. John was able to hit all goals and achieve high customer satisfaction ratings by structuring his department to its optimal performance with little additional resources. Most of what was covered in this story relates to the examples used in this lesson.

Quick Lesson Summary

- You need a solid plan and the methods needed to succeed to obtain the goals and objectives.

- You need to make sure both you and your employees fully understand the mission, goals, company products, what is expected of them, and what is expected of you.

- Carefully analyze all aspects within your department before making any changes. Get with key members of your staff and discuss all options.

- You need to get the right people to do the right job. You might need to reassign them for optimal performance.

- You need to set up a timeline whenever a major project, task, or structuring takes place. The short-term plans must coincide with the long-term objective.

- You need to provide the right materials and training. A lack of materials and training will result in a lack of efficiency.

- You need to know how to use programs such as spreadsheets to monitor your department's performance and correct issues as they arise.

LESSON 3 - HOW TO MANAGE YOUR EMPLOYEES & BUILD A STRONG TEAM

Introduction: Get the most out of your employees including working as a team

The definition of a team is a group of individuals who clearly know what is expected of them both individually and as a whole. They know the objectives and have a common goal while working interdependently. To have the best team, however, you also need to get the most out of the individuals. You can get the most out of your employees by learning how to best manage them. Once you get the most out of each individual, a strong team will start to develop with respect and purpose. You do this by giving them clear expectations, motivating them to hit those goals, recognizing the good work done, evaluate their performance and if they did a good job, rewarding them with a merit increase or other meaningful awards.

Great managers need to make people function in a collaborative fashion. This can be quite a challenge when you have so many different personalities to manage. You need to mold them to think as a team, and motivate them to exceed the level of performance they normally would under another manager who's not of your caliber (after all, the skills you are developing will separate you from the rest). Your employees will recognize your managerial and leadership capabilities and you will be respected.

In this lesson we will give you the necessary tools to build strong and motivated individuals, who will in turn work as a great team. Putting these tools into effect will not only benefit your department, but also the company as a whole.

Shape the individual and build the team in 5 steps

By following these 5 steps, you will be on the right path to building a strong team. You will get the most out of your staff and also develop a strong spirited department:

1. Create and Develop a strong team with solid expectations
2. Motivate Professionally and with respect
3. Recognize and Praise great work
4. Evaluate and Appraise employee performance
5. Compensate and Reward a job well done

These 5 steps will be discussed in much greater detail throughout this lesson. The goal is to build the best team possible so you, your staff, and the company succeeds. To have your employees performing to the best of their abilities, they must know:

- Exactly what is expected of them (Creating and Developing)
- Exactly what it is they will be doing (Creating and Developing)
- That they will be trained (Creating and Developing)
- That they will have the right tools (Creating and Developing)
- That teamwork is essential to success (Creating and Developing)
- That high morale is key (Motivating Professionally)
- That they will work in a great environment (Motivating Professionally)
- That they will be continually challenged (Motivating Professionally)
- That they will be noticed when they have done good work (Recognizing and Praising)
- That there will be affirmation of good work (Recognizing and Praising)
- That they will take full responsibility for their work (Evaluating and Appraising)
- That their performance will be reviewed (Evaluating and Appraising)
- That there will be rewards and gifts given for exceptional work (Compensating and Rewarding)
- That there will be monetary incentives for a job well done (Compensating and Rewarding)

Step 1 - Create and Develop a strong team with solid expectations

You need to create a team atmosphere within your department with a sense of mission. You need to share your vision of what the company can be, so they have a common purpose. To get a group of individuals to think as one positive team, they also have to see you as a positive, good spirited and motivated hard worker.

Here are 19 ways to help create and develop a strong team with solid expectations:

1. **Make sure the team is set and ready to go.** You need to first make sure you have planned, organized, and structured your department to its maximum potential. We talked at length about organizing and structuring in Lesson 2. Once structured, you will most likely have sub-team goals such as that of a Tier 1 and Tier 2 group. In most cases you will have at least one team lead or SME. This person must have the people skills in order to handle any individual issues in their group. Even though a person might be technically inclined, they may not know how to deal with the everyday people issues that are commonplace in the work environment. The ideal is to have a technically competent person who is also a people orientated team lead. The point here is to have someone in the group, or in the sub-teams, who can help build teamwork by being there to help their team address the everyday type of issues. This person might just be you if the department is not very big. If you do have your department structured in a way that has sub-teams, make sure everyone within the whole department understands the goal of being part of one big team.

2. **Start off with a fresh approach**. Are you a new manager with old staff? Old, meaning they are settled in their bad habits. When trying to create a team, you need to start with a fresh approach and positive attitude. You might be asked to rescue a dying department. If so, if you cannot make the old staff see the new light, you might need to clean up shop. This also goes

for employees with bad attitudes who are unwilling to change. A few changes like these can turn around a department's performance and morale almost overnight. All it takes is a few bad apples to spoil the lot. You do have to first try to rectify the situation before making any drastic decisions. Lesson 5 goes into detail on how to deal with difficult employees. However, if you have done all you could, you sometimes have to make the difficult, but needed decisions. It's important to make your mark right from the start. People want a manager who will bring in a new and fresh approach to an old and stale department. If there are no problems, then leave it alone. That's a fresh approach in itself; not changing for changing's sake.

3. **Create a one or two paragraph mission statement.** This should be sent out and posted on the wall and should contain the company's and departments values. When we say mission statement, we are not talking about some corny poster on the wall that no one reads. This is what you want the department to be known for, and what you want engraved into the minds of every employee. The department's goals and mission must have meaning for your employees. They should be involved in creating the mission with simple declarative sentences. The mission statement should come across, as making it seem like their job is truly important to the success of the company. Make them feel connected to the company rather than just a place to pick up a paycheck. The goal is to make them feel like they "fit in" and is a good part of their life. The best words you can ever hear from someone is, "I like this company so much that I plan on working here until I retire." Here are a couple of ideas to use depending on the type of company you work for:

- If your company provides a service that is making a positive contribution to the community, then you should promote something like, "Our contribution to the greater good makes the world a better place."

- If your company provides a service that is making a positive customer experience, then add something like, "Our every action can lift the customers spirits and soul."

- If your company provides a value towards customer service, then you can add something like, "Providing world class service will set us apart from the rest of the competition." You might want to add something like, "We will win the customer over by going the extra mile."

Try to consider things like:

- What is the value of the company that the customers pay for?

- What is the competitive advantage?

- What kind of quality is expected?

At the end of the day it's all about profitability, however, with stringent control and practicing ethical practices. In other words, you do not want to make a statement such as, "Do whatever it takes to make the sale."

The mission statement should be short and general, yet has a powerful punch. You might want to throw in some team guidelines, or "Norms," on team interaction as well. It is also important to regularly review the goals with your staff associated with the mission.

Actually make it a point to test the mission statement. Make sure people perceive the way you're leading and managing the organization as being consistent with the mission statement itself.

This statement might even be used as part of a marketing campaign or posted on the company's web site, so make it good.

4. **Periodically walk around the department.** Take the time to sit down with your employees in their environment. Have a small impromptu meeting with one individual or a couple of people every once in a while. Bring a notebook with you and clearly show that you are documenting some good ideas, requests, issues, etc. If it's not something you can answer or resolve at that very moment, tell them you will look into these suggestions and comments and follow up as soon as possible. They will be surprised that you truly listened and followed up even if you could not fulfill the request or idea. They will know you tried and you will earn their respect.

5. **Periodically hold team meetings**. For example, hold weekly meetings to go over the goals and share the direction in which the team is heading. Go over items such as performance based stats, sales, customer compliments (and complaints...), needed materials, training requests, and any other pertinent information. Also announce upcoming events such as new projects, new products, visiting VIP's, or structure changes. You want to always keep your team well informed and not left in the dark. This is also a good chance to gain ideas for improvement, and if needed, how to ease any tension in the group. Make sure to set up the meetings in your Outlook calendar to re-occur for at least 6 months. You can update each meeting request with an agenda with items you would like to discuss. Also make sure you have all of the needed paperwork to pass out to the team, or show in a PowerPoint presentation. This will show you are serious about your expectations. See Lesson 7 for more advice on holding effective meetings and giving presentations.

6. **Make sure everyone is fully trained and has what they need**. Although training was already mentioned in Lesson 2, it is worth mentioning again. Always be aware of any training the team needs to accomplish the goals at hand. They also need the right materials to do the job to its optimum.

7. **Teach them how to work as a team**. Talk to your employees about how important it is that there is support amongst team members with respect for one another. Team members need to rely on other team members to accomplish the work or the goals of the team, which is the basic principle of team spirit. They will listen to you as you are their manager and more importantly, especially in this aspect, their leader.

8. **Show how the goals of the team tie into the organizational goals**. Explain to the team why their part in obtaining the departmental goals are also part of the big picture within the company's goals. When they perform to or above standards, the company is more likely to succeed. Keep in mind that even though you do not want your department to be the weakest link within the departmental chain, you should still want to see other departments succeed. You will have a solid company in which to work, and a very happy upper management team. This should be stressed to the team as well.

9. **Make their opinions count and always follow up**. If someone brings a training idea, talks to you about furthering their career, or confines in you about how some improvements can be made, make sure you follow up on everything that has been brought to your attention. If you can provide what was requested, you will not only build that persons morale, but it will inevitably get around the department that someone approached you with and idea and you followed up. People like being taken seriously and if an idea is implemented, a strong sense of pride happens which can be contagious amongst other team members. Stress that you want your team to be innovative and that you're always willing to do whatever it takes to improve any process, procedure, or make any functional improvements. Even if you cannot accommodate the request, or it is something they do not want to hear, at least they know you listened and took them seriously. Just make sure you always follow up with the reason why.

10. **Support the differing strengths of your teammates**. Allow each person to bring their unique qualities to the table. There can be some new and innovative techniques and processes that can lead to doing things in new and different ways.

11. **Sometimes let the team decide**. Encourage the team to come up with improvements to existing processes, ideas on troubleshooting, equipment they need, etc. If you build the right type of team, you can trust what is presented to you, and you can give it your blessing. This is a great motivational tool as well.

12. **Make sure your team members are not afraid to speak up.** If no one speaks up or contributes anything during a meeting, there are potential ideas that will not be shared, or even worse, there may be problems that are not identified. You want any ideas or concerns to be dealt with right then and there. Make sure you stress that you want people to share even if they might create some waves. You also want to make the timid people feel comfortable to participate. Let them know that their contribution to the team is just as important as anyone else's opinions.

13. **Make sure everyone understands what is expected.** Just saying we need to work as a team and leave it at that does very little and sounds like a corny cliché. You need to give clear details of the expected goals, and potential consequences if the goals are not achieved. Clearly defined roles and responsibilities for each team member is key.

14. **Demand the needed attention to detail.** Express the importance to become a world-class organization by striving for perfection. Make sure to

stress the importance to "dot every I and cross every T."   Inspire the team to make it their goal to treat each situation they find themselves in with absolute professionalism. Customers and upper management knows the difference between good and great, or even great and brilliant performance. Strive for brilliance in making sure every possible detail is given full attention. You have to be excessively meticulous or else the flaws will become acceptable. Once your team knows the attention to detail that is expected, you will see excellent results. The higher quality the team, the better the teamwork.

15. **Stress that the customer is right, no matter how wrong they are...** When you are creating your team, you need to make sure they understand this simple core value. Always tell your staff, and yourself, that without the customer there is no company, thus no paycheck. You do not have to be quite so dramatic, but this is basically the truth. Teams work a bit harder and are a little more patient when they remember this fact.

16. **Try to curb any negativity about customers or other departments.** It's so easy to complain, criticize, and always find faults in customers or people in other departments. A prime example is how customer service is always bashing a salesperson. Even if it's justified, you as manager do not want to add fuel to the fire. You can always have a lighthearted thing to say like "Sales sure seems to pass the buck," but follow it up with something like, "but we need sales to sell or else they will not bring income into the company." Then follow up with letting the team know that if it gets too out of hand, you will meet with the salespersons manager (and you should truly have a brief discussion with the sales manager). Your staff might have a common grief about a customer or company employee, but watch it closely and don't let it get out of hand.

17. **They should act as if a camera is filming them.** Have them pretend that a camera is filming their actions when working. They will find themselves treating the customer like gold or precisely producing a product. This little tip will always keep them in check (try it sometime...).

18. **They should act like they are Ambassadors for the company**. If an employee and team feel like they truly represent the company in their actions, words, and attitude, they should feel like ambassadors to the company. The team will feel their contribution to the company means something. As ambassadors, they should feel like a true part of the success in the growth of the company.

19. **Team Building is not a one-time activity.** Be prepared to continually work on improvements, ideas, functions, etc. Just calling a group of people a team does not necessarily mean they are working in harmony as a team. This should be looked at as a continuous ongoing project.

Points to keep in mind:

- **Strong teams do not need to be micromanaged**. Even though micromanaging was mentioned in lesson 1, it is worth mentioning again.

- **Make sure you know what they know.** Just saying "do it" without knowing what needs to be done is a morale killer that will destroy teamwork. You should be able to do the basics of each individual's job in your department whether it is answering a phone, taking an order, making a product, or technically supporting a customer. Besides, your confidence level will also rise if you understand the work being done by your team.

- **Balance is key.** You want your team to be happy, but at the same time not acting goofy. You want them to be serious, but at the same time not stressed. You want them to communicate openly, but at the same time not always complaining. You want them to be easy going, but at the same time not flaky. You want them to be communicative, but at the same time not so much of a social butterfly. You want them to be independent, but not disrespectful. Always make sure there is balance in the air and be prepared to counter-balance as soon as possible.

- **Project teams within a team.** This is a temporary team used for a specific reason. For example, you might need to have some of your testing software updated. This would not need the whole teams participation, but it is too big of a task to delegate to just one or two individuals. In this case you would pick a small team whose task would be to work together on the project until the mission is complete. Be sure to communicate exactly what is expected and in what timeframe.

Step 2 - Motivate professionally and with respect

To motivate you need to be positive, honest, encouraging and direct. To be honest, motivation starts at home. If you are truly motivated, it is easier to spread that enthusiasm to others. Share your vision and mission with confidence. Your attitude, the way you handle yourself around others, and the way you talk to each individual will subconsciously build morale. Do not come to work stressed out and miserable, and yet expect your department to be happy and enthusiastic.

Some people work hard and do good work for pay and recognition. It is your job to give them monetary increases and praise a job well done. Some are lazy and do bad work, yet still expect to get paid. It is your job to get them motivated and show where they need improvement.

Motivating a team uses a "one for all and all for one" approach. Motivating an individual is more of a one-on-one approach to get your point across and to inspire. The people you are trying to motivate must be truly motivated themselves. They are motivated in different ways:

- By the actual work they perform
- Their pay
- The work environment
- A helpful manager when needed
- Not micromanaged when all is under control

Whatever you do, don't patronize your staff with silly gimmicks such as balloons, bells, and whistles for ordinary work done. This just makes it look like you are treating them like children in a kindergarten class. Motivate professionally with maturity and respect.

Although monetary increases, rewards, praise and recognition are big motivators, we will first look at 23 other ways in which to motivate professionally and with respect:

1. **Be a solid leader.** Be the person who can make decisions, solve problems, has an open door policy, knows how to delegate, and provides regular feedback. People are motivated when they trust their leader.

2. **Give clear instructions.** A person and team are more motivated to do a good job when they know exactly what is expected of them. No one likes to be given daily tasks or a project with little to no direction. People are more motivated when they know the exact goals to reach, both individually and as a team.

3. **Show how much you value everyone in your department.** This especially holds true for the good workers. Quite often you should take them aside and truly communicate to them your appreciation. When they know you know how hard they work and how valuable they are, it makes them feel great and continue to be motivated. A simple pat on the back, shake of the hand, or a simple thank you goes a long way, much more than you would know. It is so simple to say kind and encouraging words. This simple people skill will get you more than just about any other motivational technique.

4. **Help people grow.** Always try to help people grow their skills and develop their careers through training, providing opportunities, and spreading the word through upper management. This will make you be the person people want to work for and be in your department. When employees feel they are learning and growing, they work harder and more efficiently. Don't let them become board and stagnant or else they will become sluggish, both personally and professionally. Challenge and empower your employees with tasks, projects, and assignments. You will both win. Coaching and mentoring your employees by focusing on the needed strengths for them to learn and grow is one of the best things you can do as manager and leader. Build their confidence when they are unsure about themselves, bring them out of their shell when they are shy, and help with reporting and process skills when they are not program experts. By helping your employees learn and grow, you will have more people in which you can delegate tasks. This in turn gives you more time to focus on other aspects of improving your department, which is a win/win situation.

5. **Encourage your employees to recognize each other for great work.** Whenever a co-employee does great work, goes the extra effort by helping out one another, or inspiring extra teamwork, try to get them to pat each other on the back. When employees respect and help one another, you have a highly motivated department. There are reward programs like "power points" that you can set up for just this type of scenario. Rewarding ideas will be covered later in this lesson.

6. **Motivate by building their confidence.** This should be done both individually and as a team. When people feel good about themselves, they work better as a team. They need to clearly understand the big picture and believe that working as a team produces better results. This will get the slower performers working faster, and the faster performers continuing to work hard.

7. **Motivate the already confident by listening and discussing triumphs.** The more you show these "self starter" type of employees that you really care about their expert skills, the more they will be motivated to keep you impressed. You would also really try to make sure you get these employees whatever they request. For example, if they ask for a software package, get it for them without asking too many questions. You want to especially build respect with these key employees.

8. **Show the team you truly care.** Showing concern and understanding for your employees are signs of management strength, not weakness. Let them feed off of your positive and caring approach. Strong leaders show they care by getting the team what they need to succeed, even if they have to work across department lines. Ask about their interests, family, hobbies, and genuinely be curious about their lives. Know the little things like how their kids did in the game. You can do this in a group atmosphere as well. Many employees who feel you are uncaring or unfair are more willing to cheat on their expected workload and think they can get away with it. They will feel like they are just a number so why should it matter what they do. So make sure you are there for them and show that you care. This really helps build harmony and teamwork and thus more productivity.

9. **Stress their importance to the company.** Let them know that what they do is a vital part of the company's success. Even an operator who just answers a phone is vital as they are the first customer touch point. If the operator comes across as a positive happy person, the tone will then be set to the person who receives the transferred call. Another example would be a support technician who not only fixed the problem, but also asked if there is anything else they can do and go the extra mile. This can result in future sales just based on the support the customer received.

10. **Create more interesting and admirable job titles.** For example, add the word "Specialist" after a normal mundane title. "Technical Support Specialist" sounds a little more important than "Technical Support Representative," yet has the same job responsibility. This also looks better in the customer's eyes. Some employees might find this a bit suspect. They will think a better title with no monetary increase is a bit dubious. It is up to you to judge whether or not this idea would work for your department. This should also be considered when writing a job description as described in lesson 4.

11. **Do not rule by intimidation.** Only short-term gain is usually achieved with this approach and a higher rate of attrition usually occurs. It is good for a little healthy fear associated with the natural approach to hierarchy and respect for the position, but that is as far as it should go. Intimidation is a morale killer.

12. **Don't raise your voice.** Show people their errors and mistakes in a calm and professional way, even if you want to scream. Calmly show them how to do it right. Morale goes down when your temper goes up. A sergeant in the army has a need to yell, as it could be a matter of life and death. A manager of a business department luckily does not have that responsibility.

13. **Don't penalize them for doing their best.** If you do not hit a goal or complete a task, don't take it out on your staff. It is your job to set a truly achievable goal, provide the right training and materials, and hire the right people. If they are doing their best but their best is not good enough, you need to re-evaluate how to achieve the goals or complete the tasks. See lesson 2 for ways to set up your department to its optimal.

14. **Focus on their strengths and try to work around their weaknesses.** There will be times when a person is better suited in another position or other duties. That is not to say that they should be rewarded for poor performance, it is more about working with what you got. Many times you will have inherited someone who has some sharp skills but are not happy in their work. For some reason, although they are sharp, they are just not getting the job at hand. You may have tried to get them trained, talked to them about the need to improve their performance and/or attitude, and you still have someone who is not performing up to speed. You can go through the discipline and firing processes as described in lesson 5, but if there is a chance to truly utilize this person, do all you can to keep them. You might first need to post the job for others to apply before you can move this person into the other position. That might be up to HR. If it works out and you keep this person after you moved them to another position, you would want to talk to them about your high expectations. This could really be a win/win situation for both of you.

15. **Really, really motivate your favorites.** This goes against conventional "all for one" thinking but lets face it, you want to keep the employees who enjoy doing the difficult tasks, who never complain about the work given, work after hours to complete the task, and is willing to do what it takes to make the company succeed, fully motivated with extra perks and pats on the back. Try hard to accommodate any of their requests. These are the people who can help you, help the rest of the team, to understand what is going on.

16. **Continually train and keep your department up to speed.** Whenever there is something new on the horizon such as a product launch, software release, or any new projects ahead, make sure you train them to fully understand the new entity. It is really important to make sure the supervisors of the department are always involved in the latest training opportunities. This is where daily meetings come into play as discussed in lesson 7. It is important to show the department that you want to make sure they have all the training they need. They might also have some training ideas or requests. This is one thing that can really earn you a great deal of respect, and show great leadership skills. Constant training builds and motivates both the team, and individual.

17. **Make the environment for the employees as nice as possible.** The environment in which your employees are expected to work should be clean and ethically pleasing. You should also make sure they have all the materials

they need, no matter how trivial, to perform to their optimum level. An unorganized department, dirty bathrooms, or not having basic supplies are fairly easy to amend and at little cost. If possible, get the best chairs and replace the old broken equipment. These small changes can enhance employee morale, and improve productivity. Give them what they need to produce, and they will produce. Even a $5.00 item can make a big difference to someone. Try not to nickel and dime everything unless absolutely necessary. Also, make sure that your team knows and sees that you are doing everything you can to improve their working environment. Even if you are unsuccessful, they will appreciate the fact that you tried. Just make sure you don't have the attitude of "this is what you get, so get use to it."

18. **Motivate the good workers by disciplining the bad.** Another way to keep the good workers motivated is to discipline the bad workers when it is truly time to do so. Putting your head in the sand when there are problem employees is a de-motivator for the good workers. You also want the poor performing people to feel a little uncomfortable so that they know they need to improve.

19. **Make your positive attitude seen.** Make it a point to at least once or twice a day, depending on the size of the department you manage, to walk around the department and say hello with a positive, feel good smile on your face. Ask how things are going or if there is anything you can do for them. Even asking them if they would like a Coke or something trivial like that helps build morale. You also want to really motivate your supervisor staff. They are your front line to all complaints and getting your point across in a daily if not hourly fashion to the team. They are the ones in the trenches with the rest of the department. This is why it is so important to meet daily, or at the least weekly, with your supervisors. In meetings, you are sharing the goals and discussing improvements all the while motivating due to the time you give each day. There will be more information regarding meetings in lesson 7.

20. **Don't let them burn out.** When you start seeing that the challenge is getting to be too much, people feel more like a number than part of the company family, are easily disappointed, stressed over changes, too much anxiety trying to obtain the goals, or just basically losing interest, you need to remedy the situation as soon as possible. Provide a bright outlook for the future, listen to their worries and concerns, let them know you care, let them know how valuable they are, provide more interesting yet related training, and rejuvenate by reducing the de-moralizing tasks and increasing the interesting work. Signs of burn out can lead to employee resignation.

21. **Have some fun.** Depending on the type of department you have, certain external team building events like bowling, paint ball, golfing, and picnics are a good idea at least one time a year. You can also have some internal fun such as a pizza lunch, have a potluck lunch, or a jersey day in which you wear your favorite teams jersey. Some people are not into after work activities, and that's fine, as long as it's a majority decision.

22. **Buy Cokes, donuts, bagels, pizza, etc for the team periodically.** For a few bucks, you will have happier employees. You may be able to expense this as well for morale purposes. Even while you are walking around the department, just ask if you can get them anything such as a bottle of cold

water. Write down the order on a notepad and maybe ask one of your supervisors to help personally pass them out. These little gestures go a long way. Don't make it a corny event, just a nice simple gesture.

23. **The Management team cooks a barbeque for all the staff**. This is both motivational and rewarding for a job well done. Employees will appreciate the fact that their manager is barbequing for them.

Point to keep in mind:

- **When you hit a plateau...** There will be times when your department does great for so long that the challenge is no longer there. When you get to this point, try to motivate by looking at beating your competitor's goals. For example, if you are at a 95% customer satisfaction rating, try to make it to 98% by focusing on every little bit of detail. Another way to motivate is by finding new training courses with certification. You can also try cross training your employees by having team members sit with other team members in different groups or even departments. Also let your boss or upper management know you are willing and capable of taking on new projects and additional responsibilities if applicable.

- **Ask a few of your most trusted employees what truly motivates the team.** There is nothing wrong with this. You shouldn't keep on throwing darts at the board hoping one of them hits the bulls-eye. Not only is it ineffective, it can make you look bad and silly trying some obscure motivational techniques. By understanding what truly provides the motivation the team needs to succeed, the quicker you are to obtaining your goals. Pep talks and fun games might be ok for short-term goals, but in the long run they have no effect. Communication, again, is key.

- **Hire nothing but the best people.** New employees who have the right aptitude and attitude tend to motivate and build morale with existing team members. There will be more about hiring the right people in Lesson 4.

- **Don't forget the people out of sight.** If you work in a 24/7 type of company or providing after hours support, you will not see the swing and graveyard shift personnel as much as you would like. They need to be motivated as well.

- **Again, do not micromanage.** If you plan, organize, train, communicate, direct and lead correctly as described throughout this course, you should not have to micromanage your staff. Continually over shadowing or controlling excessively and not letting them have a chance to prove themselves is very demoralizing. Looking over someone's back is very uncomfortable unless they ask for the help. This does not mean that you shouldn't monitor the work going on in your department. It means to trust that your staff is capable of doing the work expected of them. If there are any problems or training issues, you handle it by meeting with the supervisor or with the individuals themselves to discuss ways in which to improve.

Step 3 - Recognize and Praise great work

People like to be recognized and crave praise for doing good work. People crave praise, but do not always like to give it. One of your jobs as manager is to make sure you give out praise as often as possible. In the workplace it really holds true because it is a place where they spend on average 40 hours a week. People want to be happy and secure in a place where they spend so much of their time. It only takes a few seconds to say, "Thank you," and "great job," but you get years of return. It's so easy, and quite effective.

Here are 12 ways to recognize and praise your staff in a professional and dignified way:

1. **Don't hesitate to acknowledge the good things**. Whenever there are events such as when a project is completed, a task is performed, monthly goals are achieved, a compliment from a customer is given, evidence of good work is seen in documentation, or a compliment from another co-worker is given, be absolutely sure you make it a priority to talk to that individual as soon as possible and give them a true hearty thank you. There might even be times when the employee already knows, for example, a customer gave a nice compliment regarding their performance. It would do so much harm if you did not take the time to thank that person. An employee, who feels they have not received any praise recently, or that their best efforts and work performed is ignored, will end up de-moralized and un-motivated.

2. **Praise in public.** Not only will the person or team feel good that you praised them, their peers or other departments will also see it. It is also contagious as the more you praise, the more they will want to receive it. There are, however, times when you should praise privately...

3. **Don't publicly praise an individual on a team related effort.**
    Depending on the situation, in most cases if you only single out one person with praise that was based on a team effort, you are going to damage team morale. For example, if the customer satisfaction goal was achieved you want to first praise the team. You can give praise to an individual as long as you first gave praise to the entire team and then added in the individual praise related to the subject at hand. However, you can and should praise the individual in front of the team if it's an individual accomplishment not necessarily tied to a team goal.

4. **Post the results on the wall in big letters and in clear view for all to see**. You and your team should take pride in achieving the goals set. There should be constant reminders around the office regarding the departments' objectives. Besides, this will also inspire and motivate everyone to achieve those goals and objectives or else all will see the dirty laundry of the department...

5. **Make it publicly known when there is something positive to share about an employee**. This is not necessarily praise for individual performance in front of the whole team, but an anomaly of sorts when something good is said or happened with a particular employee. Don't

embarrass the person or make the other team members jealous, but do it in a way that shows how this contributes to the overall success of the team and department. For example, an important customer who normally is hard to please gave a compliment to a particular individual. This good news should be shared. You should also periodically share good news with the senior management team. It's a win/win situation because it also makes you look good as the manager of the individual. *Note: If there are any negative comments about an individual, you should never broadcast that information to other employees. This should be a one-on-one conversation with the individual only.

6. **Create a storyboard on the wall to show motivational achievements**. Every time you get a customer compliment, one employee recognizes another for extraordinary work, or an exceptional task was completed, you should document and post it on a "Celebration Wall." It does not have to be elaborate and will cost next to nothing. Document the achievement with the employee's name, or team effort, in big print and pin it to the wall. Continue doing this and before you know it, your wall will be filled with inspirational comments. The more stories that are posted, the more people will want to be included in the storyboard. If you run out of room, continue it on another wall. There does not need to be any big fanfare, just a posting on the wall. You should, however, have already given a personal note of gratitude to the individual or team as well.

7. **Recognize and praise quickly.** It you wait too long to tell someone about a recognizable event, it will lose its effectiveness. It can also create a certain anxiety, as the employee would have thought up to that time, that you did not notice the exceptional work.

8. **Give Praise, recognition and positive feedback on what means the most to the individual and team.** Be sure to praise correctly. Praising a job well done on a specific skill or true attained goal is meaningful. Generically praising for praising sake, especially if you are missing the important point, looks bad on you and you will lose respect. For example, a technician troubleshot and fixed a very difficult repair. Instead of focusing on the technician's excellent troubleshooting skills, your praise was related to a lack of typing mistakes. Sure that's important, but it missed the true mark. This is why it is important to fully understand just what it is that your employees do related to their job functions. Using the example above, if you do not realize how difficult the troubleshooting was done to fix the problem, the technician will be demoralized thinking you do not realize just how good they are and how hard it was to truly resolve the issue.

9. **Admiration of a person's skill is a show of respect and recognition**. Sometimes the most important way to recognize good work is to be in true awe of an employee's performance. This can be based on their skills, knowledge, attitude, etc. True respect for the team or individual is truly meaningful.

10. **Go into detail regarding the recognition.** Follow up the "thank you" with more in depth comments about the good deed done. It will show you truly mean it and understand the positive impact that was made.

11. **Write a letter, forward the e-mail, or write the e-mail yourself**. Proof of a written compliment is very powerful. You can cc the team and if desired, upper management. Simple, but effective and so easy to do.

12. **Have someone in upper management take the time to acknowledge the individual or team**. Ask your boss or someone else in senior management to personally thank the individual or team. This simple gesture goes a long way. It also makes upper management feel good about what they are doing, and makes you look good for suggesting it. Another win/win situation.

Points to keep in mind:

- **The effect of giving praise is a very powerful and productive tool**. The individual or team not only feels better about themselves, but will most likely think, "I can do it even better." So chances are their performance will improve to an even higher standard. Studies show that positive feedback releases the chemical "Dopamine" which is a stimulant of excitement. Interestingly enough, you will also feel more positive about yourself.

- **Don't start with praising, and end with a lecture**. If you approach someone or the team with the intention to praise, don't then turn it in to a time to focus on the negative. It's like a child who is proud about getting an "A" on their report card, but you then quickly focus on the "C". There is a time and place to talk about the "C", but not at that moment.

- **Praise when praise is truly due**. The team or individual needs to earn praise, not just get it because they all showed up to work on time or just doing normal daily tasks. If you praise for the expected things, it will lose effect on the exceptional things.

Step 4 - Evaluate and Appraise employee performance

Giving feedback, whether positive or constructive, can truly be effective if done timely and correctly. Effective feedback is specific, not general. For example, you would not just want to give positive feedback like, "Good job on fixing the problem." You would want to go into specifics like, "Good job on the troubleshooting skills you used to determine that the problem was a customer router misconfiguration." Make this positive feedback timely, specific, and frequent. Recognition for effective performance is a powerful motivator. Most people want to obtain more recognition, so recognition fosters more of the appreciated actions.

The same holds true if work done was not up to standards. In this case you would make a constructive observation. Constructive feedback is not criticism, but alerts to an area in which performance could improve. It is descriptive and should always be directed to the action, not the individual or team. The main purpose of constructive feedback is to help people understand where they stand in relation to expected, and productive, job behavior.

By sharing information and observations, when done sincerely and honestly, will help the individual or team on specific actions or behavior that they can do something about. It is a good idea to approach the situation by saying something like, "I would like to give some feedback on how you troubleshoot if that is ok with you?" This way it will come off looking like you want to help rather than scold. After you have provided the feedback, make sure they fully understood what you said by asking them a question or two or by observing their behavior.

Employee evaluations can be a positive, encouraging, and a good synopsis on how they are doing in the many categories of their job responsibilities. On the other hand, it can also be considered a waste of time and doesn't work if neither you nor your employees take it seriously and just go through the motions. Many managers hate having to do these evaluations. Managers usually just want to get the necessary info together as fast as possible and are happy it only comes once or twice a year. Depending on the amount of employees you are evaluating, this can be quite a big task. However, if your department has been managed right, it could become a rewarding experience. Evaluations, also called performance appraisals, are important and most companies perform them so they will be discussed here.

Performance reviews can be an effective tool but only if you and your staff take it seriously. This is not just a snapshot of how they are doing at the moment of the appraisal, but a review of the past 6 months or year. You need to have the necessary data to back the appraisal, and everyone needs to understand what is expected and how they are appraised.

In general, most appraisals cover the set goals and objectives including:

- Volume or production levels
- Thoroughness and attention to detail
- Accuracy
- Attitude
- Teamwork
- Attendance and punctuality
- Corporate values
- Future goals
- and Final notes

When developing a performance review:

- Be sure to meet with your employees and review the performance appraisal goals, values, and expectations.

- Meet with them at the beginning of the year or evaluation period and establish the timeline. Most companies perform these appraisals once or twice a year.

- Make sure you and your supervisors have detailed records of each employee's performance. Outline the recent accomplishments as well as improvements needed. You need all of this data for the review itself and to back up the review if questioned.

- When it's time to do the performance review, make it a priority to eliminate any employee anxiety. Don't put it off.

- Once the review has been discussed, be sure to come to terms together on the evaluation rating and goals going forward. Short-term and long-term goals should be established whether for growth or improvements.

- End the review on a positive note. If there are any issues, be sure you have discussed and offered training, counseling, and coaching to help improve on the needed skills and remedy any deficiencies.

You want the review to be thought of as professional and an inspirational experience. Reserve plenty of time for the meeting with no interruptions. If performed correctly, your employees will feel you truly understand their strengths and weaknesses, and will leave with a positive outlook for the future. It will also establish your credibility as an effective leader. To help create a successful outcome, here are 19 valuable tips to think about when performing employee evaluations:

1. **Evaluations keep a written record to support pay increases.**
   Documentation of the employee's performance lets the employee officially know where they stand in the company and what you think about their performance. You want your team to feel like you really do want to take the time to let them know what they are all about. It will inspire them to perform better and they will respect you more as manager and leader. The goal is to make them feel as if they have had special attention, whether it is praising or encouraging. This same mindset should always be used for everyone you evaluate. It is their scorecard to see how well they did and if tasks were achieved or completed on time. It can also be thought of as a report card. The evaluation process makes sure that you are utilizing the talent in your organization that not only benefits the employee, but you and the company as well. So you can see, even though these types of appraisals are usually thought of as a waste of time for many managers, there is some important underlying value.

2. **In most cases evaluations have a set of core job objectives and corporate values.** The core objectives would basically refer to the overall job performance expectations. The corporate values refers to open communication such as working with others to produce the best result, a caring culture treating others with mutual respect, or unmatched service & support taking personal responsibility for customer satisfaction. They are based on a scale of something like 1 to 5 with 5 being best. There can also be statements such as "exceeds expectations, meets expectations, and below expectations." These ratings would be for each job objective and each corporate value along with an overall score.

3. **Appraisals, at the very least, lets the employee know that someone at work is thinking about their job performance.** When employees know they are working hard and doing a great job, they want it put in writing. Your

employees should be well aware of what is expected of them as long as you put the lessons learned in this course into place. This is because you have communicated, coached, and guided your individuals and team to achieve their goals, objectives and values. This will also make it much easier to create the appraisals since all of the goals, objectives, tasks, responsibilities, and corporate values have already been well communicated to the team.

4. **Hopefully because you have managed the department so well**, you will have mostly "meets" or "exceeds" expectations. However, this does not mean they all "walk on water." If you give a score of "exceeds expectations" or a "5 out of 5", they truly need to be considered your star performers. A common mistake is rating people too high, know matter how they performed, which does not give a clear way for improvement. It does not mean you should be necessarily be giving more negative reviews, just keep it balanced. If they truly are a star performer, give them top marks.

5. **Be sure your supervisors also follow these guidelines.** If they are performing the reviews with their direct staff, then they need to have the same mindset as you have. In most cases, depending on the size of the company, you would review your supervisors and you supervisors would review their direct reports.

6. **If you expect or anticipate complications with a particular employee performance review...** You need to make sure you have all documentation and data to back up your evaluation. If they are confrontational, and indeed not happy with the appraisal or the amount of the raise given, make sure you stay open and understanding. Prepare to discuss and stay professional at all times. Do not be confrontational or take a hard line approach. You do, however, need to be decisively direct. Stay focused to the points at hand. Have the confidence that you have truly previously communicated your vision, goals, objectives, and values to the individuals and team, and have coached all you could have up to this point. Stand by the fact that your appraisal will be fair and accurate, and that you're not coming across like you are on a witch-hunt.

7. **If you have an employee who is performing below expectations...** You need to find ways to coach and provide training for improvement. This could be because they are still fairly new, were previously a good employee who is losing their way, or recently promoted and still growing. You might want to give a 30 or 60-day action plan to improve along with a follow up meeting to discuss. If, however, you have an employee who is just non-retainable even though you've coached all you could, repeatedly spoke to them about their bad attitude, or their performance is just not acceptable anymore, it is time to terminate the employee. You should deal with this as soon as possible. It does neither of you good to prolong the issue. Lesson 5 deals with this subject in much more detail.

8. **Whatever you do, make sure you complete the performance appraisals on time.** You should even strive to be ahead of schedule if possible. It will not only make you look efficient as a leader who cares about their department, it also makes HR and upper management happy. Some people really do care about these evaluations and work hard all year just for this moment. This is another time to really thank the good workers, and try

to get the bad workers to become inspired within themselves. The last thing you want to do, is do an "11th hour" rush or miss the deadline. Whenever money is involved, you need to do all you can as quickly and efficiently as possible. The good news is if you are consistent and have communicated your vision and goals, you should be able to complete these in a timely fashion. Most companies already have an appraisal form for you to use along with directions.

9. **It is better to focus on the positive rather than the negative.** Start out with the positive. People tend to take the positives lightly, but the negatives heavily. If you start off with a negative, the positive will practically be ignored and forgotten. Only bring up the negative if it relates to the performance review. If the negative is performance related, this would be a perfect opportunity to coach the individual and create actions to improve.

10. **When discussing appraisals, be sure to tailor each one to each person's personality.** You should know what makes them tick and to get the most out of the evaluation. A "cookie cutter" approach just wont cut it... You want to stay consistent with the documentation and expectations for all, but unique with the verbal presentation for the individual. See the managing different personalities section in this lesson for more on how to deal with particular personalities.

11. **Make an outline of the significant items to cover.** By creating a cheat sheet of sorts, you can be sure to hit the important areas like:

    - Important contributions the employee made to the company
    - Personal interests
    - Making or missing a specific goal
    - Accuracy issues
    - Attitude
    - Potential growth possibilities

12. **It's a "bit of an art" to encourage someone with poor performance.** During the evaluation, when you are dealing with a poor performance related situation, stay confident but not intimidating, serious but not scary, and make your point but not be disheartening. You also cannot be sheepish and intimidated such as hiding behind jokes, passing it off as no big deal, etc. If you act like it's not a big deal, even unintentionally, then your employees will think it is no big deal and will continue to perform badly.

13. **Do not compare the employee to other employees.** This is demoralizing, hurts teamwork and will not accomplish anything but antagonism towards the compared employee.

14. **Encourage open communication.** You want your employees to always feel comfortable to be able to talk and share any issues, concerns or ideas. You should welcome as much input as possible. The same goes for you as manager towards your employees. Be open and not defensive if your employees make comments like, "I'm not advancing quick enough" or "my salary is not at the level as the work I perform." Use the skills taught throughout this course to be able to communicate efficiently, no matter what the topic.

15. **Treat each appraisal with the same mindset and professionalism of a job interview.** You have to always keep in mind about any possible anti-discriminatory issues that can arise. Although they have already been through the interview process at one point, and you most likely feel much more comfortable with them than you did in the beginning, you still need to be "politically correct" and careful on what you say and how you act.

16. **Stay on track and keep to the specifics.** You have to know when to move on to the next subject once the point was made, discussed, or debated. There is nothing wrong with a good debate, but when you hit a brick wall or the subject has been exhausted, there is no use in continuing on with that particular conversation. You need to make the decision to move on with confidence. Try to find a nice segue into the next talking point.

17. **Focus on the significance of each success and failure.** This should be looked at as it pertains to the company's possible successes and failures. The importance you add to each objective looking at the big picture adds more impact.

18. **Always make sure the employee leaves knowing what is expected in the future.** This goes for both good and bad performance reviews. Just saying something like, "Good Job, keep it up," is not enough. You need to embellish what is expected in the future besides "keep up the good work." You should have a plan to enhance the individual's goals and keep them wanting to continually strive to improve. You've got to always be looking forward and never just settling on the "status quo."

19. **Always be sure you did everything you could before terminating an employee based on the performance appraisal.** Sometimes it comes down to the point where there is just no saving an employee based on such poor performance. You do, however, truly need to make sure you've done all you can to coach the person, help improve their skills, or help with any personal issues. If you can look yourself in the mirror with no trepidations, then you know you did all you could and are making the right decision.

Points to keep in mind:

- **If you have an employee who is disruptive, has a bad attitude, or is a "bad apple..."** you need to deal with the person as soon as possible. It only takes one bad attitude to spoil the team. You should never pretend this problem does not exist or hopes it somehow corrects itself. You will lose the respect of your team if you do not deal with the situation. Bring the person into your office without making a big scene, and make it as private as possible. Be upfront and discuss what you are seeing and how important it is to have the whole team working in "harmony." This also goes for the employee who is not performing up to standards. Don't wait until it comes to the point of no return. Many times issues blow over without incident and things get worked out without intervention, however, you need to be aware of any growing concerns, especially if it affects team performance. Lesson 5 will cover how to deal with problematic employees in more detail.

- **Measure the goals and show proof**. You need to visually show your staff on whether or not you hit your targeted goals with statistical reports, customer surveys, or any other type of pertinent data. By showing the results in your weekly or monthly team meetings, the clear directions and specific time frames you give to them will have more meaning. Examples of these types of reports are shown in lesson 2.

- **Make sure they feel accountable and take responsibility for their work.** You want them to feel proud of what they do, and not take any short cuts or perform sloppy work. You need to instill into them that they should take pride in their work. They should also know that poor work will not be tolerated and that they will be held accountable.

- **Lets face it; it's mostly about the money...** When it comes to appraisals, sure it's important for you to get your point across, praise and encourage, and let the employee know what's expected in the future, but when it comes down to it, it's all about the money. If possible, it would be best to be able to discuss the merit increase during the appraisal meeting. It is usually an hourly increase based on the overall evaluation score, which is normally a certain percentage increase of around 3% to 5%. It can be as high as 10%, or as low as 1%. Sometimes it is nothing. In many cases you have to wait a few weeks after the initial appraisal to inform them about the merit increase. Just let them know to be patient and that you will get back to them the moment you have the information. Also, always make sure you let each and every employee know they should never discuss the increase amount with their fellow employees. This goes with their hourly rate as well.

Example – Employee Appraisal Form. This is an example evaluation form that has the goals and objectives expected of the employee.   In this case you can check whether the employee exceeded, was able to meet, or fell below targets and expectations. Each goal is also weighed by a percentage. This example just shows the goals and objectives. The full appraisal also contains corporate values, notes, comments, and a place for signatures. This should be presented in the beginning of the year, or appraisal period, so that the employee understands how and when their performance will be appraised.

Sample Corp - Performance Appraisal

Performance Year: 2009	☒ Goal Setting		☐ Mid-Year Review			☐ Year-End Review	
	☐ Self-Assessment		☐ Manager's Assessment				
Name: Customer Care agent name	Title: Representative, Customer Service						
Date: 1/11/09	Department: Customer Care						

Performance Ratings: ETE = Exceeds Targets & Expectations, MTE = Meets Targets & Expectations, BTE = Below Targets & Expectations							
I. Performance Goals & Objectives	**%**	**ETE**	**MTE**	**BTE**	**Actual Performance**		
Core Job Objectives							
Customer Care – Order process time: 95% to 100% of all orders opened are completed within Order guide lines = rating of ETE 90% to 95% of all orders opened are completed within Order guide lines = rating of MTE Below 90% of all orders opened are completed within Order guide lines = rating of BTE	30%	☐	☐	☐			
Customer Care - Time in Order queue: Average answer time under 30 seconds = rating of ETE Average answer time between 30 seconds to 60 seconds = rating of MTE Average answer time over 60 seconds = rating of BTE	30%	☐	☐	☐			
Order input quality including proper documentation and use of report and closing codes in company database.	20%	☐	☐	☐			
Total	80%	☐	☐	☐			
Special Job Objectives							
Back up Tech Support with basic troubleshooting							
Total	10%	☐	☐	☐			
Individual Development / Leadership Objectives							
Multi-tasking abilities, works well under pressure							
Total	10%	☐	☐	☐			
Overall Performance Goals & Objectives Rating	**100%**	☐	☐	☐			

Step 5 - Compensate and Reward a job well done

Kind words go a long way, but rewarding with money, gifts and awards goes even further. Compensating and rewarding employees goes a long way in helping retain employees for good job performance. This is also a chance to really reward the best of the best. Depending on the company and budget, you can be creative in some aspects, and traditional in others. You as manager will sometimes need to come up with reward expenses and increased pay percentages out of your budget (see lesson 8 for more information on budgets). On the other hand, you have to always be striving to keep costs and expenditures down. It's a fine balance, but one that can, and should, be achieved.

To begin with, you should have a full list of everyone's salary within your department. You will most likely have a salary range for each position already established, if not you should set levels so that you do not have employees performing the same job functions with too much difference in pay. Look to see if some employees are obviously underpaid for what they are doing, and others who are at a capped level of pay. Past and present performance reviews are a good way to capture someone's exceptional work in a way that justifies a larger than normal increase in pay.

Here are 16 ideas for you to incorporate regarding compensation and other rewards:

1. **Try to pay them what they are worth.** When it comes down to it, if you offer an above-market wage, the employee usually matches it with more effort in their job performance. HR or upper management usually sets the rate of pay for employees, so you need to be creative in order to get a raise for your best employees.

   The catch 22, when it comes to motivating, training, praising, and getting great results, is now you have employees who are much better than they were when they first started. The better they are, the more they are in demand. Usually you can give somewhere around a 3% to 5% increase during their annual performance reviews, but there are times when you need to give more to certain individuals who truly deserve it. You don't want to lose them to the competition. This is when you need to do some creative talking to your boss or upper management. With all of the positive data you have regarding the employee, it should be easy to at least state your case.

   Hopefully there is room in the pay scale to give them an increase. Here's a typical scenario: The yearly salary for the position is set at $30,000 to $40,000, and the employee currently makes $35,000. You ask to move the rate of pay to $40,000. That would be a little over a 14% increase. Most companies do not give more than a 10% increase at any one time. Even though $5,000 may not sound like a huge jump as far as dollars are concerned, it is regarding the percentage jump based on the existing salary. It is up to you to present your case and see if you can bend that rule. If you cannot get $40,000, and only get the 10% increase (which would bring it up to $38,500), at least your employee will know that you tried and will still appreciate the increase, even if it was not exactly what they were hoping for...

The main goal here, besides the obvious increase in pay, is to show the employee that you and the company are eagerly looking out for their best interests, which in return, the employee should be looking out for the company, by exceeding job expectations in their work performance.

2. **A raise based on the Employee Appraisal/Performance Review**. The better the review, the higher the increase should be in pay. It may be by only a percentage or two, but at least it is something. A great review shows how much you value them, even if the reward is just a small increase in pay. The most you will usually be able to give your employees, based on yearly performance reviews, ranges from 3% to 5%. What usually happens is you have an overall department percent average that you cannot go over. For example, if you cannot go over a department average of 4%, you could give one person 8%, one person 6%, one person 4%, one person 2%, and one person, due to extremely poor performance, 0%. You would still be on target as the overall average is 4%. This is why performance reviews can be so important.

   Your employees will no doubt know how the raise percentage is structured. If you give a raise to your best employees that are above the average percentage, they will feel justified and happy. In turn, you would give a lower than average raise to the under performers. If you have been doing your job right, there should be no surprises. If just about everyone in your department is above par, then you will most likely be giving average raises to most of the department. They should understand, as they will realize that their co-workers are of equal caliber.

3. **Promotion is the reward**. This might seem obvious, but this is the best reward. A good team member, who is motivated, continually praised for good work, and exceeds expectations on appraisals, might just be worthy of being rewarded with a promotion. You should always be looking out for these possible growth opportunities for your top employees.

   There also comes a time when an employee is at the top level of pay, or capped, for the position they hold. You want to give them more money, but there is just no more room for them to grow in their current role as far as money is concerned. The answer could be to promote them to another position. There might even be times when you need to create a position just for this cause. For example, you determine a lead technician is needed in your department. Although you might be tailoring this position for just this one individual, chances are you will need this position in the near future anyways.

   If you promote someone to a position that requires the supervision of others, start off on the right path using a personal development program. Don't just throw them off into the deep end and expect them to pick up the necessary skills needed to be successful. Make sure you train the person on the skills associated with:

   - Thinking strategically.
   - Establishing priorities.
   - Giving and receiving feedback.

- Developing communications skills.
- Conducting effective personal interviews.
- Conflict Resolution.
- Understanding the full scope of the company strategy, policies, and procedures. This is very important and is usually a mystery to people.
- The use of the latest technology, tools, applications, and programs such as Excel Spreadsheets, Word Docs, and PowerPoint's.

4. **Try to have the power to give on the spot raises**. In most companies HR will not allow such a thing, but if it's possible, strive for the ability to give an increase at your discretion as long as you do not go over budget. You can let upper management know that you will not abuse this power, and that performance levels will rise because of it. This is because employees will tend to work harder knowing you have this capability. If not, they might only put in the extra effort right before appraisals are due.

5. **Do your research when it comes to requested increases in pay.** Be sure the increase is truly due, and is justified through past performance results. By checking the employees history of performance and pay levels, you can either be extremely confident when pursuing getting the increase, or content in denying the request.

6. **Give small gifts such as movie tickets**, gift certificates, credit cards with a limited amount, and even cash. For only a few dollars, you can give a small award for a job well done. Do not make it a predictable thing or else it will lose its impact and become expected. Be creative. Try things like taking them out for lunch, letting them go home early, or giving them a $50 voucher. The only potential problem would be a complaint that one gift is better than the other. Maybe you can give them a choice?

7. **Employee of the week parking space**. Simple, but effective, especially in the bigger sized companies.

8. **Move the person to a better office or desk.** This is a nice reward, which is also motivational.

9. **Bonus for hitting the goals**. This is quite common and usually a semi-annual or annual event. This is why setting clear expectations and goals with the stats to back it up are so important.

10. **Paid time off and unpaid leaves**. Letting people go home early when it is slow, and still get paid, can be considered an award. This can also go for longer lunch hours and extra vacation time. Some people are happy to just go home early, even if it is unpaid. *Keep in mind that company rules and/or state laws can be a factor on the legality of these types of rewards.

11. **Awards such as plaques, trophies, or certificates**. An employee of the month engraved on a plaque might work, but don't be surprised if it gets a bit old after a while, especially if the same person always wins. Another problem could be if it's the same manager who always does the picking, it will look like favoritism. Use something like this for a true major accomplishment or

achievement that is more of a yearly type of recognized reward. If it is truly treated as something truly special, it will be much more effective.

12. **Employee points used towards company provided gifts.** This would be for company merchandise such as hats, shirts, jackets, or even a product the company sells. Have a program in which employees can award points to other employees for a job well done. You can also give out these points. Once you get a certain amount of points, you can redeem them for merchandise. As long as it's not abused, it is a fun and simple program. It lets everyone decide who is deserving of a recognition award. An example of abusing the program would be best friends who award each other just, because they think the other has a good attitude, etc.

13. **Annual recognition banquet** held for award events and ceremonies such as employee of the year. Major awards like trips or cash, grossed up to cover taxes, can be given. This can be a fun event for all, not just the winner.

14. **Make sure to reward as quickly as the achievement was accomplished.** Giving a reward out months after hitting a targeted goal does not go over very well. Besides, at that point they are most likely already focused on the next target.

15. **Match the award with the person.** It is better to give an award out that means something to someone, and that they will truly enjoy. If they like music, then give them a certificate to a music store. If they like fine dining, then give them a voucher for a great restaurant. When you get to know your employees, this will not be so hard to figure out.

16. **The reward should compliment the achievement**. The better the achievement, the greater the reward. For example, don't give the same $20 gift certificate for a person staying late one night to finish a task, as you would for a person who saved an important account through months of extraordinary effort.

Points to keep in mind:

- **Reward programs require a lot of planning and preparation**. Don't just wing it. Take it seriously so that your employees take it seriously. You should get some kind of reward committee to help.

- **Don't make rewarding predictable**. It will lose its effectiveness and not taken seriously after a period of time.

- **Do not reward if the goal was not achieved**. Seems obvious but it happens all the time.

- **When it comes to compensation you need to be careful**. Most of the time people do not know what the other is making, even when they are in the same department performing the same job functions. You need to try and prevent employees discussing their rate of pay. Some companies have a set rate of pay, so this will not be a problem. You may need an interpreter or union representative with you when discussing pay. Don't make promises you cant keep, it not only demoralizes, but can also turn into a lawsuit.

- **You will have your favorite employees.** You most likely will, if truly deserved, promote them at one point. You might even take them out to lunch or dinner. The important thing is not to show too much favoritism in front of your department. You need to make sure the whole department knows you are setting the same standards and goals for all. You need to show that when it comes to business, you treat the people you don't really like the same as you do with those you do like. Just make sure to treat everyone in the same professional manner. That is the key, always be professional to everyone, equally, to eliminate the possibility of being accused of favoritism.

Managing Different Personalities

You will encounter many different types of people during your management career. If you are managing a group of around 20 or less, you really should be able to get a feel for each individual's personality. Even if you manage a group of 100, you should still be able to know the key players personalities. It helps when you know what makes each one of them tick, especially when communicating one-on-one. When dealing with different personalities, be tolerant of styles different from your own. Always try to adapt to their personality to get your point across, or to get more out of them.

You can't use a cookie cutter approach with every employee. In most cases, you will need to change your communication approach with each individual. For example, you will not get your point across if your too direct and data oriented with a touchy-feely kind of person. In the same token, you would not want to be too touchy-feely with a no-nonsense type of person. This is also important when delegating any projects to individuals or as small teams. If a person or team is too analytical, there will be little creativity. If a person or team is too sensitive, fewer decisions will be confidently made. Here are some ways to deal with different personality traits:

- o The **"Considerate"** are nice, calm, and like to think things through. They usually have an optimistic "glass half-full" point of view. They are agreeable, but might take a bit longer than others to get the work done. They might need some help in making decisions. The good news is usually the work is more complete with fewer errors. Let them know calmly, yet directly, what you need from them. However, also spend some time to talk about family and other non-work related topics. This would be a good person to do long-term detailed oriented type of projects. Give a lot of encouragement and praise to get the most out of this type of personality.

- o The **"Aggressive"** likes to take control and do things quickly. They are not afraid to make decisions. They are usually good at what they do, and know it. Just make sure they do not try and control you. They can produce a lot of good work for you, but every once and a while you need to make sure they know whose boss. Be direct, straightforward, and use a no-nonsense approach to business. This would be a good person to use to put out any fires that need immediate attention.   Make sure you give this person a lot of praise when praise is due. If you don't, they will be upset.

- o The **"Analyst"** will always try to find flaws in the system. They will also play devils advocate. If you say, "Do this," they will say, "why don't we do it like that?" Sometimes it's a good thing because there might indeed be a better solution, but most of the time it's just someone being too critical. They tend to procrastinate when making decisions. Listen to what they have to say, but if you feel it is going nowhere, take their suggestions and move quickly onto the next subject. This would be a good person to give projects like finding possible trouble producing trends that requires deep analytical investigation. This is more of a "just the facts" type of person. Don't waste either of your time to chat about subjects of little importance.

- o The **"Sensitive"** takes any type of confrontation too personally. They do as they are told, but do not like making decisions. They are usually very nice and pleasant but their feelings get hurt too easily. Try not to be too direct with this type of personality. Use an encouraging type of approach when dealing with any performance related issues. This would be a good person to give projects that are more "touchy-feely."

- o The **"Talkative"** tend to be more feelings oriented and will show more emotion, whether positive or negative. They have a strong interest about people and are usually the "social butterfly" of the department. They usually like making decisions but want conformation just in case. Try using a lightened-up approach and some humor to get your point across to this type of personality. This would be a good person to help plan social events or any projects that require some animated personality.

- o The **"Brainiac"** will use knowledge and sarcasm to get what they want. They will try and dance around the basic topic. They will also dance around making any type of decision. Make sure you keep this person on track as they can lose focus on the task at hand very easily. If needed, make them repeat themselves in terms everyone can understand. This would be a good person to give the projects that are more "data-oriented."

- o The **"Quiet"** is one who very rarely talks at meetings, seems to have low self-esteem, and is continually sub-conscious of their actions. Not only should you try to bring this person out of their shell, they just might have some brilliant ideas that you can incorporate. There can be power in the quiet person as they might be the ones with the most compelling ideas. We tend to give our attention to the commanding personalities and ignore the quiet and soft-spoken. On the contrary, the quiet people are the ones you need to seek out.

- o The **"Results-Driven"** tend to focus solely on targeted metrics but sometimes lose focus on the big picture. They feel like they are doing a great job because of meeting an important goal, however, they are doing a poor job on another aspect of the job. You need to get your point across by being direct. You have to stress the importance of the big picture and to use common sense. For example, this is the type of person who will stop troubleshooting a problem, even if they are close to fixing it, because they went over the average call handle time. This person is usually more suited for simple straightforward tasks that do not require thinking outside of the box.

o   The **"Loner"** just wants to do the job and not get involved with company picnics, break room conversations, or any non-work related subjects. They do not like any interaction with fellow employees. You should talk to them about the importance and reasoning of the team approach. It is to their benefit if the team exceeds, not only for job security, but also for any possible rewards you have in place. With open and honest communication, you should be able to get them to understand and work as a team member. This does not mean they have to be everyone's best friend; they just need to be supportive and reliable. The problem with a person who does not want to be part of a team usually ends up not fully understanding the expectations of the group, and will have the type of excuse like, "Nobody told me…" or "I did not know I was supposed to do that…" etc. This person might be a diamond in the rough and if they just do not fit in to the current team, see if there is another position that would be better suited for them. This might look like you are rewarding someone because of a personality issue, so be careful how you handle this as it could create conflict amongst your team. You, and most likely HR, will have to determine the outcome of such a move. Still continue to try to get this person out of their shell, and try to give them projects that do not demand a team effort.

o   The **"Overly-Confident"** feels like they know everything and can do no wrong. Sometimes they act confident even when they don't know what they're doing. You need to get your point across by being very direct. You might want to humble this person every now and then. Make them repeat exactly what it is they are supposed to be doing. Give them projects that can easily be tracked to make sure they are not headed in the wrong direction.

o   The **"Curmudgeon"** thinks of everyone but them self as incompetent, and does not take supervision well. They tend to be grumpy and sarcastic. They have a pessimistic "glass is half-empty" point of view. You do not want to approach this type of person with your tail between your legs. State the facts and let them know exactly what is expected of them. Use a matter of fact approach and try to give them projects that do not demand too much creativity or touchy-feely.

o   The **"Mean-Spirited"** makes it known that they are not happy with work or the people around them. In many cases it is due to problems that are not work related. If you feel that it is affecting employee morale, you should talk to this person and make sure they understand that you need a department that works in harmony. That the goal is to a have everyone work in a pleasant atmosphere in which there are no personality conflicts.

o   The **"Bad Attitude"** is a major problem. You need to let this person know that their attitude is affecting morale and is unacceptable. See lesson 5 for ways on how to handle this type of difficult employee.

A short story about building a strong team

John knew that although his department was structured perfectly, he had to make sure his employees were willing to follow the plan. He explained that the changes he made were necessary for the department and company to achieve the goals and objectives. He had chosen the right people, let them know what was expected, trained them, got them the needed materials, and created a good working environment, but still had to find more ways to keep them motivated. He needed a strong and happy team in place or else it would all fall apart.

By making his employees feel like a true team, he decided to let them work as a team. He found ways that inspired teamwork. They knew that by working as a team, they would not be micro-managed. He let them be involved in making decisions and really listened to their suggestions and ideas. He also made it a priority to always acknowledge exceptional work done and in a timely fashion. He made sure that everyone fully understood that if the goals were achieved, they would be rewarded both in pay and other small gifts of gratitude. He developed a performance appraisal that was based on statistical reports that documented whether the goals were reached. He also documented their strengths and weaknesses in order to always keep them challenged and to improve. He would always look at ways to help them grow, and promoted his exceptional employees. Basically, John showed his team that he cared about them as people. He got to know them personally and supported them 100%. He did know, however, that it only takes one bad apple to spoil the lot, so whenever he felt there was conflict, he dealt with it immediately before it affected the group.

John had built a solid, unified team with the same goals in mind. They wanted to work hard because they knew they would be recognized and praised for a job well done. The harder they worked, the more John would show his appreciation. The skills they obtained were truly recognized, and even upper management came by to talk to the team about their success. John's department was not only physically and logically in place, but now with a motivated team who was happy to follow the processes and procedures, he had created.

Epilogue: Your employees work better when they are happy and feel they are part of a team to reach a common goal. It gives them a purpose and they will feel like an important part of the company. You want them to want to look good in your eyes. By implementing the skills taught in this lesson, you will have a strong team who respects your management skills and sees you as a leader who cares.

Quick Lesson Summary

- The five steps needed to develop a great team are:

    1. **Create** and Develop a strong team with solid expectations
    2. **Motivate** Professionally and with respect
    3. **Recognize** and Praise great work
    4. **Evaluate** and Appraise employee performance
    5. **Compensate** and Reward a job well done

- These same five steps can be also used as building blocks to develop the individual.

- A strong team knows exactly what is expected of them, and what it is they need to do. This includes the goals they need to achieve. A strong team also does not need to be micromanaged.

- Continually look for ways to motivate the team to increase job performance. Do it in a way, however, that does not insult their intelligence.

- Show appreciation of their good work by making it a point to recognize and praise, when *true* praise is due. Know the value of their exceptional skills.

- Care about your team and their interests. Let them know you always have their best interests at heart.

- Evaluate and appraise their work by documenting it to be used in a performance review.

- Give them the raise they deserve based on their job performance, while staying within budget. Even small rewards mean a lot when you show respect towards the team and individual.

- The key to managing different personalities is to take the time to get to know the people, and find out what makes them tick. You have to know how to deal with aggressive, sensitive, quiet, and mean personalities, just to name a few. You will be able to get the best out of them, by managing the personality, rather than using a generic approach. Be tolerant of styles different from your own, and try to adapt to their personality to get your point across.

LESSON 4 – HOW TO HIRE & RETAIN THE RIGHT PEOPLE

Introduction: The goal is to hire and keep the best people

The most important aspect when looking to hire someone is to have the mindset to hire and retain the best and right person for the job. Try to recruit people who will thrive under your management approach. In most cases you will inherit your staff and department, which is obviously out of your control. So when it comes to hiring someone new, you get a chance to make a fresh start and hire nothing but the best. And, once you hire the right person, you do not want them to leave. Nothing is worse than hiring someone, provide training, and as soon as you feel comfortable about the person, they leave. This is why you need to determine up front if the person you hire is going to be around for the long run. The ability to spot the perfect candidate is a necessary skill in management, and it is easy to learn.

Be patient when you are hiring, and whatever you do, don't just hire for hiring's sake. You might get lucky and find someone right away, or interview 20 to 30 people before you find the right candidate. You will have to live with the people you pick, so it is imperative that you make the right choice. Once you hire a problem employee, you will have a lot of work and stress ahead of you. It is also a morale killer when you bring in a bad apple, and it makes you look bad as far as judgment goes. Hopefully, you will work, or currently are working for a reputable company that pays well. People are drawn to the better companies and you will most likely get more applicants. If not, you might need to look into other ways to get the message out to the public. Some advertising ideas will be discussed later in this lesson.

Once the individual is hired, you will need to set clear expectations, evaluate the person's performance, and compensate and reward when the goals and objections are met, as described in lesson 3. It is up to you to hire the best people and keep them happy. This lesson will show you valuable information and ideas to use during the interview and hiring stage. There will also be some ideas and ways keep them in your company for a long time.

First off, do you really need to hire someone?

Many times, a new hire is replacing someone who left, or you have an opening available in your budget, so you feel you have to fill the spot. You need to carefully examine exactly what you need before hiring someone. Being overstaffed can cause boredom, and even worry, because of the reduced workload. When there is little work to do, there is more of a possibility of future layoffs.

You might even be asked from the team to hire some more help, but the solution is not necessarily to throw more bodies into the mix, but to re-examine processes and procedures that are in place. It is up to you, and expected of you as manager, to determine this conundrum. When you do not replace an employee just because they left, which is sometimes part of an acceptable attrition rate, you might just be doing everyone a favor, not to mention less cost to the company thus higher profit. You might even be able to shift the current responsibilities to another department. Keep all of this in mind when thinking about filling a new or existing position.

Only fill the position if truly needed. It's understandable that you might feel if you do not hire someone right away, you will lose that position forever. This is quite common, but you have to weigh out the pros and cons.   One pro is you will have another employee under your belt, thus a better chance to hit the goals. One con is you are costing the company more money, thus your management skills might be in question. Create a list, think about it very carefully, and then make your choice.

Creating the right job description to find the right person

You need to create a job description that truly focuses on the exact skills and qualities you are looking for in the potential new hire. You need to define the right job responsibilities. You want this description to be truly in synch with what they will actually do, and the skills they actually need. This way when you are evaluating resumes, you will be able to spot strengths and weaknesses much easier. The performance evaluations should also be in synch with the skills and responsibilities within the job description. You will have to update the job description from time to time if there are any additional responsibilities, new skills, or new product experience needed.

Items that should be on the job description are:

- General Description: Basic overview of what you are looking for in a candidate.

- Primary Job Functions: Brief description of the type of work performed.

- Required skills: The "must have" would be on top, the "should have" in the middle, and "nice to have" at the bottom.

- Desired skills: This would be skills you wish the applicant had, but not absolutely necessary.

- Experience: Type of work experience the applicant must have, and the amount of years doing this type of work.

- Education: Needed or desired. This can be anything from technical certification to a master's degree.

- Work status: Full or part time.

- Travel: Enter a percentage if there is any travel associated with the position.

- Reporting: The positions direct report. It might be you or one of your supervisors.

For example, if you were looking for more of a Tier 1 support technician with lower technical capabilities than a Tier 2 technician, you need to be clear on the expectations in the description which will justify the lower rate of pay. You would create it around the skills needed for the position. You would not want to make a description with too many high-end requirements for a lower type of position. It might put off some potential good applicants. The opposite is true if you are looking for a higher end type of position.

You also need to keep in mind whether this is a *non-exempt* position (paid on an hourly bases) which would include overtime and is typically on the lower end of the pay scale, or *exempt* (paid on a salary basis) which is usually on the higher end of the pay scale but with no overtime.

The following screen shot is an example of a basic job description for a Tier 1 technician with somewhat lower expectations than that of a Tier 2 technician.

Example – Job Description. Data Repair - Tier 1 Technical Support Engineer

---

Sample Corp

Job description: Data Repair - Tier 1 Technical Support Engineer

General Description:

Technical Support Engineer for the company's family of Internet based products. Candidate will possess a broad technical knowledge of analog, digital and VoIP voice services; IP networking; and data service provision. Candidate will be highly experienced in providing excellent customer service and problem escalation/resolution.

Primary Job Functions:

Provide Tier 1 support to end users, dealers and distributors. Provide troubleshooting and technical support via phone, web based tools and email. Advise customers regarding the product's proper use and address specific user issues. During problem escalations, act as a liaison between customers and Tier 2 support. Candidate will assist the customer base during installations.

Required Skills:

- Strong understanding of Ethernet, TCP/IP routing, Network packet analysis tools use and configuration.
- Strong technical and analytical skills.
- Solid experience in problem analysis and resolution of software problems. Proven ability to function in a self-directed environment.
- Must excel in a fast-paced, agile environment where critical thinking and strong problem solving skills are required for success.
- Innovative thinker who is positive, proactive, and readily embraces change.
- Ability to handle clients professionally during all interfaces.
- Sales support to help resellers and end users select, optimal installation configurations in a complex network environment.
- Strong written and verbal communication skills.

Desired Skills:

Experience troubleshooting and correcting Jitter, Latency, and Packet loss across public or enterprise networks using network analysis tools.

Experience:

2+ years of Telecom and Networking experience in a technical support/help desk environment.

Education:
Network+ and/or CCNA certification (preferred)

Work Status:
Full time

Travel:
Position requires 0% travel.

Reporting:
Reports to the Manager of Customer Service Technical Support

How to find the right person

The first place to look for the right candidate is to search within the company. Most HR departments insist on this anyway. HR will most likely perform a pre-interview for both internal and external applicants. The good news is if you implement all that is taught throughout this course, you should be known as a good manager that people want to work for. You would post your position internally for a period of time, and then look outside the company if you could not fill the position. Hiring from within is the best bet, as you will already know the person's character, background, and realize that they already know the company's goals. It also reduces costs.

You will also have the benefit of talking to that person's supervisor or manager. They will be able to answer any concerns you might have. Keep in mind this manager might oversell this employee because they want to get rid of that person. You will then inherit a problem, and also realize you cant trust that manager ever again...

The next place to look for a possible candidate would be through any or all of the following. The costs will be in parenthesis:

- **Online job finder** (minimal cost) such as <u>monster.com</u> or <u>careerbuilder.com</u>. You just go to the Internet site, sign up, and fill in the necessary info.

- **Post on the company's website** (none to very minimal cost) – the possible candidate will also have a chance to see what your company is all about.

- **Newspaper ad** (minimal cost) – Post an ad in the classified section of your local newspaper. You will need to provide the title of the position, a brief opening regarding the company name and what they are all about, the qualifications needed including years of experience, the salary if desired and contact info. Even if it costs a little bit more, make the ad big enough to catch their attention. Try not to make it look crammed up. Many times this same add will appear on the newspapers web page as well.

- **Recruiter or Headhunter** (medium to high cost) – This is a person or *search firm* who you ask to look for the right candidate based on the job description criteria you gave them. In most cases they will take a one-time fee of a certain percentage of the yearly salary once you hire the candidate. For example, they might take 5% of a $40,000 a year salary, which would be $8,000. This would be considered paying the recruiter on a "Contingency" basis. The other payment method would be considered on a "Retainer" basis in which you pay the associated percentage whether you hire someone the *search firm* found or from another source. In this case the recruiter gets paid either way.

- **Networking** (none to very minimal cost) – Word of mouth or certain blogs on the Internet can be very effective, and inexpensive.

- **College or trade school bulletin board** (none to very minimal cost). This is a simple way to get perspective students in the same field as yours to apply.

- **Employment agency** (medium cost) – This is an agency that assists job seekers in finding work. Companies such as kellyservices.com and appleone.com are a couple of online examples.

- **Radio or TV advertising** (medium to high cost) – This will depend on your location and if it is viable.

- **Temp (Temporary) agency** (low to medium cost) – An agency that places jobs for temporary work. This is a good way to determine if the position is really needed, and if you do not like the person, you can ask the temp agency for a replacement. Some agencies would expect an extra fee if you hire the person full time. There could also be a waiting period before the person is eligible to be hired full time. This is also a good idea if you are busier only during a certain period of time such as Christmas. An example of an online temp agency would be roberthalf.com.

What to look for in an interviewee

Much of the hiring phase is based on how well they answered the interview questions, but what gets their foot in the door is based on key words and experience from their resume. When screening and reviewing resumes you will develop a quick eye for:

- Key phrases
- Acronyms
- Familiar companies in the genre of your company
- Over qualified or under qualified
- Bounces around a lot

You should have a "yes," "maybe," and "no" pile. Calling the "yes" and "maybe" candidates yourself for a pre-interview helps both you and the candidate so you don't waste each other's time. You might even strike up a good rapport, which will make the live interview that much more interesting. You should create a list of quick and to the point questions for the telephone interview. Ask about experience, education, desired salary range, and general information. Use this same list for all pre-screenings to help keep the telephone call to a short and formatted way. You can go into more detailed questions during the live interview.

You also need to develop a sixth sense and follow your gut, although don't hire based on gut alone. Try not to pre-judge based on stereotypes, such as, thinking a man with long hair must mean he will be a troublemaker. After performing a few interviews, you will start to build confidence on exactly what you are looking for and need. You might also want to have one of your employees, like a supervisor, to be in the interview with you. Their impressions count and can help determine if the person will be a right fit for the team.

Here are 16 things to look for when interviewing and evaluating a person to join your company:

1. Natural talent. Getting someone who you know has the aptitude and attitude is just as important than experience, intelligence, or determination. You can always train for skills.

2. What the person has really done in previous jobs. Resumes are most often quite embellished.

3. Knowledge of your industry or product without going off track.

4. Emphasis on a great education and hoping you do not notice the lack of experience.

5. How long they spent at each job based on their application and resume. If they tend to bounce around a lot and spend just a few months or one year at each job, you might be in for some trouble. It usually takes a few months just to get someone trained to be able to fully perform the job functions. The last thing you want is someone who gets trained and ready to go, but leaves just a short time later.

6. Are they over qualified and only applying because of a slow economy and high unemployment? This employee, although qualified, might be desperate for a job. They might leave the moment something better comes along.

7. A nice and good personality. Remember this adage, *"You can train a nice person to become skilled, but you can't train a skilled person to become nice."*

8. Integrity and honesty with a strong work ethic.

9. Comfortable eye contact.

10. Nervous mannerisms showing they have something to hide.

11. Someone who can articulate clearly and speaks well.

12. Excellent attendance and dependability.

13. They way they are dressed. A dirty look says a lot about their personality.

14. A person with a team attitude who will fit in with the rest of the team. Think about how much energy will this person bring in to the department.

15. Someone who wants to go the "extra mile" to ensure top customer satisfaction.

16. Someone who looks like they will appreciate the job and opportunity and will have fun at work.

Job interview questions to ask

First create a guide form to use on all interviews, which grades each of the questions given below. Grade it on a level of 1 to 5, with 5 being best. You should have at least 10 skill related questions. You will want to make many copies to use as a guide for future interviews as well to help stick to the same outline. Have a comments and notes section, as well as a name and date. This can then be attached with the application and resume. Make sure you have a few "how and what" type of questions to verify what they claim. See how quick and correctly they answer the question. Many times if someone does not know the answer, they will go off track and talk about something they do know.

The more prepared you are, the more respect you will have already developed if you decide to hire this person. With respect comes trust, and they will look forward to working for you. The opposite is true if you seem like you are just bumbling around during the interview. Also make sure you give your full attention to the interviewee with no interruptions. Put the applicant at ease by making some non-threatening small talk, and not jumping right into the question/answer phase. They are going to be nervous and blow the interview if they feel threatened or intimidated. You goal is to find the best in this person, and watch out for the worse.

Here are 14 questions you can ask during the live interview. You may have already covered the basics if you did a pre-screening interview over the phone:

1. **Ask about their experience**. You are looking for what they did, time spent at jobs related to the position you are trying to fill, and how well that experience qualifies them for the job.

2. **Ask about their education.** Related college courses or certificates are highly valued and shows that they are taking this career choice seriously.

3. **Ask about their skills.** You are looking for their top job related strengths.

4. **Look at the application and review the salary range** at their previous or current employment. This will give you an idea if they are in or out of your pay range, and the opportunity for them to give a desired amount. They should not ask up front what the pay is for the job. It shows impatience. You should provide the opportunity.

5. **Ask a couple of questions to see if there might be some potential conflict** or attitude issues down the road. Ask, "Who was their favorite manager and why?" then ask, "who was their least favorite manager and why?" The second question is the trick question. You can get some valuable information from a person who you might suspect as dubious. Listen for the negatives that could end up haunting you, if you hired the person.

6. **Ask what they liked the most about their last job**. The type of answers you want, relates to learning, growth, respect, and loyalty. If you get answers pertaining to non-job related duties, such as making a lot of friends, or got to go home early when it was slow, you might have more of a social butterfly who is not focused on the true meaning of a job.

7. **Ask what they least liked about their last job**. If you get complaints that are related to the day-to-day running of a business, you might have someone who doesn't like structure. You want comments that are more justifiable like, "A lack of structure or direction." You might not get a negative comment at all, which is ok.

8. **Ask about the best praise or recognition they've received** and what made it so good.

9. **Ask about their greatest strengths and weaknesses**. To help determine strengths, ask them about their best day in the past year and what were they doing and why they liked it so much. To help determine weakness, the same applies for their worst day and why they disliked it so much. This is a bit of an uncomfortable question to answer, but it can determine the overly confident from the sheepish person. There might be some great value for you to learn in both the strengths and weaknesses on how they answer this question.

10. **Ask what is the best way they learn** and when in their career did they learn the most and why. This can help you determine how best to train this person if you hire them.

11. **Can they multitask and perform well under pressure?** Give a few different scenarios related to the position. For example, there is an outage that is affecting customers, and the lines are ringing off the hook. Customers are on hold for a long period of time even adding to their frustration, and you still need to enter the notes from the previous call. Should you quickly take care of the customer to get to the next call? Should you let the customer know that you have been inundated with calls and that you are doing the best that you can? The answers to these types of questions can give you insight on how well they handle stress. You should also ask the interviewee about a couple of stressful times they've had in previous jobs. If they answer that they have never had any type of work related stress, then they are most likely lying or never had that type of position.

12. **Are they a team player and will they fit in?** You have to think about the rest of the team and determine if this person will benefit or hurt the team spirit and production.

13. **What makes them feel they are more qualified than the next person?** This is a hard question to answer. They will worry if they come off as too confident or too humble. But you can still get some valuable insight from the answer to the question. If they say something like, "I'm the right person because I know the type of idiots who are out there," then you know you've got trouble. If they come across as unsure about themselves, you've also got trouble. You want someone who feels comfortable enough to answer the question with a simple but clear statement like, "The best way I can answer this question is to tell you that I really love doing this type of work and will not disappoint you." The answer might be rehearsed, but it is still worth a try.

14. **If you have a company website with your product line,** you can ask them if they went to the website before the interview. If they did and

answered some questions based on information from the website, you know you have someone who is ready to take the initiative to learn. If they didn't go to the website, it shows that they weren't even willing to take the time to do their homework for the job they are seeking. Unless they state that they do not have an Internet connection or are not computer savvy, there is no reason why they couldn't have visited the website.

If applicable, also have them perform a quick typing test to show speed, spelling and use of grammar.

Be sure to find out what shifts and possible hours they can work. Also, if they are going to be working a swing or graveyard shift, make sure you have them on a normal shift for the first few months so they can get all of the training and support they need. You do not want to throw them into the deep end with little to no support.

Don't be surprised if you get questions asked from the interviewee.
Depending on the question, this is not a bad thing and it shows they have a true interest in the company and where it is going.   Be careful not to mislead, or give job security type of comments or commitments. Tell them that a decision will not be made until all applicants have been interviewed. When in doubt, have them talk to HR for all benefit, and salary type of questions. This includes how and when they will be notified if they got the job.

If they ask questions that show more interest in not working than working, you should be concerned. Here are a couple of questions that if asked, should be considered dubious:

- When can they take a vacation and for how long?
- Will they get paid if they take off the day before or day after a holiday?
- Is working overtime mandatory?
- Is working on the weekends mandatory?
- Can they only work the hours that are required?
- If it is slow, can they leave early?
- When will they be promoted?
- How long do they have to work in your department before they can transfer to another department?
- When will they get a raise?
- How late can they be before it is considered a tardy?

If they are asking these types of questions now, who knows what they will be asking in the future.

Use your time wisely, however, try and ask questions that give the applicant a chance to talk about their experience and skills, rather than asking only yes or no type of questions. You want to ask as many open ended questions as you can. It gives you a chance to see how well they know the subject at hand, and gives them a chance to relax a bit.

Let them do most of the talking during the interview. Many managers talk too much and come across as intimidating or bragging. You can also learn a lot about someone on how they react during uncomfortable silence. Do not jump in and try to finish their sentence. You should also find some common interests to break the ice, just make sure you do not cross any possible discriminatory lines.

Questions you should not ask

You need to be familiar with topics that are not permissible as interview questions to avoid possible discrimination lawsuits. Examples would be race, ethnicity, gender, religion, age, health, illness, disabilities, and national origin. Stay away from all questions and conversation that is not related to the job unless they are just some nice pleasantries like hobbies or the weather. Absolutely refrain from making any illegal type of statements or asking discriminatory questions. Go to this link to help find out what are considered illegal questions to ask during an interview: U.S. Equal Employment Opportunity Commission http://www.eeoc.gov/.

***It is a good idea to have at least two people responsible for interviewing and hiring applicants. Not only will you get a second opinion, it can help support the decision not to hire if the unsuccessful applicant files a discrimination charge.

Checking their references

The candidate might seem very trustworthy, but to ease your mind and to fully justify hiring this person, take the time to check both the professional and personal references. Think about it, if they are lying about their references, you never know what else they might be lying about. In many cases HR will perform a background check, which will help as well. You want to be assured that the person you hire can do the job, contribute to your growth and development, and have no past history of violence that might one day endanger your employees.

Also keep in mind that you might be liable if you failed to do a background check on a person who then attacked another in your workplace. That alone should give you reason to not ignore this important part of the hiring process.

Many companies you call will only verify the employment dates and not job performance. At least you will know they did indeed work at the location they stated, and at the same timeframe that was stated on the application.

How much should you pay?

In most cases, HR will have already determined the pay rates. If you have created a new position, you will have had to work that out with HR before even posting the position. You can always try to use your management influence and change the rate of pay due to the expertise needed. Just make sure you have your boss's blessing, and you have the budget to cover the change. Just be careful not to make waves with HR. You need them to be on your side. You will have years of heartache if you do not have a good relationship with HR...

If you are able to set the rate of pay yourself, check around and see what the competition pays. If you can pay the same, or even slightly more than your competition, the better the chance for a long-term happy employee. Look for the average rate of pay for the experience required in your city. It would also be a good idea to use some well-known companies rate of pay as a benchmark, even if it is nationwide. You want to find the range of the highs and lows. Hopefully you will at least be in the middle. Just remember, you get what you pay for.

If you have a range of pay for the position, you can try to balance it out by hiring the least experienced and not as technically skilled at the lower end of pay, and the more experienced with higher skills at the upper end of pay. However, if you do this, you need to stress to your employees to never discuss their rate of pay with their peers.

Making the final offer

HR will most likely present the offer to the candidate. It really is best as they will be able to answer questions associated with benefits, first paycheck date, etc.

If possible, it would be a good idea to set a probationary period of 90 days. This would give you the right to let someone go if they are not performing up to standards. You should find out if this is possible before making the final offer. If not, you should try to lobby this idea for future new hires.

Employee on-boarding and orientation process

You want to make the first days on the job as stress free and exciting as possible. With the right approach, you can have your new hire "chomping at the bit" to get to work and be productive. You want them to know that they will be trained, given clear directions and expectations, understand the goals of the department, and will be part of a team. You want them to feel comfortable, and not feel like they are in the way. Make sure you give the employee who will be training the new hire plenty of advance warning. This shows respect for both individuals. Make sure the trainer takes it easy for the first couple of days, and encourages the new hire as much as possible. Do not let the new hire train with someone who is too busy, or will share any ill feelings they might have with the company.

Here are 10 tips to use whenever dealing with the new employee:

- Gladly welcome the employee the moment they arrive. Shake their hand with a hearty welcoming tone.

- Chances are they will be nervous and already stressed by filling out all of the new hire forms with HR. Offer a cup of coffee or something to help make them feel at ease.

- Walk the employee around the building, and introduce the new hire to your staff as a welcomed addition to the team and company.

- Give a brief history of the company and where you feel you're headed. Explain how it works, described the products and/or services you provide, talk about the competition, etc.

- Go over the department and company's goals and objectives.

- Go over the job functions and responsibilities.

- Give absolute clear expectations of the employee's role in your department and company. Stress for attention to detail on every aspect of the job, for example, you expect nothing but world-class customer support with excellent documentation. If you have set up a probationary period, now would be a good time to discuss immediate expectations.

- Cover any rules or regulations that HR did not cover. This includes any safety policies and procedures.

- Talk about the schedule, the person or people who will be doing the training, seating and computer arrangements, etc. This is also the responsibility of the employee's direct supervisor.

- Make sure a positive and welcoming feeling has been established, and shake the employee's hand with a sense of value and ensuring confidence.

Employee Retention

Now that you have hired the right person, you want them to be a part of the organization for many years to come. The less turnover, which is the coming and going of employees, the better. It reduces costs, keeps morale high, and you get full return on your investment. You need to keep your new hires, and existing staff, happy and content as discussed in lesson 3.

Finding the best people who can fit within your culture, and contribute within your organization, is a challenge and an opportunity. Keeping the best people, once you find them, is easy if you do the right things.

These 16 specific actions will help you with recruiting and retaining all the talent you need:

1. **Be known as a great company to work for.** If your company has the reputation as being the best, people will not want to leave. Why would anyone want to leave a place they love? A place where people envy and wish they were able to work?

2. **Be known as a great boss to work for.** You want your employees saying, and truly meaning, that you are the best boss. Implementing all of what is taught in this course will surely help make that happen.

   Point to keep in mind; it is more common for people to leave due to quality of supervision than any other reason. You do not want people leaving because of you, or your supervisory staff.

3. **Always provide the right tools and training**. The easier a person can do their job, and the more they know about their job, the more likely they will be comfortable and not want to leave.

4. **Continue to promote the best.** You want your employees to know that when they strive to be the best, they can be promoted and grow with the company.

5. **Pay better than the competition.** Although this is fairly obvious, and has already been mentioned earlier in this lesson, it is still worth mentioning again.

6. **Use your influence to have, and keep, the best benefits package**. This helps you personally, helps retain your employees, and helps the company as a whole. People will not want to leave a company with a great benefit plan. Even if the competition pays better, knowing you are secure in benefits can outweigh the other. This includes medical, dental, life insurance, and retirement. Matching 401k's are also a big incentive to stay with the company for the long-term.

7. **Have a company bonus plan**. If the employee knows that they will get a bonus if the company hits the yearly goals and targets, the more likely they are to stay. Even if the company missed the year-end bonus target, there is always the hope for next year. That right there just helped retain an employee for an additional 12 months.

8. **Offer stock options.** This is a great way to keep people for 4 or more years, due to most options are fully vested by the 4th year. For example, 25% vested after year 1, 50% vested after year 2, etc.

9. **Offer tuition reimbursement**. As long as they are with the company, and are taking a course that is related to their position within the company, it's a win/win situation when the company pays for tuition fees. This helps retain the employee for at least a year or two, and people tend to stay with a company that treated them so well, even after the course is through.

10. **Competitive vacation package.** The longer you are with the company, the more vacation time is added. For example, you get two weeks vacation after years 1 and 2, three weeks vacation after year 3, four weeks vacation after year 4, and max out at five weeks vacation after year 5 and beyond.

11. **Provide cross training**. Employees who learn what others do usually want to aspire to learn more and train harder. It takes time to learn new skills, which means they will stay with the company for quite some time.

12. **Inspire employee feedback**. An employee who is afraid to share ideas and concerns is more likely to explode with bottled up emotions, and then look elsewhere for a job. There will be employees who are quiet and seem content, but inside they are fired up. They do not say anything because they are afraid of retribution. Encourage openness as described throughout this course.

13. **Parity amongst departments**. If one department is getting all of the perks and recognition, and the other departments are ignored, you will have some disgruntled employees. First off, don't let the ignored department be yours. Second, make it a point that fairness and equality is established. You might need to explain that certain department's function differently when it comes to commission and perks. For example, the sales department gets paid by commission, and might get a better reward than you can give to your staff as customer service manager. Your job as customer service manager is to make sure your staff is aware that if sales do not sell, they do not get paid. The trade off between a steady paycheck that your staff receives, and the possibility of a great reward that sales might receive, should offset one another.

14. **Do not rule by intimidation.** When people feel intimidated and threatened by you, you might achieve short-term gain, but the employee will leave the moment an opportunity presents itself.

15. **Keep to your commitments**. People do not trust a boss who is all talk with no substance, thus will want to leave. Always follow up no matter what the circumstance. Always keep to the meeting you have scheduled, the events you have planned, or the promises that you made. Even if you give information that the employee does not want to hear, the fact that you respected their idea enough to follow up will earn you respect. When they respect you, they will not want to leave you.

16. **Make sure they feel like they are part of the "in crowd."** Treat your employees like they are special and that working for you is cool. They should feel they are part of a team that is looked at as "the best of the best" with respect, and even awe.

Your goal is to make it to where there is no reason for your key employees to leave other than that of a brand new experience or relocating. There's not too much you can do about that. The chances of high retention are also higher when you hire the best as described throughout this lesson. This is just another reason why hiring someone with a good attitude who shows integrity is such a good thing to do.

Key employee retention is extremely crucial to your department and the company's success. Retaining your best employees ensures a solid future along with customer satisfaction and higher sales no matter what kind of department you run.

A short story about hiring and keeping employees

Sample Corp was growing, and more support was needed to provide the kind of customer service that was expected of John and his department. Because John had structured his department to it's optimal, it was easy to add an additional person, both logically and physically. John updated the job description and put an ad in the local paper and online for a Tier 1 data repair technician. He was so excited to add another person to his head-count; he ended up hiring one of the first people he interviewed. This person had the right skills and seemed like a good enough person, but after just three months of employment, the new employee quit.

John was upset. It cost the company time and money to bring in a new employee, not to mention the time and money invested into all of the training that was needed. John thought, "What kind of person starts a new job and quits after just three months?" He decided to investigate to see where he went wrong and if there was anything to learn from this poor hiring decision.

John pulled out the employees resume and quickly spotted that this person jumped around between companies more than he had realized. In just three years, this person had five different employers and the reason for leaving was because a better offer was made. To make things worse, John did not call any of the previous companies or references for employment verification and character assessment.

From that point on, John added job history and time at each company into his new hire checklist. He knew that it was pretty easy to spot someone with the right skills, but it was harder to spot someone who is still searching for what they want out of their career. He also made it a point to call references and verify employment.

It also made John realize that if his existing staff sees people leaving for other opportunities, they might leave as well. Luckily, he already had a motivated staff, due to setting clear expectations along with recognition and rewards in place. However, he just knew not to take that for granted. He decided it was time to discuss some new retention ideas with his fellow managers and upper management. After a few meetings, they came up with a new vacation policy that rewarded those who stayed with the company for over four years, with 4 weeks of vacation (the previous policy was 3 weeks). It was also decided to provide tuition reimbursement for job related studies. Just these two changes greatly reduced attrition, not just in John's department, but also throughout the entire company.

Epilogue: You have to really do your homework when it comes to hiring a new employee. You not only have to look at their skills, aptitude, and attitude, but that they will be around for the long run. Always look for ways to retain your employees and do not be afraid to discuss ideas with upper management. The points discussed in this lesson should help greatly when it comes to hiring the right person and keeping your employees for many years to come.

Quick Lesson Summary

- You have to hire the right person, not just a body to fill the seat. You will have to deal with all that comes with the "wrong person." It is better not to hire at all, than hire a problem. Remember, *"You can train a nice person to become skilled, but you can't train a skilled person to become nice."*

- Make sure you truly need to hire a new employee. Don't just hire for hiring's sake. You don't want to lose the opening, however, you also do not want to be overstaffed. Make the right decision.

- Create a relevant job description and always keep it up to date. Focus on the most important job skills first, and then add the desired qualifications.

- For a successful interview, have a good list of questions to ask and points you want to discuss based off of their resume. Look for aptitude and attitude, as they are the most important qualities. Provide a professional, yet friendly atmosphere to put the applicant at ease. Make sure you know what questions you <u>cannot</u> ask during the interview process.

- Check their references and employment history before making a decision

- Set the rate of pay as competitive as possible.

- Set the right tone by making the on-boarding process a positive one.

- Always look at ways to retain your employees. Motivating, recognizing and rewarding are very good ways to keep your best employees, but there are also incentives like tuition reimbursement, longer vacation time, and bonus plans to keep them around for the long run.

LESSON 5 – HOW TO DEAL WITH CONFLICT, PROBLEMS, DIFFICULT EMPLOYEES & FIRING

Introduction: The toughest part of the job...

You, as manager, need to do your best to make sure your department is running like a well oiled "team-machine" as discussed in lesson 3. However, just when you think everything is going along smoothly and under control, the inevitable conflicts, disagreements, and differences of opinion start to escalate, and harmony within the team is disrupted. There might be legal consequences in certain situations. In some cases it's time to fire the individual.

Your job as manager goes beyond just making sure you hit the numbers. You sometimes need to be a counselor or mediator. In most cases, using good old common sense will get you through the issue at hand. You should be the first line of defense, as you might be able to handle the situation by just listening and showing some compassion. You should, however, never be afraid to ask for HR's help whenever needed. This lesson will deal with all of these issues and more.

Dealing with Conflict

In some cases, the conflict can be a good thing like process improvements or better ideas to service the customer. This can be part of the "open communication" that is encouraged within the team. However, in most cases the conflict is more negatively based. Examples of conflict are:

- A personal problem with two or more people. It could be based on issues such as values, beliefs, a friendship gone sour, flirting, sexual harassment, or vulgarity. These incompatible situations can lead into arguments and even worse, physical fighting. There is also the chance of termination, especially when dealing with sexual harassment. The two most common sexual harassment categories, both of which are considered as part of the 1991 Civil Rights Act as illegal employment discrimination with punitive monetary damages, are:

  1. Asking for sexual favors in return for providing a raise, promotion, etc. (Quid pro quo).
  2. What a woman perceives as a hostile environment like unwanted touching, pin-up calendars, sexual jokes, sexual comments, leering, inappropriate photos, etc.

  Your HR representative will most likely be involved if these types of situations were to occur. See the U.S. Equal Employment Opportunity Commission http://www.eeoc.gov/ for more information.

- A perception of one working harder than the other.

- One person blaming another for past mistakes.

- Rebellious jealousy because it looks like you are playing favorites.

- Not happy or thinks it's unfair with the type of work assigned to them.

- Personality clash. For example, a systematic vs. unorganized approach to the job, or a sensitive person vs. insensitive person.

- Disagreements – one person feels it should be done one way, and another feels it should be done another way. This could be based on ideas, goals, process discrepancies, etc.

- Inappropriate dress for work. It might be too revealing or unprofessional.

- Personal hygiene.

You should have your radar on at all times to try and prevent these conflicts before they escalate. You should take the time to learn and understand the laws associated with the EEOC http://www.eeoc.gov/. This includes understanding the policies regarding Affirmative Action, as you or your supervisor's personal attitude can make or break your organizations EEOC and affirmative action policies. If you create an atmosphere of equality, and help facilitate understanding and tolerance among all employees, you should be able to avoid any conflicts associated with the EEOC and affirmative action.

Keep a tight rein on any individuals who are problem talkers and deal with any outbreaks immediately. Also as manager, you should never joke around about any sensitive subjects. You have to always use common sense and never make comments that could make some laugh and hurt others. That is not to say you should not have a sense of humor, as in many cases your sense of humor can help build team morale and help eliminate stress. Just be careful on what you joke about. Never joke about anything dealing with racism, sexism, religion, etc.

You also need to be careful not to make promises you cannot keep. For example, telling someone they will get a raise or a promotion if they finish a project on time when you are not 100% certain it is even possible. Unless you are 100% certain, never make such a claim. An innocent type of comment like this can become the basis of a binding employment contract.

Another concern deals with being a member of management in an unionized organization. You have two job functions as you need to perform your normal management duties by getting the most productivity out of your workers, and you need to be aware of, and adhere to, management's commitments under the union contract. The National Labor Relations Act http://www.nlrb.gov outlines unfair labor practices that can affect you as manager. You should be well aware of the main issues like blocking an employee to form or join a union, attempting to influence a labor union, and discriminating against members of a union. These legal and actionable offences can lead to your dismissal along with a great deal of cost to your company.

When it comes to anticipating potential conflict, look for signs such as tension in the air, off handed comments, backstabbing, manipulation, a normally outspoken person is now quiet, a normally quiet person is now outspoken, facial expressions, and undermining. You need to react immediately using the managerial skills described throughout this course and not let it simmer. If, however, an interpersonal issue does occur, do not put your head in the sand and hope it all works out. You must make it a priority to get involved and resolve the problem. Conflict resolution, whether resolved by you, or you acting as a mediator, is essential. Even if you do nothing but let the parties work it out themselves, it's ok as long as it truly gets resolved. If the conflict is not resolved, you might run into emotional issues leading to withdrawal and also possible resignation. You need to get involved, but how involved you get determines on the severity of the conflict.

Determine the type of conflict and the severity. The types of conflicts determine the type of approach that should be taken. Here are three questions to determine the type and the actions you should take based on the severity of the conflict:

1. *Is the conflict an issue that is shared by all on the team?* These conflicts can be issues creating disharmony with the team such as problems with the processes and procedures that are in place, other departments that are not doing their job correctly, or customers unhappy with the service or product thus creating friction amongst the team, etc.

   - If **yes,** then you should ask all of the, who, what, when, where, how, and why type of questions. Find the points of failure causing the friction and show your team that you are doing all you can to correct and remedy the situation.
   - If **no,** then proceed to question 2.

2. *Is the conflict due to one individual?* These conflicts can be issues such as personal hygiene, an employee inappropriately dressed, or an individual complaining of the work assigned to them or thinks it's unfair, etc.

   - If **yes,** here are some ways to deal with the issue:

     o If it is a *dress code* issue, first see if there is a dress code in place by HR that you can easily find in the handbook. If there is, explain that this is corporate policy. If not, then you need to talk to them in private and be honest and upfront by stating that, in your opinion (do not say another individual is complaining), what they are wearing is not appropriate. You might determine that the problem is due to such issues like safety, causing disruption in the office, or because it might make people feel uncomfortable. In most cases the employee will feel a bit embarrassed and understandable. If not, then you need to state that part of your managerial responsibilities is to make sure the department works in harmony, and that you cannot afford any disruptions of any kind. If needed, you can ask for HR's help. Don't be surprised if the employee compares what they are wearing to what another employee is wearing. If so, just say that you will look into it and will deal with any situations that need attention. You might truly have to address that issue as well.

o If it is a *hygiene* issue, first off speak to them in private and say that you have something that is somewhat uncomfortable to talk about, but needs to be addressed nonetheless. Ask them to please do all that they can to make sure their personal hygiene is taken care of before coming into the office. You can state that part of your managerial responsibilities is to make sure the department works in harmony and that you cannot afford any disruptions of any kind, including hygiene related issues. You do need to be careful as the hygienic problem might be medically related. You might want to suggest they see a doctor about certain hygienic issues if the problem continues. Just make sure to let them know to please do all they can to control their hygiene as much as possible. If it does not improve, you should talk to HR about the next steps that should be taken. You might need to move the person to an area away from the group.

o If they are *not happy* with the work assigned to them, or think it's unfair, then you need to ask them why they feel this way and be prepared to discuss all possible options. If for instance they are complaining about the work given to them, find out if other staff members also have the same complaint. Also compare this person's workload to the other staff members. If this person is indeed working harder, then you need to address the issue with your staff.   If not, then you need to tell them that the workload is part of the overall job responsibilities. Let them know that you will look into possible process improvements or if it is possible to hire more staff.

Another example would be if someone is complaining because of the extra workload the late shift has to perform, which has less people and added responsibility. You should remind them that they agreed to work that shift, however, you should give them the option to move into another shift. If another shift is not available, let them know they will be on the waiting list. At least they can see the light at the end of the tunnel and that you understand their predicament.

- If **no** then proceed to question 3.

3. *Is the conflict pertaining to more than one individual based on personal issues, personality clashes, disagreements, etc?*

- There might be times when the problem rectifies itself before you get involved. It might be too trivial to worry about and the best solution is to postpone setting up a meeting and let the issue die down on it's own. For the simple conflicts, your serious involvement might just be throwing more salt into the wound. However, you need to be 100% sure that all is good by monitoring the situation for a while.

- If you feel there is a true problem, then you need to meet with all of the individuals involved at the same time. Do not meet with them separately or else you will probably get over exaggerated and potentially untrue comments.

You will most likely be acting as a mediator, so your job is to let each person briefly state their issue with no interruptions from anyone else in the room. You would only intervene if it starts to get out of control. After hearing both sides, you need to sum up each other's point of view to be sure everyone is on the same page. At that point, you would ask each of them what it would take to appease each other. The overall goal is to have all parties commit to making the necessary changes to resolve, or at least reconcile, the conflict. Let them know that you expect and have the confidence that they will make every attempt to resolve each others differences with respect for one another. You should also follow up after a week or month to make sure all is on track. Here are three common conflict examples between two or more people:

- o **Friendship problems**. It is inevitable that strong friendships will develop between co-employees, and that's fine. People are happier when they have a true good friend at work. The problems you may see is too much socializing when they should be working, other team members getting jealous which can create a bad atmosphere, or if they get in a fight which creates tension. In most cases, the good out weighs the bad. However, if there is a problem, fix it as soon as possible. If you do not personally see the conflict, you can spot these types of situations through performance appraisals, comparative stats, the rumor mill, or passing comments. Your job as manager is to make sure they fully understand that their friendship cannot affect their work. Let them know it also affects the work and morale of any other team members. Most of the time it all works out and gets resolved either during the meeting you have with them or right after.

- o **Personality clash, differences in life styles, different beliefs and values, etc**. The saying, "Oil and water don't mix," holds true in the workplace. Some people just do not see "eye to eye" and that creates tension. In most cases, there is nothing you can do to make them like each other. If the conflict came to the point to be discussed in your office, the best thing you can do is to let them talk it out. You can also share your views of the overall goals of the department and the type of teamwork needed. It does not mean they have to be friends, but they both need to understand the main objective and that you cannot have it any other way. They need to walk out of the office with a sense of mutual respect due to the same goals you instilled upon them.

- o **Disagreements or mixed expectations**. Issues like; how one person does not like they way the other person enters data, how one person troubleshoots differently than another, how one person tells another how to do their job, or how one person expects a report at a certain time and does not get it, are all classic examples of disagreements and mixed expectations. This may be process related in which you need to fix. However, most of the time it is just the point of view or misunderstanding of one person towards another. After hearing both sides, examine and work it out to where there is a compromise. Based on these examples, some compromises would be; there should be more detailed data entered, but it does not have to be a book. There can be a few more troubleshooting steps, but the overall performance is acceptable. A person can help another, but should never act like the boss. And finally, the report can be guaranteed to be ready at 11:00, instead of the unrealistic 9:00. These are the type of creative compromising ideas you need, to be able to resolve the minor problems. Unless it is an absolute work related problem that defies the company's values and job expectations, little compromises like these usually resolves the issue.

✓ *Steps to take when dealing with conflict:*

1. **Counsel and Verbal warning:** First, send a simple e-mail asking them to stop by your office at a given time. Do not go into details or specifics, just a simple invite. You can also verbally ask them as well as long as it's done privately. If there is a problem with the scheduled time, simply move it to a time that is good for all. Try not to make the meeting seem mandatory or else you will already start off with a negative approach. The point is to make the meeting as indiscreet as possible and also gives them a chance to prepare for the discussion.

   When you meet, after you say your hello's, say the reason you ask them to visit you is to discuss something that is difficult to share, and a bit uncomfortable, but needs to be addressed. You can also start off with something like, "I understand there is a problem that needs some attention." Do not bring any person or persons names up, or that there is even a complaint from anyone. This is straight from you, which is part of the job of being manager. You want to make sure that it is understood that you are the one who is bringing the matter into the forefront. Use a lot of "I" statements like, "I want to make sure we do everything possible to resolve this issue," or "I understand what your are saying, but..."

   Be straightforward, simple, and to the point, yet empathetic, which strengthens and deepens the relationship and rapport. Do everything you can not to embarrass the person. When dealing with a conflict involving more than one person, you will be most likely acting as a mediator. You want to resolve the conflict by "reasoning together." Be sure to have each of them briefly describe the problem and to not interrupt each other. Always try to focus on the positive aspects of each other's statement. Once each person has had a chance to explain their side, you can ask how we as a team can correct this situation. You should mostly be listening to them work on trying to resolve or reconcile the issue at hand, which is exactly what you want. If tempers flare, be sure to intervene and make sure everyone is calmed down before proceeding. Make sure everyone sticks to the point, but is able to get everything out. Make sure to follow their statements and solutions with clear and precise summation. By repeating back what has been said solidifies the solutions.

Keep a cool head and remain in control of your own emotions. Employees might be irrational with no common sense, uncooperative, mean, and disrespectful. Use a calm tone and make sure you present yourself with an understanding attitude. Let them know that you do care and will do all you can to help resolve the issue. Just never talk to them with a condescending tone. Also, always bite your tongue before you say something you might regret. Certain words can set someone off on a tangent. Also be careful using certain actions such as hand gestures, crossing your arms in a defiant way, confused facial expressions, demoralized posture, too much eye contact, or sounds and grunts of discontent. You will get your point across more effectively if you keep it professional at all times. Keep your advice to yourself and let them work it out mutually. You should only get involved with advice or solutions when there are no other alternatives, or if you are asked for your help in the matter.

Make sure all parties make an agreement on the direction and steps needed to solve the problem, or create the opportunity. You need to make sure that everyone is focused on the big picture and on the future. There should be no more blame game. Your goal is to find a win/win situation where all parties involved are satisfied with the outcome. A compromise is good, but if you can have them leave with the feeling of a change for the better, you've reduced the chance of future conflict. Also remember, the quicker you help resolve the issue, the less chance the conflict spreads throughout the whole department.

If you think the problem may take some time to resolve, then you need to get all parties involved to reach an agreement on a timeframe when this will be resolved. In most cases the issue can be rectified immediately.

2. **Written warning, suspension or termination:** If the issue is not resolved after implementing step 1, then you will need to explain possible disciplinary action. The nature of the discipline depends on the issue and HR policies. Issues dealing with conflict are not as clear-cut as job performance or attendance problems, which are described later in this lesson. With those types of problems, there is usually a process like a verbal warning, then a written warning, then either another written warning or suspension, before finally resulting in termination. With conflict issues, depending on the severity, you might need to go to suspension and/or termination stage right away.

Always remember that you should be:

- **Well prepared.** Have all your ducks in a row and all necessary documentation, important notes, and facts to discuss with confidence.

- **Non-judgmental.** Make it known that you are not taking sides or made any pre-conceived judgments. Remain objective and see each person's perspective. You goal is to only find resolution, or at least reconciliation. You want to be decisive when you need to confront, however, you will mostly be listening and mediating, especially when dealing with more than one person.

- **Documenting everything!!!** This cannot be stressed enough. You will need documentation to prove future disciplinary actions if the conflicts cannot be resolved.

Dealing with Violence, Bullying, and Anger in the Workplace

Violence takes on many forms. It can be a threat of force, shove, fistfight, etc. In extreme cases, it can involve the use of a gun. Whatever the form, it's potentially dangerous. Even the bully who intimidates is a threat of sorts. These situations create low morale and damage productivity. They can also be costly to the company due to a lawsuit brought on by the victim of the violence.

Try to look for signs of violence before it occurs. If you or your staff sees emotional outbursts, co-workers confronting each other, employees confronting authority figures, or even unusual social behavior, you need to address the situation as soon as possible. First try talking to the individual in private to get an understanding of the emotional outburst. It might be related to the stress of the job, which is something you can control. If it is an emotional issue beyond your control, get in touch with HR. They may be able to help provide some intervention. You might want to let the person go home early, or even take a couple of days off to deal with the emotional situation.

The main point here is to defuse the situation before it escalates. Bring the person into your office and talk it out. You do not need to be a psychologist, just be there to listen and provide as much insight as you can. Again, do not be afraid to utilize HR if it is something beyond what you can control. If it comes to a point where serious violence can take place at any moment, get in touch with security. If you cannot get in touch with security, call the police. You do not want it to get to a point of no return, and you especially do not want any serious violence to take place in the office. At the very least it should be taken outside.

You also want to defuse the bully by establishing the fact that such behavior is not tolerated as part of the company's values. State this calmly and not let in to what the bully is seeking, which is intimidation. In most cases a person is a bully because of their own fears and low self-esteem. The best thing you can do when dealing with a bully is to never let them succeed by getting good performance results due to the bullying of others. If they truly do good work that is not the result of intimidating others, praise the good work as you normally would. If the bully sees that you are monitoring and recognize good results, based on true achievement or by intimidation, the bullying should subside either way. If not, the situation should be treated as any other difficult employee issue. How to deal with difficult employees will be covered in the next section of this lesson.

The best thing you can do is maintain a positive, calming, anger-preventing attitude. The leadership tips in lesson 1 can help, as well as much of what is taught throughout this course. You might not always spot the people who are ready to explode, but you will decrease the chances if the environment you create is a positive one. By treating everyone with a true caring attitude, you will reduce explosive situations. If you manage and lead with an explosive authoritarian personality, your employees might want to explode as well. This also goes for dealing with angry people in your department. They might not be violent, but the negative emotions the angry employee is generating affects morale nonetheless. When someone is showing signs of anger, find out what triggered the emotion and find a solution to the problem.

Whether a person is violent or just angry, you need to always protect yourself and your team members from harm. Defuse the situation. Take the person outside or in your office to keep others away from your conversation. Calmly discuss the issue, remove the person from any tools or machinery which can cause harm, let them take the rest of the day off to get a hold of their composure, and if needed, get HR and/or security involved whenever the situation is beyond your control.

Whenever you speak to an employee, whether it relates to bulling, anger or violence, always be sure to document everything that transpired. You would need to give, at the very least, a verbal warning. Depending on the severity, an incident report is usually written up by you or HR.   Depending on the nature of the act, suspension and/or termination is highly possible.

Dealing with Difficult Employees

Unfortunately, even when we try to hire nothing but the best, create a strong team environment, train, coach, and motivate, there is still the chance you will have a difficult employee or two. One who:

- Calls out sick and rides the time off policies to the very edge.
- Does the absolute minimum work expected, but just enough to fly under the radar.
- Testing and criticizing the office policies in place.
- Gossiping, but not to where it can be seen in the office.
- Backstabs fellow employees.
- Controls a situation by using negativity.
- Has a bad attitude.
- Conducts themselves poorly.

The worst thing is that they do not have enough infractions to suspend, let alone terminate. They know how to work the system. They are the "bottom of the curve" employees.

Everyone can't be a star player, but they should at least be average. With the difficult employee, there is no enthusiasm, drive, and usually a bad attitude. Just when you think there is a chance after some private motivational conversation, they will pull the rug from underneath you once again and leave you wondering why you have this employee. It affects the morale of co-workers and of those who work hard and follow the rules. It tests your ability as a leader and manager, and starts to poison the well with the teams' lack of faith in management.

Chances are, this type of behavior has not only worked for them in the past, but is simply part of their personality. They feel like they are smart enough, and even smarter than their co-workers, to beat the system. They become so difficult that managers and co-workers just start to put up with it, which makes the person feel like they won. They feel they can get away with anything and even have a look about them that says, "What are you going to do about it?" The good news is there are some things you can do to correct this type of behavior and start holding them more accountable.

No one likes to have to deal with these types of problem employees, but when you have an employee who is disruptive, has a bad attitude, or is quite frankly a "bad apple," you need to deal with it as soon as possible. You should never pretend this problem does not exist, or hope it somehow corrects itself. You will lose the respect of your team if you do not deal with the situation. You need to deal with this type of issue immediately with a "zero tolerance policy" once you start to see the cracks. Don't wait, it will only get worse. It may even get beyond repair on what has already been broken.

✓ *Steps to take when dealing with difficult employees:*

1. **Counsel and verbal warning:** Get all of the facts and bring that person into your office without making a big scene. Be honest, and upfront, and discuss what you are seeing and how important it is to have the whole department working in "harmony". Simply ask if there is anything wrong, or if there is something happening in the workplace that is causing what is perceived as "a person with a bad attitude who is unhappy at work." Listen and show empathy if the conversation is headed that way. There may be some personal issues that they just need to get off of their chest. If you get a sarcastic, "Nothings wrong with me," then you need to state that is not what you see. You have to be strong, but not attacking, and let them know that the behavior shown is not acceptable and needs to improve.

   Be sure you are focusing on the problem, not the person. You are seeing a behavioral issue that you are concerned with, but do not make it seem like it is a personal attack on the person because you do not like them. Stay calm, let them do the talking, and be sure you are letting the person know that you are truly listening by being able to recap the conversation.

   Point out their strengths, and try to first focus on the good aspects of their performance rather than a perceived bad attitude. The goal is for the boss, and co-workers, to try to see the positive, and not the negative.

   Use a lot of "I" statements like, "I need to make sure the department is working in harmony," or "I cannot accept bad behavioral problems in the department." Do not focus on the person and say, "You need to..."

   Document and date this conversation as a verbal warning. This is not a written warning, but shows that you did talk to the person about difficult employee issues. The more you document, the easier it will be to terminate if it gets to that point. The biggest mistake is to not document. Documentation and building a case is the proof that shows you talked to this employee many times but to no avail.

2. **First and second written warnings:** Continue to confront until the behavioral problems are eliminated. The employee might feel like they are under the microscope and you are on a witch-hunt, but this is the only way to fix the problem for good. It might take some time depending on the situation, but you need to show you will not give in until you are completely satisfied. Also realize you do have to show equality for all. For example, if the employee is always just a few minutes late but within the grace period, you need to make sure if there are others with the same bad habits that they are dealt with as well. If the issue is not resolved, then you will need to explain possible disciplinary action. The nature of the discipline depends on the issue and HR policies. The problem may or may not be as clear-cut as job performance or attendance issues. Again, make sure you document the overall conversation.

   You may need to ask for HR's help as well. There is nothing wrong with this. You do, however, need to make sure you have truly done all you can before it gets to this point.

   The overall goal is for the employee to fully understand the problem at hand, what the solution must be, and what the consequences are if the behavioral problems continues. You should obviously never reward anyone for bad behavior, but if the person truly shows vast improvement, you can give the recognition deserved. It cannot be seen to the team that "if you have a bad attitude, you get what you want." It should be seen as you had a situation that needed to be dealt with, they've seen an improvement in the person's attitude and performance, and you are doing what is best for the overall good of the department. Do not discuss any personal issues, or even what was said to the employee, with the rest of the staff. If they ask you any questions, even in private, just say that you addressed the situation and what was said and done is confidential. They might be a bit disappointed not to hear the juicy gossip, but you will gain more respect in the long run for keeping all employee related issues confidential. This goes for the employee who is asking as well.

3. **Suspension and/or termination**. If it gets to the point where you have tried everything mentioned in steps 1 and 2, and the employee is still not willing to change behavioral problems, then you need to begin suspension and/or termination procedures in accordance with your company's policies.

Dealing with Poor Job Performance and Required Expectations

You have given them training and clear expectations, but the employee is not performing up to standard. This may be related to the difficult employee just described. It may be an employee with a great attitude but is lacking the skills needed. It might be a personal issue. When you see an employee whose work is poor, or misses a deadline due to procrastination, making up excuses, or blaming others, you have a problem. It can simply be a lack of confidence or direction. Maybe it is just too much of a task for this person to handle. You will be able to track job performance through performance reviews as discussed in lesson 3, unfortunately, however, performance reviews are usually held annually or semiannually. If you do not have a monthly performance review in place, there's a good chance that problems could occur between reviews.

✓ *Steps to take when dealing with poor job performance:*

Before anything, show confidence in the employee's ability and that you recognize they are trying and are willing to solve the problem. Ask the individual if you can help in any way. Approach the situation with a positive and ensuring attitude. If they are defensive or showing an obvious lack of care, go directly to step 1.

1. **Verbal warning**: If there are signs of cracks, bring them into your office as quietly as possible without embarrassing the employee, and just verbally discuss the issues at hand. Let them know that this is more of a heads up and not necessarily going to be a write up. Focus on the problem or behavior that needs improvement, not the person. Ask for the employee's view of the situation. Is the problem related to:

   • The employees' immediate supervisor?
   • A process issue?
   • A lack of training and/or is the training relevant to the job at hand?
   • Insufficient or a lack of tools?
   • Personnel issues regarding co-workers?

   If so, the responsibility is yours and you need look at ways to remedy the situation. Discuss potential solutions to the problem or improvement actions to take. Ask the employee for ideas on how to correct the problem. Offer suggestions so that the employee knows you are prepared to do what it takes to help them improve.

   If it's a personal issue, you should show your concern and suggest they should talk to HR. Make sure they realize how important they are to the company and how it is imperative that they're performing up to job expectations.

   Let the employee know you will have to give a written warning if their job performance does not improve. Agree on a written action plan that lists what the employee will do to correct the problem or improve the situation, and what you will do if you need to provide more training or better tools of the trade to use. Document and date this verbal warning. This is not a written warning but shows that you did talk to the person about performance related issues.

2. **First written warning:** If the problem is still occurring, and assuming you have done all you can on your end to remedy the situation, bring the individual into your office again, but this time showing how serious the situation has become. Have examples prepared to be able to discuss. You should also already have the written warning filled out to give to the employee once the meeting is over. Set a date and time for follow-up. It would be a good idea to set up a checkpoint so you or the employees' immediate supervisor knows how the employee is progressing on the plan.

3. **Second written warning or suspension:** If there are still problems at the follow-up review or soon after, this would be a time to either give a second written warning or suspension, which is usually between 1 and 5 days. This all depends on the HR policies already established. If the employee refuses to improve, they should be terminated. It is extremely important to always document any conversations and coaching performed that is related to the issue at hand. You will need this documentation if it gets to the point of suspension or termination.

4. **Suspension and/or termination:** If no improvement in performance occurs, you should proceed with a temporary suspension without pay. The intention to suspend should be confirmed in writing with details of start and end dates. HR will be involved and your presence may or may not be required. It is imperative that you have documented every meeting with exact detail. This might be needed if it ever goes to court.

   If it is determined that the employee should be terminated, the employee should be advised that as a result of poor performance, they will be dismissed. At this point, HR policies regarding pay and benefits will be discussed.

Dealing with Attendance issues

People take days off and are sometimes late for work. That is a given. The most common problem is when people take days off when they are not sick, such as wanting to stretch the weekend into 3 days, but when they really are sick, they come into work because they have run out of sick days. This is not good for the employee or other employees as they can become sick. The real problem, however, happens when they call out sick after they have exceeded the sick days allowed for the year. You can't turn a blind eye to this behavior and it is unfair to those who make it a point to come to work everyday and are on time. It is usually just a couple of employees who are the culprits. It is especially hard to deal with attendance problems with a person who is otherwise a great employee. Nonetheless, you have to deal with it, and with equality to all.

Here are eight points to keep in mind on how to control and possibly reduce attendance issues:

- **Make sure your employees understand your view towards attendance.** Make it a point to share your passion towards having a low absentee and tardiness department. Your supervisors also really need to fully understand the attendance expectations as they are on the front line and will see the infractions much more easily than you. If HR has not created one, have an attendance policy that clearly lays out the guidelines. Also lead by example by getting to work a bit early, leaving a bit late, and rarely, if ever, call out sick.

- **Have your employee's call you direct instead of their immediate supervisor**. They might think twice knowing you, the manager, will answer the phone or hear the voice mail.

- **Maintain accurate records**. There are easy to use software programs to track attendance. You can even use something like your Outlook calendar to make a note of each infraction. Create easy to use codes to not take up too much space. For example, instead of John Doe called out sick or John Doe was 15 minutes late, use something like JD-S or JD-15m.

- **Look for trends.** If you see an employee call out on a Friday or Monday, chances are they are taken advantage of sick days for pleasure. If you see an employee call out at the end of the month when your department is at its busiest, you most likely have someone who is not a team player. If an employee is always around 5 to 10 minutes late, it's not just a one off traffic jam but someone who just is not making the effort getting ready and to work on time. You might even see repetitive signs of sickness or tardiness with the employee looking like they have been partying all night. You want to address these trends as soon as possible.

- **Individual problem - have a one on one meeting. Multiple people - hold a team meeting.** When you have an individual or two who are repeat offenders, you want to deal with them separately. Don't punish all for a few problem employees. However, when you are seeing a trend with multiple members of the team with attendance issues, you need to hold a team meeting and show the statistics. Stress how it can damage the achievement of goals. Reducing absenteeism might even turn into a goal in itself. This will show all that you are serious about attendance, and how their attendance is important to the overall success of the team. Stress that you should not have to hire more people to achieve the goals due to poor attendance. This will put on certain peer pressure that can work to your benefit, especially if you offer a reward to the team if they achieve an attendance record you have set.

- **Allow for personal business.** It is better for your employees to be up front and tell you the truth. There might be a few occasions when someone needs to take some time off in the day to handle something that can only be dealt with during business hours. Just make sure they do not take advantage of this gesture.

- **Create an award program for those who do not call out or are tardy for a certain period of time.** It can be a paid day off or other ideas that were given in lesson 3. It shows that even though you are a stickler regarding attendance, you want to show your appreciation to those who make it a point to show up to work and being on time.

- **Have them make up time missed to make up for time lost.** Depending on state laws and company policy, this may be an option. If not, can they use some of their vacation time, or get no time if they have already used up all of their sick time? The "no time" means they would not get paid for the time missed. It would affect hourly/non-exempt employees much more.

✓ *Steps to take when dealing with attendance problems:*

1. **Counsel and verbal warning:** E-mail, or get their attention privately as to not embarrass the individual, to meet in your office. Start off by stating you are concerned over the absences or tardiness. Establish the reasons and determine what needs to be done to improve the attendance issues. If the problem does not appear to be a major health issue of any sort, you should advise the employee that an improvement in attendance is expected, or the next step in the procedure will be taken. There should be no more attendance problems for the following 6 months. Monitor the attendance monthly and proceed to step 2 if the problem continues. Document this meeting and consider it a verbal warning, not a written warning. You should notify HR if there are any medical issues that can possibly keep the employee out of work for any length of time. If the doctor confirms fitness for work, the employee needs to be warned about the consequences of continued absence.

2. **First written warning**: If the employee's absences continue, set up a second meeting. State the purpose and be prepared to discuss the reasons for the absences. Talk about the implications and how it affects the team and department, not to mention the company, and warn that if the problem continues, employment may be suspended and/or terminated. This all depends on how HR has set up the attendance policy. Document this meeting and consider it a written warning. Monitor for improvement, if there are still problems, go to step 3.

3. **Second written warning or suspension:** If there is still no improvement, consult with HR on what should be done next. If you can, and would like, set up another meeting with the same criteria as described in steps 1 and 2. Listen to what the employee has to say, and let them know you will get back to them to determine the next step. You can either give another written warning stating the next infraction is automatic suspension and/or termination, or go straight to the suspension stage. Again, this is determined on the existing HR policy.

4. **Suspension and/or termination:** If no improvement in attendance occurs, you should proceed with a temporary suspension without pay. The intention to suspend should be confirmed in writing with details of start and end dates. HR will be involved and your presence may or may not be required. It is imperative that you have documented every meeting with exact detail. This might be needed if it ever goes to court.

   If it is determined that the employee should be terminated, the employee should be advised that as a result of excessive attendance issues, they will be dismissed. At this point, HR policies regarding pay and benefits will be discussed.

Before you take drastic measures with all that has been discussed so far in this lesson, make sure the problem is not morale related or some other underlying issue. The fault might be yours due to departmental cracks, which you will need to find out what is wrong and fix as soon as possible. There might also be a problem with the time clock, parking situation, or scheduling that you should do your best to fix, or come up with an alternative solution.

Dealing with Firing or Laying off an Employee

One of the most difficult tasks you have to face as a manager is firing employees. This is the part of the job that most people dread. You should not fire anyone unless you are absolutely certain that it is deserved, however, most managers wait far too long to finally fire an employee. If you have provided clear expectations, and have implemented the associated steps and tips that have been discussed in this lesson, you will be justified in the decision and it should come as no shock to the employee. By utilizing all of the leadership and management tools taught in this course, you will have behaved ethically and legally, and again, justified in your decision to fire. Besides, if you do not fire an employee who truly deserves to be let go, you will lose respect within your department.

The employee who, breaks the rules, is not performing up to job expectations, has a poor attendance record, or causes difficulties in the workplace, needs to be let go. It is not good for the organization, and in many cases, it might just be the right thing for the individual. There are times when an employee is almost subconsciously begging to be let go to venture out to new things, but does not want to quit due to job security.

As stated many times throughout this lesson, documentation is an absolute necessity. Even when it is just a verbal consultation, it needs to be documented. Without the proper documentation, you may see yourself in a wrongful termination lawsuit.

HR is your best friend at this juncture and if you have provided full documentation and followed the company guidelines, you will not only look good in their eyes but the firing process will be that much easier. The same applies for laying off an employee, as only a few steps would need to be modified.

✓ *Steps to take when firing an employee:*

1. Hold the employment termination meeting. This is the time when you tap the employee on the shoulder and have them come into your office immediately. Even if they are in the middle of something, once you made the attempt to talk to the employee, it needs to happen right away so that there won't be anytime for the employee to think about what's to come. The employee's supervisor and/or a HR representative should also be present. The IT department needs to be notified as well to lock them out of their computer.

2. Don't be tentative and dance around the subject, just be straightforward, look the employee straight in the eyes, and let them know that you have to let them go.

3. Even though it should come as no surprise to the employee, you will probably
    be asked the question, "Why am I being fired?" State the reason for the
    employment termination. Have some quick notes prepared to be able to
    touch the main points. Be calm, quick to the point, and compassionate.
    Don't say more than you have to or else the focus might be on a moot point.
    Keep this termination process as short as possible. You can say something
    like this:

    > "As you know from our past conversations, we discussed the
    > importance on meeting the required standards (you can modify as
    > needed to the subject at hand). I think the way we approached and
    > tried to rectify the issue was fair and reasonable. I think I made it
    > pretty clear it was imperative that you met those standards. I don't
    > believe it was any lack of effort on your part; however, we are going
    > to have to terminate your services as of today. I really wanted this to
    > work out but unfortunately it has come to this point."

4. The employee might want to ask a couple of questions. You will be so
    prepared that you should feel comfortable to discuss how it got to this point.
    Don't discuss it for too long, you want to answer the questions and end the
    conversation as soon as possible.

5. The employee might be acceptable and want to end the experience as soon as
    possible. If that is the case, you do not need to lengthen the process by
    continually talking. HR will take it from there to discuss any possible
    severance pay, last paycheck, vacation balance, health coverage, etc. If,
    however, the employee is upset and lashes out, don't lose your cool. Let
    them get it off of their chest, but just for a short period of time. Make sure
    you maintain composure, no matter what the employee is saying, and know
    when to say, "I understand you're upset, however, we gave you many
    opportunities to improve so we would not have to be in this position." Stay
    compassionate and respectful, and then give a nod to HR that you've said all
    what you have to say and let them take over. They will most likely bring the
    employee to their office.

6. If the employee is not showing any signs of being too upset, you can give
    some advice on how they can further their skills or find another job through
    an agency, online, etc. Tell them about their strengths, for example, that
    they are a team player and should look into a position that utilizes their nice
    and compassionate personality. If you can build their self-esteem with the
    employee leaving on a positive note, you have done a great job during this
    tough assignment.

7. If the employee needs to go back to their desk to pick up some personal
    belongings, you, and preferable a security guard, should be with them at all
    times. You do not want the employee to explode on the floor, so you want to
    get in and out as soon as possible. The computer should have been locked
    down, but just in case, do not let the employee touch the computer. You do
    not want a company wide e-mail with slanderous remarks going out to
    everyone. You can always offer to pack up the employee's belongings and
    they can pick it up after hours from the HR office.

8. HR will most likely meet with the individual in their office to discuss possible severance, when their last paycheck is coming, when benefits terminate, and any information regarding extending their health coverage or any other details. HR will also collect the employees badge, swipe card, and any other needed material. Due to the employee being terminated, this would be considered the employees exit interview. At that point the employee will be walked out of the building.

9. Your department will be talking about what they saw and will be anxious to find out what is happening. Explain to the team that the individual is no longer with the company, without going into too many details. Leave it at that. They will figure it out for themselves and you want to be seen as a "quietly strong leader."

If you have to layoff employees, you can use the same steps as just described, you would just have to modify steps 3 and 4 to fit the reason. This reason for the layoff might be due to your company being part of a merger or downsizing due to financial reasons. It could be because you are just overstaffed. In tough economic times, it should come as no surprise. It will still be quite a shock and you will need to show extra compassion during this tough time.

This might be a little tougher on you, because you might really like the person, and they are being let go for no fault of their own. On the other hand, it might be considered easier to layoff someone because it wont be due to an attitude issue, poor performance, conflict, etc. In some cases, people actually want to be part of a layoff in order to get severance pay. They might want to start over on another career path or just retire early.

If an employer calls you for a reference from the terminated employee, just state the title and dates of employment. If you give any more information, you might be drawn into a libel suit. Most likely HR will answer these questions, and if the call comes to you, it would be best to just transfer the call to HR.

In some circumstances, firing an employee is an immediate necessity for the safety and well being of the rest of your employees such as:

*   Is physically violent.
*   Brings a weapon to work.
*   Arrives to work under the influence of drugs or alcohol.
*   Views pornographic movies on work computers.
*   Steals company property.

You may need to confer with HR first, however, these types of situations need to be dealt with as soon as possible. If you feel that the employee is violent and could be a danger, utilize the same advice given earlier regarding violence in the workplace.

Point to keep in mind. If you work in an organization that is part of a union, the employee should be advised that they are entitled to be represented by a union representative for any requested discipline meetings.

A short story about conflict in the workplace

John had a great team, but one employee in particular just had a bad attitude. This was an employee John inherited when he became manager. This employee was always negative, did not act as part of a team, and was arrogant in everyway. John talked to this employee to try and inspire and encourage (including documenting this verbal warning), but after a short period of time, the employee fell back into their usual ways.

Only a few weeks after John spoke to the employee, a loud disagreement between this employee and another happened on the main floor. It was loud enough to have people stop in their tracks wondering what was happening. John immediately went to the floor, and calmly asked each employee to stop by his office. He talked to them about how conflict in the workplace is unacceptable, gave a verbal warning for one of the employees, and a written warning to the employee with the bad attitude stating that if this behavior continues, suspension and/or termination would be the next step taken. These warnings were done separately as not to embarrass each employee.

It was a bit of a shock to the employee with a bad attitude that a written warning was given, however, John made it perfectly known that this was not the first time they met because of this team-affecting behavior. John also was not quite as caring as he was at the first meeting. He took out the notes from the last meeting and went over what was discussed, including that a written warning would be given if the behavior continued. With this documentation, the employee had no choice but to accept the written warning.

That put a scare into the employee, who from that point on had no more attitude issues. The employee's personality and character stayed the same, but there were no more negative comments or further disruptions.

Epilogue: When you have an employee who is disruptive in any way, they need to be dealt with before it becomes habit forming. Don't wait until the bad apple has spoiled the lot. Talk to them right away. State that their disruptive behavior is disrupting harmony in your department. If this did not work, the employee will most likely disrupt the harmony again, however, this time you can give a written warning with more of a stern approach. Warnings of possible suspension or termination are usually quite effective.

Quick Lesson Summary

- You got to take the good with the bad. Setting up a department, hiring great employees, and motivating and rewarding are the positive parts of management. Unfortunately, you have to be prepared to deal with the negative side as well.

- Always be ethical, legal, caring and compassionate. These traits will keep you out of trouble. You should try to inspire your staff to act the same way.

- Know how to determine and deal with conflict as soon as possible. Use both knowledge obtained and common sense to work out the issues with the individuals. Know the severity of the conflict, as you might need to get HR involved.

- Conflict and difficult employee situations differ from poor job performance and attendance issues. You need to approach the conflict and difficult employees on an individual case basis. Nonetheless, you need to always document every infraction.

- Although firing an employee is not the most pleasant thing to do, when necessary, it is the right thing to do. When you know that you have done everything you could to help the individual, followed HR guidelines, and gave verbal and written warnings with absolute clear expectations, you can feel justified and confident in your decision. Besides, your department is counting on you to deal with the major problem. Many times it is actually the best thing for the employee as well.

- Don't hesitate if you have to deal with a violent employee. Get security, or even call the police, if anyone, including the violent employee, is in immediate danger.

LESSON 6 – HOW TO DELEGATE, MANAGE YOUR TIME, SOLVE PROBLEMS & MAKE THE RIGHT DECISIONS

Introduction: Know how to get it all done with the least amount of stress

Managers usually have to juggle many tasks, projects, and meetings daily. If you try to take on every project yourself, you will most likely end up missing deadlines and ineffectively prioritizing. You need to multitask, but you can only do so much. You will end up stressed out. You will be rushed for meetings and somewhat ineffective as your thoughts will be on the tasks at hand rather than the subject meeting. Your staff will also feel a bit demoralized, as they will feel you do not trust them to take on the tasks and projects you are working on. All together, it is a lose/lose situation.

This is why delegating is one of the most important aspects of being a successful manager. It might seem like you are passing the work on to others so you don't have to do it, but that is the wrong way to think and it is untrue. When you delegate, you are able to multi-task more effectively. This helps manage your time to be more prepared for things like upcoming meetings, dealing with internal issues, and prioritizing upcoming projects. It will also help reduce stress. Your staff will be motivated, as they are participating in ways that will help the department and company. All together, it's a win/win situation.

An important part of delegating is making the right decisions such as, who will be best suited for the project? How many people are needed? How long it should take? Managers need to make decisions on the problems they are faced with everyday. Some problems are small and require little decision making, some are detrimental to the department's success and requires a well thought out and sound decision. You solve problems correctly by making the right decisions up front.

This lesson will cover how to effectively delegate, focus on how to multi-task, manage your time, and making the right decisions to solve the problems, all the while keeping your stress levels down.

Delegate Confidently

A sign of a good leader is how they are able to delegate. You need to get the work done through others. This is the best way to accomplish more every day. The basic definition of delegating is "assigning duties to another person or persons while still being held accountable." The most important thing is to know whom to delegate to and when. You should make sure you know exactly what needs to be accomplished before you give the task to someone else.

Don't feel like you are passing the buck. This is expected of you as a manager. It is vital that you let your staff take on most of the tasks, projects, etc. This gives them a chance to show what they can do. It breaks up the monotony of the day and gives some excitement to the individual or team.

Some managers make the mistake to not delegate because they think that if they hold all of the cards, they are indispensable. On the contrary, you are more indispensable when you show your leadership skills by delegating. You are more likely to get praised or even promoted when you show your leadership skills, and not because you know something that someone else doesn't know.

Successful delegation of authority might seem like it takes time and energy, but it's worth it. It helps employee empowerment and gives you a chance to focus on larger and more pressing issues. It's worth the time and energy to help employees succeed and help them in their development. They will more likely be able to meet your expectations, and you build the employee's self-confidence and self-esteem. Employees, who feel successful, usually are successful. This will also open up future delegation opportunities. The more you delegate, the easier it becomes. The tighter you hold on, the harder it will be to let go.

Do not be intimidated when it comes to delegating. You might feel unsure and timid when approaching another to do the work. Use your leadership skills to confidently delegate with a "matter of fact" approach. Again, the more you do it, the easier it becomes. In fact, you will be respected for your delegation skills.

You get power, when you give power. Help your employees grow, teach them well, and be happy in their success. The best compliment you can get is a compliment given to one of your employees.

Before you delegate, first ask yourself these three questions:

1. Can this project or task be delegated and do you have the staff that can honestly do the work required?

2. Should it be delegated or is it too critical and truly needs your involvement?

3. Do you have enough time to delegate the job effectively and explain the expectations and outcome?

If you can say yes to the three questions just asked, utilize these eight tips and points when delegating:

1. **Pick the right person best suited for the task**. Match the task with the person closest to the responsibility. Some tasks can go to a lower rung employee, or some might need to go to a supervisor. They just need to have the knowledge and skills to do the job.   You want it done right. If the project is successful, the employee gets the credit. If it fails, you are accountable.

2. **Make sure the person can work independently**. What tends to happen is the unsure or savvy person continually asks questions to the point where you end up doing most of the work. This is called "reverse delegation." Through time, you end up taking on some if not all of the duties you gave

the person. You end up spending more time on the project than you would if you have just did it yourself from the beginning. You get questions like, "Can you set that up for me?" even though they should be able to do it for themselves. If you come across this type of situation, instead of making the decision for them or taking back the task, go over the various possibilities and put the ball back into their court. If you ask for something and somehow you walked away with the responsibility, you have experienced reverse delegation. Don't give in unless the person truly cannot do the task asked of them. If needed, assign the task to someone else without demoralizing the person.

3. **Make sure the person understands exactly what it is you want them to do**. Set clear and objective goals. Let them know exactly what you want. Do not just say something like, "Don't worry about it, I'm sure you will be able to figure it out." Ask questions, watch the work performed, or have the employee give you feedback to make sure your instructions were understood.

4. **Get the agreement and commitment of the employee**. You want them to commit to you that they will perform the duties to the best of their abilities. If they are overwhelmed, or if they are already working on previously delegated tasks, chances are the project wont get the attention it deserves. You will also be stressing out the employee.

5. **Give the person the authority to take control of the whole project**. This will show you trust the individual and not look as though you just dumped all of the work on them, yet take the credit. They should be able to attend meetings associated with the project even when upper management is involved. Make sure you stand by the person and their decisions. Also make sure they use their authority wisely and not abuse the power given.

6. **Determine what tasks will need more monitoring than others**. It is up to you to determine the strengths and who can get the job done quickly. The good news about delegation is having someone you trust do the work, however, you are still held accountable for the outcome. Give a deadline when you expect the project or task to be completed. Set up a daily or weekly meeting to review if you feel it's needed. Whatever you do, do not micromanage and watch over the employees shoulder every few minutes. You need to let them make, and correct, mistakes. It's all about balance. Give them the space to be able to utilize their abilities to the best effect, while still monitoring and supporting closely enough to ensure that the job is done correctly. It is also their responsibility to report to you on the progress of the project. You should not have to ask for updates.

7. **Motivate them by discussing how the success of the project will make a positive impact.** The positive impact refers to the company and to themselves. Let them know that what they are doing is truly important, and that they will be recognized for a job well done. This will help build commitment to the project as well.

8. **Once the project or task is completed, carefully review.** Make sure all was done correctly and to your satisfaction. If you accept incomplete work or a lack of effort, you will be hurting yourself and the employee. They will

not learn, and you will always get the same results. It might take some extra time upfront, but the reward is a better future. Be sure to praise, when praise is due, when the job is completed up to standards. The easiest and simplest reward to give is a compliment to the completed delegated work. You both walk away feeling good and satisfied about the accomplishment.

Here are three different possibilities to consider, before a task or project is considered complete:

- *Do you need to make the final decision that the task is completed?* The employee reports to you when the task is finished and you decide whether or not it is completed.

- *Do you need to review with the employee and the two of you decide that the task is completed?* The employee reports to you before making the final action to finish the task, which then is considered completed.

- *Do you let the employee make the decision that the task is completed?* The employee just lets you know that the task is finished and has decided that it is completed.

The levels of delegation needs to be understood by all in the same way when setting clear goals and objectives. Also, when you delegate, try not to always pick the same person. Spread it around to those who show interest. If you have your eye on someone to promote, delegating to that person is a win/win situation. Just be careful that you do not show favoritism as you could run into Human Resource issues.

By implementing the points given, you will be able to confidently delegate with successful results.

Multitask and Prioritize

Unless you're managing just one or two people, it's inevitable that you will be involved with many issues and tasks all at once. Some need immediate attention, while others are less important. Multitasking is about knowing how to juggle several issues or tasks at once. Prioritizing is about knowing which of the issues or tasks are the most important and need to get done first. You need to be able to combine multitasking and prioritizing expertly. This is a bit of an art, but it can be learned.

Even though the pressure might be on, you always need to keep a cool head. The saying, "Never let them see you sweat," is perfect when it comes to multitasking. Exude a sense of calm and control. This is a show of strong leadership.

Here are six ways to help you with everyday multitasking:

1. **Delegating,** as previously described, comes into play the most when multitasking and prioritizing. Without delegation, proper multitasking would be almost impossible. Make sure tasked priorities are shared with your team. They will want to see the project succeed as long as they know the goal.

2. **Chart it out on the whiteboard** and make a list of the tasks and its importance. Separate the tasks into three groups:

   a. Group 1 needs to be done immediately or at least by the end of the day.

   b. Group 2 would need to be completed in the next couple of days.

   c. Group 3 would need to be completed in the next week or month. Just make sure you never lose sight or put the tasks from group 3 on the back burner for too long.

   The point here is to not only make a list of tasks, but to schedule based on importance rather than just having a "to do" list.

3. **Focus on the critical items.** Postpone current tasks if needed, and put full attention on the critical task. Sometimes you need to make the right decisions like canceling a meeting in order to get the task completed in time. A good leader can adapt to changes and break routine in order to address the issues at hand.

4. **Work smarter, not harder.** This cliché works well when it comes to multitasking. This basically means reducing or eliminating redundancy by improving workflow. This thought should be used for all aspects of your department including processes and procedures. Utilize tools that are in place to reduce the time spent on each task, thus reducing the amount of open tasks on your plate. Use automation whenever you can to reduce time and redundancy. It is worth the investment to develop automated tools, especially if most of the tasks are regular and in common. This can include how you set up your e-mail such as utilizing task manager in Outlook.

5. **Set a part of the day to focus on the "non-informational" tasks.** This would mean turning off instant messaging, close your e-mail, and only answer calls when absolutely necessary. Part of multi-tasking is knowing what tasks you do not need to do such as real time response to all e-mails, always on your IM, etc.

6. **Make multitasking a game**, and try to keep your mind as clear as possible with the tasks at hand. Instead of letting it get to you, try and make it fun and challenging. The quicker you accept you have to "do more with less," the easier it gets to get on with the task at hand.

Try and stay motivated and not lose sight of the big picture. Know when to pay close attention to detail, and when to take short cuts.

Keeping Stress under control

Stress is inevitable. It happens at home as well as at work. No matter how well things are going, there will always be some problems that come your way. As a manager, you might find yourself trying to cope with staffing shortages, recent layoffs, too many errors, missing goals, newly added goals, turnover in senior administration, etc. If you're new to the job, you will have enough stress with learning the ropes let alone all of the other possible contributing factors.

Stress cannot be avoided and you cannot always control what happens, but how you react to the situation can make all the difference in the world. That's the secret to keeping stress under control. You need to know the cause of stress, how it affects you, and how to adapt. Here are 12 ways to help adapt to stressful situations:

1. **Know your trigger points**. Think about the most common trigger points that get you stressed. For example:

   - *Is it when you are going into a meeting?* If so, take the time to be well prepared so that you can have confidence when going into the meeting.

   - *Is it when you are not making your numbers?* If so, get with your top people and figure out how you are going to correct the situation.

   - *Is it because of poor employee attendance?* If so, let your staff (or just the offending employee) know that you recognize the problem and will be keeping a close eye on future attendance issues.

   - *Is it when you lose focus on a particular project?* If so, change the scene for a while and focus on another project or task. When you come back to the original project, you will have a renewed focus.

   - *Is it when you have too much coffee or cola*? If so, only have one cup of coffee in the morning and one coffee or cola in the afternoon. Caffeine can help trigger stress.

   The point here is for you to figure out and recognize your hot spots so that you can take the necessary steps to reduce or eliminate the problem situation. When you see it coming, quickly focus on a calming scene like relaxing at the beach or being with your family, and most importantly, stay cool. Always deal with stressful situations in a calm, yet controlling matter. Be professional and do not run away from the situation. Play the part of a wise and calm leader, and never let them see you sweat. Always give the impression that you have everything under control. Losing your cool and control will only add to the stress that is already there. When you're under stress you will start panicking and talking too fast. When you see stress coming your way, control the panic and slow down your talking. This will instill calm to those around you. If you're not losing your head, they wont either.

2. **Stop and take a deep breath**. A common response to stress is shallow breathing. Breathing shallowly deprives the body of adequate oxygen and will

prevent you from thinking clearly and functioning properly. The next time you feel stressed, try these breathing techniques:

- Take 2 or 3 deep breaths – in through your nose and out through your mouth.

- Press the side of one nostril with your finger, breathe in slowly and deeply through the other open nostril, and hold it for a one second. Release your finger and use a finger from your opposite hand to press the side of the opposite nostril and slowly let out all of the air through the previously closed nostril. Now do it in reverse. Do this exercise 2 times.

Your body will respond with reduced muscle tension, lower blood pressure and a slower heart rate. These are very calming breathing exercises.

3. **Time management**. Using your time efficiently will reduce stress. Set and prioritize your daily objectives. Concentrate on what is important to you and set aside the less important issues. There will be a more in-depth discussion regarding time management in the following section of this lesson.

4. **Reduce the stress by dissecting the issue.** Calmly break down the elements that are causing the stress into a couple of manageable parts. Get some help from your team members or co-managers when needed.

5. **Take a break and take a walk.** Exercise plays a key role in reducing and preventing the effects of stress. It can help to relax muscle tension and improve sleep. When stress is at its peak, get up and move. Take a walk around the parking lot, get a glass of water, or do some stretches at your desk.

6. **Laugh more often and lighten up.** The old saying, "Laughter is the best medicine," is especially true regarding stress. Laughter helps reduce stress by releasing endorphins into your body that can lower your blood pressure, stimulate your brain, release tight muscles, change your emotional outlook and thinking, and increase your oxygen intake.

7. **Make some Feng Shui type of changes in your office or cubical**. A few changes such as less lighting and adding plants can help keep you calmer. Include items that can help your mind and alleviate stress like a favorite CD, picture, quote or poem.

8. **Keep a notepad and a pen by your side at all times**. This will allow you to jot down notes, appointments, and deadlines for work assignments. Keeping notes of all expectations helps you plan more properly and stay more organized, which helps reduce stress.

9. **Take care of your health**. Try to get at least eight hours of good sleep every night. Eat properly to provide your body with the essential nutrients for living a healthy life. Exercise at least 20 minutes a day. This is obviously good for your health and will also help you during stressful situations.

10. **Talk it out with your family or friends**. Talking to family or friends helps you to vent and relieve tension. They may even come up with a solution to

the problem that is causing you so much stress. This also helps put things into perspective. Sometimes just talking about the problem makes you realize it's not that big of a problem after all.

11. **Find a hobby and do more fun things outside of work**. The more you relax outside of work, the more you will be able to adapt to the stressful situations inside of work. Try to find time to relax with your family and friends.

12. **Keep a positive attitude**.   A negative attitude can have a negative impact on accomplishing your goals. Keeping a positive outlook can give you the energy and momentum you need to get through the workday. Your positive attitude is contagious. The same can be said for a negative attitude. Don't walk around with a frown, have a smile on your face. When your staff sees you as a positive leader who has everything under control during a stressful situation, they will be instilled with confidence. Focus on the positives of the big picture so that you can fix the smaller negative problems. Also, try to stay away from any negative situations such as gossiping.

By following these tips, you can lessen the amount of stress at work and improve your health.

The good news for new managers is that what is considered stressful early in your career, will seem trivial once you have some experience under your belt. All new managers get stressed out with their new job responsibilities, but it will get better. Just remember to have confidence in your abilities.

You also need to make sure your employees are not stressed. By utilizing the structure and teamwork philosophies taught in lesson 3, your staff should be relatively stress free. You should still keep an eye on your employees to make sure they are not stressed out too much. The less stressed they are, the less stressed you will be. If you see signs of bad attitudes, back stabbing, work areas in disarray, absenteeism, high attrition, a feeling of fear, and just an overall look of stress on their faces, hold a meeting with your staff as soon as possible and address the issues. The two questions to ask are, "What's wrong with the department," and, "what can we do to fix it?" Focus on the matter at hand and make sure you set the ground rules of no personal attacks. Express that you all want the same thing, which is to work in a positive stress free atmosphere. Listen to what everyone has to say, write down all of the points brought up, and don't stop pursuing the issue until you have an answer to the problem. Make sure you close the meeting on a positive note.

Time Management

Part of being a successful manager is to know how to manage your time, as the demands on your time will increase. You can be sure that just when you are at your busiest, a 2-hour meeting is scheduled, or you might be ready to work on a process and realize you need to join a conference call.   These types of conflicting duties will happen, and quite often.

You need larger blocks of time so you can concentrate on writing the process, meet with you staff without feeling rushed, or attend the conference call and give your full attention. You can't expect to write a process that will take a couple of hours, if not days, and expect to do it in 10-minute increments. It will drive you crazy and you will lose focus.

Here are 15 ways that can help you manage your time and make the most of your day:

1. **Start your day off right.** Arrive a little early to work, get your coffee or tea, get into your office and immediately:

   - Make sure all e-mails have been answered or sent.

   - Look at your calendar to see what meetings are scheduled so you can work around them.

   - Determine the best time to take your lunch break.

   - Reflect on what needs to be done and write out a list of every task that comes to mind. Put a line through each completed task with assurance. If it was not done that day, carry it over to the next days list. This list process drives you to incorporate your company's goals into your daily work, helping you to stay efficient and on strategy. Use the same notepad for meetings so you can add to it as needed.

   By implementing these tasks, which should take around 30 minutes, you will already be starting the day with the right focus. This can be considered your quiet time to get yourself settled. It will also reduce stress and clear your mind so you can be ready for the day ahead.

2. **Set clear expectations of the goals.** This helps in time management due to everyone, including you, knows exactly what needs to be done. This way, you do not waste time always trying to establish what needs to be done.

3. **When you are holding a meeting, stick to the agenda.** Try not to go over the allotted time. You not only hold up other people, you're interfering with your own time management.

4. **Delegating helps time management the most**. The more you delegate, the less interruptions and multitasking worries.

5. **Give members of your team more responsibility.** For example, if you have a member of your team represent your department at a meeting, you will have just given yourself some more time. You will also be showing confidence in your employees, which will increase morale. Don't make a habit out of it, just do this every now and then.

6. **Make sure your previous responsibilities have been 100% taken over**. For example, if you have just been promoted, you should not have to worry about what you used to do. You have enough on your plate, let

alone getting calls throughout the day asking questions on old responsibilities. You can help out for the first couple of weeks, but then you have to let go.

7. **Even though you have an open door policy...** If you feel a one-on-one meeting might go on for some time, state that you really want to continue the discussion and in order to give your full undivided attention, you would like to schedule another meeting to further discuss.

8. **Whenever possible, start and finish a project or task in one session**. You can immediately erase it from your list and have a sense of accomplishment. The more half-open projects you have going on at once, the more haphazardly the approach, along with additional stress.

9. **Read over reports and important materials while away from the office.** Do this during your lunch break, in a cab, in the waiting room, and especially when traveling by plane or train. You can get in a lot of good study time during these "away from the office" periods. Also, some of your best ideas might come to mind when you are away from the office. That is why it is always good to have a pen and paper ready to use at any moment.

10. **Organize your computer files and folders**. A lot of time is wasted looking for files, not to mention it adds stress. Take the time to put the right file in the right folder and keep it that way. Also clean up your desktop from both your computer and physical desk. A clear desk helps in creating a clear and focused mind.

11. **Keep a pen and paper near your bed**. You will find that many ideas and solutions come to you right before bed, and sometimes even in the middle of the night. Write down these ideas and go back to sleep. You will not regret it. There might even be times when you can send out an e-mail in the middle of the night. Not only will it be effective, it will show people just how much you care and are willing to do to run an efficient department. They will notice the time the e-mail was sent... This will help manage your time because you will start the day off with a true focus. Your mind will be clear and will end up saving you precious minutes, if not hours, in the office.

12. **Again, as stated in multitasking, work smarter, not harder**. Find ways to reduce time when working on a project. For example, if you are creating a flow chart using a word processing application instead of a program like Visio, it will take much longer to complete, not to mention it wont look as good. Try to utilize the best tools for the job such as using Outlook to schedule your time, not just for the day, but also for the week.

13. **Don't be afraid to say "no" to your boss.** When you have enough on your plate as it is, sometimes the best thing to do is just say no. Don't state it in a defiant way, just let your boss know about your current projects and if you were to take on a new request, it would put you behind. If this request is a priority, then by all means do it. If all of your workload is priority one, maybe this request can go to someone else without it looking as though you did not want to help.

14. **Politely let a friend or family member know you will get back to them as soon as possible.** Unless it is important, don't take time away from an important task on a non-work related issue. They will understand and even respect you, just make sure you do it in a polite way and truly get back to them when you can.

15. **"Under promise and over deliver."** Although this has already been stated, it is important enough to state it again. You can manage your time much better if upper management is not waiting on a project that you promised, but could not keep.

Always look at ways to utilize your time more effectively. Try to eliminate waste whenever possible. Examples of wasted time would be time spent procrastinating, web surfing, or too much socializing. If you find yourself taking a lot of time on the same type of task daily, there might be a chance you can delegate, work smarter, or even eliminate the task (e.g. does the statistic that takes an hour to formulate really matter?).

Time managing a project can vary. Project management can be as simple as putting the tasks in order to prepare for a release of a new product, or as complicated as the construction of a 20 story building. If for example you have a project to get your staff trained on a new product, you first need to:

- Determine what needs to be trained.
- Determine when the training should take place.
- Determine where the training should take place.
- Determine how long the training should last.
- Determine the amount of people who need to take the training.
- Determine how many people you can afford to take the training without losing production.
- Determine how many people can be trained without affecting the customer's immediate needs.
- Determine the cost of the training and materials.

True Project Management, such as construction work, is another course in itself. However, the basics for all projects are the same: *Resources, Time and Money*. We will discuss some of the basic tools to use for managing a project in lesson 9.

Problem Solving and Decision Making

Much of what managers do is solve problems and make decisions. Decision-making is a key role of a manager and leader. Some managers find this to be one of the most difficult tasks to perform. They have a fear of failure, and procrastinate mainly because they have a lack of a structured approach. One of two things usually happens, they either put off making the decision in the hopes that someone else will bail them out, or even worse, make a decision using a knee jerk reaction.

It is best to think of making a decision, as drawing a line between two points. If you can't draw a straight line between the two points, then that decision should most likely be rejected. When the line goes off into tangents, there might not be a realistic link between the proposed action and outcome.

New managers often try to solve problems and make decisions by reacting to them before they fully understand all of the possible factors. They feel that the quickness of a decision is more important than the long-term outcome. There are times when a quick decision is needed, such as dealing with a violent act in the workplace. However, most decisions are not needed immediately and you do in fact have the time to make the right decision. That is the key, making the right decision. Just be careful to not let decisions accumulate, or else you will have a backlog of both small and complex decisions to make. You need to find the perfect balance of knowing when to make quick and easy decisions on the fly, and when to take time with the complex decisions.

Don't be afraid to talk to your boss or upper management about major problems or needs that concern you. You do not want to be known as a manager who "keeps secrets" because you are scared of the possible repercussions. It is better to be upfront and honest, while at the same time showing you are diligently working on the resolution. You may even find yourself working with other department managers to rectify issues affecting your department. There is nothing wrong with this as it shows your commitment to your department and the company.

Define the problem or need before you make the decision. Ask yourself, and others if needed, the following who, what, when, where, how and why type of questions. In lesson 9 we will discuss cost-benefit and task management tools, however, here are 12 steps to follow to use as a guideline when making important decisions:

1. **Who should make the decision?** First of all, you might be looking at a problem or need that is not your decision to make. Be sure you are not stepping on anyone's toes, even though your heart is in the right place. If you are the one to make the decision, go to the next step.

2. **What makes you think there is a problem, or why the need?** Before you can start to make any decisions, you need to be absolutely clear the problem or need is valid. Make sure you consider those who will be affected by the decision. Talk to some key staff members to make sure you and your staff fully understands the nature of the problem or need. You want people who will speak up, are efficient, take necessary risks, have somewhat opposing views, and are strongly motivated. There are times when it seems like the problem or need comes at you like "the sky is falling," but when you take the time to truly investigate the problem or need, you might find it is overly exaggerated. This happens quite often as emotions take over logic. For instance, is it one person complaining about a particular situation or does everyone feel the same way? Is there a common complaint from your customers or just one or two disgruntled people who will never be happy? Is there a common trend or is it just speculation? Do you really need to invest in a new database or can you work with what you've got? Dig deep to find if there is a true problem, and then start on finding ways to improve. You don't want to fix something that is not broke. If you indeed suspect there is a problem, follow steps 3 through 12:

3. **Where is the problem or need?** Is it internal or external? Is it in your department or somewhere else? Is it only in certain areas of your network? Is it one employee or the whole group? You need to know where the problem or need lies before you can begin to make the right decision to fix or buy.

4. **When is it happening or needed?** Is it certain parts of the day? Is it when there is over usage? Is it when shifts overlap? Is it always at the end of the month? Is it every time there is a new software release? By pinpointing when the problem happens, it helps greatly in detecting the root cause of the issue.

5. **What is causing the problem or need?** Is the problem process related? A lack of training? Old and slow computers causing longer handle times, which in turn is affecting customer satisfaction? Are there not enough employees to handle the amount of calls? Is it a design or engineering flaw? Is it quality control issues? You need to get with key staff members to truly determine the root cause of the issue. Determining you have a problem is useless if you, or another department, cannot find the cause.

6. **How complex is the problem or need?** The more complex the problem or need, the deeper you will have to dig. Don't be afraid to go back to the drawing board until you are fully confident with the choices you have made.

7. **What is the urgency and how should you prioritize?** Some problems are more important than others. You would not want to work on a complex minor issue when you have an easy major issue that should be dealt with immediately.

8. **What is the ideal outcome?** When you are faced with a big decision, it is easy to get lost in the detail and circumstances. Write a list of pros and cons, advantages and disadvantages, and short term and long-term goals to make sure the outcome has the desired effect. Think about the objectives, alternatives, and risks. You need to be absolutely clear on exactly what it is you are expecting to achieve. Review the facts at hand then absorb them into your subconscious mind. Let these thoughts simmer for a while before going to the next step.

9. **What are the possible solutions to the problem or need?** Brainstorm with your key staff members for solutions to the problem or need, unless you are dealing with a confidential or personal issue. Note all of the ideas and alternatives on your whiteboard and then screen out the top solutions. Go over the pros and cons once again with everyone. Know the cost and risk associated with each alternative, and then be prepared to decide on what it is you are going to do.

10. **Make the final decision.** You should now know the direction you are going to take. Commit to your final choice or course of action. Recognize that you cannot know with 100% certainty that your decision is correct. You can't predict the future, but you can do everything possible to assess the problems or needs along with the benefits and risks. So make the decision, don't worry about the "what ifs," and don't look back. Do not prolong or deliberate about the decision any more. Trust yourself to make the decision. You will be able

to deal with any consequences appropriately and with confidence because you did your homework.

11. **Plan and implement the final decision.** Now that you have decided on what you are going to do, you need to determine how and when you will make it happen. Be realistic in your approach. Can you accomplish the task now? Do you have the resources? Is it in your immediate budget? Are there any time constraints? Do you have the facilities? What steps need to be taken? What systems or processes should be changed in your organization? Once you have a plan and know how to implement the solution to the problem or need, it is time to put the plan into effect. Write a schedule that includes the start and stop times, and when you expect to see certain indicators of success. If you are delegating the task, make sure the person realizes they are responsible for ensuring the implementation of the plan. Make sure the plan is communicated to all involved, including your boss and upper management if needed.

12. **Monitor and verify whether the problem or need has been solved and/or is effective.** It is a good idea to set up daily or weekly meetings to make sure all is well. Make sure all is going according to plan and is on schedule. You can then move to monthly meetings until you are 100% the problem or need has been solved. You will find out very soon how successful you are by checking reports, surveys, comments made in meetings, and whether there is any tension in the air. Use this opportunity to learn how to avoid future related problems. If you are still having problems, or your expectations have not been met, call in your key players again. Look at whether the plan was unrealistic, if you had the right resources, was it communicated enough, and did you prioritized correctly. If needed, the plan should be changed. Go through the steps again until you fully resolve the issue and find the exact solution.

A short story about delegating

When John first started out as manager, he thought that he needed to prove to everyone that he could do it all. After all, he was promoted because of his great attitude and technical abilities, so he wanted to make sure everyone knew he was deserving of this promotion. What John soon found out was, in his old job he only had to focus on one particular project at a time, rather than having to juggle five projects all at once. He also found that he was not providing the needed direction to his staff because he was so busy working on all of these projects. John was getting stressed out and also knew he needed to let go of some, if not all, of his old responsibilities.

John stopped what he was doing, listed all of the projects on his whiteboard, and prioritized them based on what needed immediate attention and what could wait. He then thought about whom in his staff could do these projects. He had a talented staff, but he would still have to go over the project details and the timeframe. He met with a couple of employees, one of which was a supervisor, another who was really good at documentation, and another who had technical expertise. To John's surprise, these individuals were excited and needed little coaching. He made it a point to not look over their shoulder, and had to trust that they would keep him updated and do the projects correctly. John had set up a couple of status meetings in advance so that he could discuss the progress of each project. The good news was that every project, with just a little coaching, went smoothly and was completed on time.

What John found out was, not only did they do the projects well, it actually motivated these employees. The more comfortable John was in delegating, the more inspiring he became. He realized that his employees expected him to delegate. He looked weak and inefficient when he did not delegate projects and tasks to his staff. Employees started approaching John more and more because they knew that he was willing to listen, and was willing to give projects to employees he trusted would do a good job. They knew that he truly wanted the best from his team and department. The best thing of all, John's stress levels decreased, he was able to multitask more efficiently due to staff that could help, and he was able to better manage his time due to the decrease in workload. He was now able to focus more on everyday managerial type of responsibilities. He started looking more like a manager who was a leader, rather than a manager who did all the tasks.

Epilogue: In management, there are so many win/win opportunities. Delegating is one of the most valuable of these types of opportunities. It not only takes projects and tasks off of the managers already full plate, it gives a chance for employees to shine. If a manager does not delegate, more stress, multitasking problems, and ineffective management of time is inevitable. Employees also do not get a chance to shine and grow, thus morale weakens. Delegate with authority, confidence, and setting clear goals and expectations, and you will be on the road to success.

Quick Lesson Summary

- A sign of a good leader is how they are able to delegate. You need to get the work done through others. Don't feel like you are passing the buck. This is expected of you as a Manager. It is vital that you let your staff take on most of the tasks, projects, etc. You get power when you give power. You need to set clear goals and expectations of the delegated project, and know when a task or project is considered complete. If you can answer yes to these next three questions, you should always try to delegate:

    o Can this project or task be delegated?
    o Should it be delegated?
    o Do you have enough time to delegate the job effectively?

- Make multitasking more of a game rather than a burden. Chart the tasks out on a whiteboard along with its importance. Separate the tasks into three groups: Group 1 needs to be done as soon as possible, Group 2 to be completed in the next couple of days, and Group 3 completed in the next week or month (just do not forget about them).

- Although stress cannot be avoided and you cannot always control what happens, your reaction to stress can make the difference on how it affects you. Know your trigger points and hot spots, always stay positive and in control, and implement de-stressing techniques when stress is building, such as deep breathing, taking a walk, or delegating. You should also keep an eye on your employees to make sure they are not stressed. The less stressed they are, the less stressed you will be.

- Always look at ways to utilize your time more effectively. Time management is key to keeping all on your plate under control. Delegate whenever possible, try to stick to the agenda during meetings, get to work a little early to address all e-mails and pressing issues, be more organized, go over reports at lunch or even on a plane, and always focus on ways to work smarter, not harder. If a time consuming daily or weekly task is really not needed, eliminate it.

- Problem solving and making decisions is one of the most important aspects of management. You should not make quick decisions with uncertainty; however, you should not let problems or needs accumulate for too long before deciding what to do next. Get others involved to help brainstorm. Find out the, who, what, when, where, how and why reasons the problem or need exists. Chart out all of the alternatives, stick to your choice with confidence, and implement the plan as soon as possible. Monitor the results until you are satisfied all is fixed, or meets your expectations.

LESSON 7 – HOW TO GET YOUR POINT ACROSS THROUGH THE ART OF BUSINESS COMMUNICATIONS

Introduction: Getting your point across clearly and concisely

There are many ways to communicate. To name a few, it can be a verbal one-on-one, a simple hallway conversation, leading a team meeting, writing processes and procedures, giving presentations, creating reports for review, talking on the phone, instant messaging, blogging, and corresponding via e-mail. Good communication skills are essential for effectively managing others, as well as working with your co-managers and upper management. The better the communicator, the better chance for management success. There are many chances each day to either succeed or fail just by the way you communicate to others.

One of the main reasons why people leave companies is due to poor communication from their supervisors and managers. Poor communication leads to poor productivity, confusion, conflict, and redundancy. Even worse, when a major change is happening within the company, such as merging with another company, poor communication leads to high anxiety and poor morale.

You need to be able to clearly communicate all of the goals, plans and changes. Communication may be the single most important skill of a manager. You can't be a leader if you can't communicate your vision. You can't motivate people if they can't understand what you want. If you think about it, all that has been taught up to this point relies on your ability to communicate in a way that they truly hear and understand just what it is your saying.

Being able to communicate effectively is not a skill everyone possesses, but can be improved through practice. Strive to be a great communicator. This lesson will cover ways to effectively communicate including business writing, communicating verbally, handling meetings, giving presentations, and dealing with change. Communicating clearly and concisely is a great opportunity for you to show off your management skills, and build respect as a leader.

Business Writing

Like everything, once you get used to doing something a couple of times, the easier it gets. The same holds true for writing e-mails, processes, procedures, or any type of written communication associated with company business. A blank piece of paper, Word doc, spreadsheet, PowerPoint, or e-mail can seem daunting at first. The hardest part is that first word or data entry. Once you get started, however, the words or figures will start flowing. You will be able to type out your thoughts and get your point across. You might run into a dry spell and have to take a break, however, it is imperative to never give up until it is completed.

The purpose of business writing is to share or request information. The information must be complete, concise, and accurate.   The information needs to be written in a way the reader can easily understand. This holds true whether it is something you're asking them to do, or what it is you need from them.

Correct use of grammar and spelling is essential. The good news is you can use spell-checks to check your spelling or go to a site like www.dictionary.com. You can even easily find words you can substitute with another through a site like www.thesaurus.com. However, when it comes to grammar, it's not quite as easy to check for grammatical inaccuracies as spelling inaccuracies. If you are uncomfortable with your use of grammar in written communications, you should find some books on grammar, or take a basic course as soon as possible. That should be a priority. You will be judged on the way you write, and you will lose respect if your grammar skills are that of a 5th grader.

When it is an *informal* subject, most likely through e-mail, write like you are talking to the person. See and imagine the conversation in your mind. You can even act out the conversation verbally, but quietly so no one thinks you're talking to yourself... If you use hard words and phrases, it will look like you are trying too hard. Just be yourself.

When it is a *formal* subject, like an important process, then you need to keep it formal. Pretend you are describing how to do the tasks in a classroom environment and document as such. Try to imagine the person who will be following this process, and how it would best read for them. Determine if it should be a step-by-step process or a flowchart process. Just remember, "less is more" in most circumstances. If you are too wordy, people will lose interest and not fully comprehend what it is you are trying to say. You might need to write a couple of drafts until you get it just right. A good idea is to have someone who you trust and understands the tasks at hand to review the process before you send it out to everyone.

You have to carefully judge the situation and the importance of each type of message you are communicating. Here are 5 steps you should follow:

1. **What type of information will you convey?** Is it a simple FYI or difficult multi-level process, etc. You need to organize and separate the different kinds of possible materials. Here are five examples,

   - *Message* - is basically just a simple object of communication. Mostly a communication of thoughts and ideas via e-mail or instant message.

   - *Policy* - describes a management decision (what should be done). When writing a policy, keep the following in mind:
     a. Write a title in six words or less
     b. Describe:
        i.   Who is (or is not) covered?
        ii. Where does (or doesn't) the policy apply?
        iii. When does (or doesn't) the policy come into effect?
     c. List management decisions and any exceptions (E.g. Management has decided that...).

    d. The name, and if possible the signature, of the person who will authorize the policy.

- *Process* - is any series of actions or operations viewed as a whole, with a start and a finish. In some cases a process might not have steps, it may simply be a continuum.

- *Procedure* - lists steps needed to complete an action in chronological order that involves <u>two or more people</u> (who does what and when). An action includes all the steps a team must take to finish a particular work or reach a goal. Every action begins with a trigger that tells the first team member to go, and a target that tells the last team member to stop.

- *Task* - outlines in order the steps <u>one person</u> takes to complete a procedure (how to do it). The key to this definition is *one person*. If the work remains in the hands of just one person for more than 5 or 6 steps, it's a task, not a procedure. A task can be thought of as a procedure for one.

- **Think about what you want them to hear, then what you are going to say.** Make sure you consider who will be reading this information and just what it will take to make sure they understand the point you are trying to get across. Make sure to use words you think they will understand.

- **Who will be the recipients of the information?** For example, is this a quick FYI to one of your employees that can be generalized, or a memo to the president that needs to be spot on? You need to tailor the text based on who will be reading the information.

- **Create the message, process, procedure, or other form of written communication**. When your thoughts are flowing quickly, write them out as fast as possible and do not worry about the spelling or grammar. You can come back to edit. When your thoughts are flowing, you will be able to get exactly what it is you want to say, and in the best way for your audience to understand. However, be aware of the length. Use enough words to make your meaning clear, but don't use unnecessary words to show off your writing skills. Business writing needs to be clear and concise, no one has time to read any more than necessary. On the other hand, don't make the piece too short. Write enough so that your meaning is clear and won't be misunderstood. Also, do not blind them with science. If you feel your audience does not know all of the acronyms or jargon, make sure to break it down so they understand the meanings. For example, you can use an acronym with its meaning once, and from that point on use only the acronym.

- **Proofread and edit before you send it out**. All it takes is one sloppy or poorly written document or e-mail for people to lose respect and not take you as seriously. Always re-read what you wrote to make sure all the words in your head made it correctly onto the document. Be sure to check for:

- Spelling and grammatical errors.

- Look for omitted words.

- Reduce the use of long words. Try to use one and two syllable words. Overuse of long words will cause many readers to miss the point.

- Make sure sentences do not run too long. Two 16-word sentences let readers grasp more than a single 32-word sentence.

- The subheading or subject line should say something of relative importance regarding the main point of the subject. This will give an indication of what is to follow in the paragraph, e-mail, etc. The subheading or subject line does not have to contain 100% of the subject, but it should contain more than just one generic word. A generic subheading or subject line can mean anything and does not set up the subject to follow.

- Try to use fewer words with active subjects and verbs. Active verbs, when the subject of the sentence is the doer of the action, cuts the length and keeps the readers awake. Try not to use passive verbs, especially when writing processes and procedures. You should write it as "who does what." If you use passive verbs, the readers won't know who's responsible. For example:

  - Active: *The data technician fixed the widget.*
  - Passive: *The widget was fixed.* [Who fixed the widget is not named]

- Stay away from vague modifiers; they will just create unanswered questions. This is especially true when writing processes and procedures. Readers want clear directions, not words like "appropriate, proper, relevant, timely, or normal." For example, a statement like "forward to the proper or appropriate department in a timely fashion" does not state the department in which to forward, not to mention in what timeframe (is it 2 hours, 24 hours, 48 hours?).

- Don't try to cram everything onto one page. A full page of crammed text overwhelms the eyes. It's ok to have plenty of white space. Besides, it also gives space for notes, etc.

- Try not to have long paragraphs. There is a certain visual and mental effort required to read them. Three short paragraphs are easier to read than one long paragraph.

- When writing processes or procedures, try to keep the width of the page to around 40 characters. Readers tend to grasp information when reading narrower columns.

- When writing directions, always list the steps in chronological order.

- Look for missing words at the end of a sentence.

- Look for improper use of heterographs like to, too, two, and there, their, they're. Also your and you're.

Try to edit as much as you can while you are proofreading. After you are done proofreading, make one more read for any additional editing. This holds true whether it is just a short e-mail to a long and involved process. You will also find that auto spell checks will sometimes make corrections that were not part of your intentions.

Here are a couple of key points to keep in mind when writing e-mails, processes, etc:

- o DO NOT CAPITALIZE ALL OF THE WORDS WHEN WRITING AN E-MAIL OR PROCESS, ETC. It is not easy to read and it looks like you are yelling out the words (unless that is the intention, which is considered rude when meant in a negative way). Only use all capitals in a title.

- o Don't come across like you are hostile in your writing. This especially holds true for sending or answering heated e-mails.

- o Before you hit the send button when creating or replying to an aggravated type of e-mail, take at least a 5-minute break before hitting send. When you come back, re-read both the original e-mail and your response. Chances are you will re-write your response in a much more controlled and professional manner. You will get your point across more effectively if you keep it professional at all times.

- o Respond to e-mails in a timely fashion, but as previously stated, be careful not to send a heated e-mail without taking the time to cool down a bit. The quicker you respond, the more professional you will look. Just like you like to get an immediate answer to your questions, so do your colleagues, employees, boss and most importantly, your customers.

- o Create an e-mail signature that has your name, title, company name, address, phone number, e-mail address and website. This should be set up as the default on all created e-mails. Here is an example:

> **John Smith**
> Manager, Customer Support
> Sample Corp.
> 123 Main Street
> City, State, Zip
> 555-555-5555
> jsmith@samplecorpemail.example
> www.samplecorpwebsite.example

o   When an e-mail is informal, ending the message with a simple "Thanks" with your name directly underneath is acceptable. If it is more of a formal message, you can use something like "Regards" or "Kind Regards" with your name directly underneath.

o   When writing to your boss or upper management, always keep it professional. Address them with respect at all times, no matter how informal the organization functions. This does not mean that you can't add some humor when the time is right. The main point is to always show respect.

Communicating Verbally

Interpersonal communication, either face-to-face or over the phone, is the most frequent communication methods most people use at work. This could be communicating with your employees, co-managers, other department personnel, your boss, upper-management, and customers. How you handle yourself during these conversations are important in how you are looked at as a manager and leader. You can also usually get what you want by communicating correctly.

Here are nineteen valuable tips to incorporate into your management and leadership interpersonal communication skills. Even though some of these tips were mentioned in lesson 1 regarding leadership, they are worth mentioning again as they directly pertain to verbal communication:

1. **Have an "open door" policy.** Your employees need to know that they can talk to you at any time. You need to have this open door policy no matter the person or issue. Whenever an employee approaches you, you always have to be ready to feel sympathetic and show you care. Here are some points to keep in mind when you are approached by an employee:

    •   Listen to what they need from you, and show them that you are willing to help. It might be about money, a conflict with another employee, or a personal issue.

    •   No matter the situation, make sure they know you are listening and fully comprehending the conversation.

    •   If you are in the middle of something important or on your way to a meeting, politely let them know that you have another appointment and re-schedule a time to resume the conversation. If it is an urgent matter, if possible drop all that you are doing and give your full-undivided attention. If you have to cancel the meeting due to the serious nature of the situation, people will understand, and in fact admire your decision.

    •   You don't necessarily need to come up with any magic solution at the time during the discussion, just make sure you get back with them as soon as possible with some kind of an idea on how to improve the situation.

- Even if the answer is not what they want to hear, they will at least know you tried and took there concerns seriously.

- Most of the time when employees are expressing concerns, it is just an opportunity to let them vent. You will however come out looking good as you did not shrug it off or made them feel stupid for talking to you in the first place.

- Do not work on e-mail or answer a call unless absolutely necessary. If you need to interrupt them, make sure you let them know the urgency of the immediate situation. You can ask if they would like to wait a few minutes, or come back in 15 minutes or so.

- If this person is a constant bother to you by continually complaining, then you will at one point need to make sure that you let them know that these continuous problems need to stop. You will have to draw the line at some point. You might suggest a meeting with human resources, which might scare them off in presenting future complaints, as they will be seen as a complainer.

2. **Be flexible and approachable**. Being laid back and approachable, while at the same time showing you have a desired commitment to achieve results, is truly a successful combination. Employees will want to communicate with you. Here are some points to keep in mind to show your approachability:

    - Do not come across like an unreasonable, mean, or sarcastic person. Intimidation might seem like it gives you more power, but it backfires most of the time. You will lose respect. People will pretend to like you, but secretly they will hate you and will leave the first chance they can get.

    - Humble yourself, but with honor, and you will get the best out of your staff, which will only make your job easier.

    - Be nice, open to new ideas (even if you know within the first few seconds that it will never work), and show flexibility. Even the smallest gesture will look big in your employee's eyes. Remember the old saying, "You catch more fly's with honey than with vinegar." You will get more out of your employees just by communicating nicely.

3. **Be open and honest.** Be yourself and act genuine. Don't play the role like you are the superior manager, but always maintain a professional persona. Let your employees know what's going on inside your head. People deal with situations, good or bad, when they feel you are being honest in a professional, yet personable way. People also trust those who are open and honest with them. You should encourage input and opinions, and be open for debate.

4. **Be absolutely clear when speaking and giving directions**. Don't try and blind people with science by using acronyms they do not know, or use confusing jargon. It will just make it look like you are trying to show off. Your goal is to de-mystify, not mystify. Mistakes from your employees could be because you did not provide the clear direction needed. Your goal, when communicating, is to simply make sure everyone understands the subject at hand, and understands exactly what it is you're saying. Speak in brief simple terms. They just might finally understand something they always wanted to know, but were afraid to ask...

5. **Listen more than talk**. You'll earn a great deal of respect and credibility by actively listening. Let them share their passion first, and then you can interject when the time is right. Show them you're interested in what they have to say by using positive body language. Asking short questions about the subject, and letting them answer at great length, also shows that you are interested in their comments.

6. **Listen with your full attention.** Know exactly what your employees need from you. If you can help fix the situation and give advise, do so. There might be times, however, when the employee just needs a listening ear. Your best approach is to listen deeply, ask questions for clarification to make sure you understand the situation, and then ask the person what they would like from you. Most of the time they realize there is nothing you can do, but they are just happy to get it off of their chest. They will most likely thank you for listening.

7. **Now make sure your employees listen to you**. If they are not listening, and do not hear what you are saying, they will not follow. If they are not following, then you are not leading. You need to establish the fact that when you talk, you expect their full-undivided attention. If you are losing their attention, stop what you are doing or saying, and let them know you need them to focus on what is being said or shown. It doesn't have to be awkward, just say it as a matter of fact, in a normal tone of voice, and get back to business. Once it has been established that you will not tolerate being ignored, it will stop happening.

8. **Be straightforward and always look them straight in the eyes**. People like an honest answer from someone they trust (even when you do not know the answer). This goes for dealing with your employees to dealing with upper management.

9. **Use the art of persuasion**. Although you might have effective open communication with your team, you still might find yourself needing to sell the new task or project. You will need to know what makes your team tick in order to know how to best persuade them that the new project is a good thing. Use your charm and positive personality to help communicate the need to meet new goals.

10. **Always bite your tongue, before you say something you might regret.** All of the respect you have gained can be lost in a single word you say. Think about what you are going to say before you say it, especially if it is during a heated conversation.

11. **Be able to take criticism.** Your actions when being criticized tell a lot about your strength in management. If they are good points, be sure to acknowledge and address them in a professional, and even thankful manner. If they are bad points, be sure to calmly state your objections and ensure them that you will take their suggestions into consideration. Make sure you do not come across as sounding sarcastic.

12. **Don't be Defensive**. You should not take a suggestion you do not like, or performance related comment, too personally. Calmly reply, without excuses, that you will look into the suggestion, or how you can improve the performance related issues. This is not to say that you should not debate a point, just don't be defensive.

13. **Don't lose your temper**. When you lose your temper, you lose respect. You can show that you are serious about something by being a little more stern and direct, but never blow your top. Have an indicator of sorts to trigger the moment you are ready to explode. It will be your "negative reaction" alert. Also, try to stay away from using foul language. You rarely see a truly respected leader cussing.

14. **Actions speak louder than words.** Even though this is a non-verbal way of communicating, it still is quite powerful. A smile with no words can go a long ways. Unfortunately so can actions like burrowing your eyes, frowning, breathing a sign of disgust, crossing your arms in a defiant manner, closing your eyes while shaking your head, shoulders slumped, fidgeting, and little to no eye contact. Even the way you sit can say a lot about you. Be careful, as these actions, even if unintentional, can be demoralizing. The same holds true with your employees' non-verbal behavior. You should analyze and react as needed. Don't be afraid to follow you gut instinct based on suspicious non-verbal actions.

15. **Continuously talk to, and get along with, your fellow managers.** Building respect and a rapport with your fellow management team members will help build your reputation among the other departments. You can also learn some valuable information, or at least let them think you are on the same wavelength. They will feel that it was a good decision made by the company to hire you as manager.

16. **Telephone etiquette.** First off, make sure you answer your calls and do not be known as a screener. Secondly, make sure you return calls as soon as possible. You need to be sure your voice sounds warm and friendly. Even when you are in a bad mood, try to have a pleasant tone. Unless the person knows you extremely well, how you talk on the phone can create a bad impression. Try not to come across too harsh and overly confident, however, try not to be too sweet and insecure. Some ways to monitor your telephone technique is to pretend a camera is filming your every emotion. This will keep you in check. Also, try to have a smile on your voice and pretend you are actually talking to them as if they were in your office.

17. **The hallway conversation**. It is amazing how many quick impromptu meetings happen when passing someone in the hallway or meeting them in the break room. These quick chats can be productive, however,

sometimes what is said can be considered a concrete decision, even if you thought it was just conversation. This is also the usual time gossip happens. Do your best not to gossip while still maintaining an approachable persona. Just use quick comebacks like, "That's interesting, I sure hope it all works out," and then quickly move on to another subject.

18. **Use your sense of humor.** Don't come across too serious and unfriendly. Just because you are a manager does not mean you no longer have a personality. Pick the right times to let your guard down and tell funny stories or a joke or two. Also laugh at stories and jokes told to you. People trust a person who has both a serious, yet funny side to them. Quickly try to tap into your memory of any stories, trivial tidbits, or quick one-liners that are relevant to the conversation at hand. Don't be shy, as part of being a manager is being a people person. Humor can help relieve tension and keep things into perspective. Just be careful not to come across as too sarcastic or say anything that can offend or be considered unethical. Also, don't come across like a clown or be too goofy. You will lose respect that way.

19. **Keep your boss in the loop at all times.** You might be known as a manager who communicates well with their department; however, you also have to continually communicate with your boss. Give them the answer before they have to ask the question. Keep them updated, even if it is just a quick stop into their office. A couple of "quick and to the point" words can go a long way. It will make your boss feel comfortable that everything is under control, which will give you more job security.

For more communication tips on how to motivate, provide feedback, evaluate, and hold difficult conversations, see lessons 3 and 5.

Holding a Meeting

Part of being a manager is holding meetings. One thing that is for certain, you need to be prepared. The meetings can be anything from a quick follow up with a couple of employees, to a formal PowerPoint presentation to upper management. Meetings can be very productive, but they can also be a waste of time. You need to make the right decision when and when not to hold a meeting. You may find that you can accomplish the meeting goals with just an e-mail or quick conference call.

Even though meetings are extremely important, ineffective meetings not only stops normal everyday workflow for little gain, it also affects employee morale. You need to know what to do before, during, and after a meeting to produce results.

If you are holding a meeting, here are 17 fundamental techniques to follow:

1. **Send out a meeting request.** This is normally done through Outlook or whatever e-mail exchange server you are using. Think about who needs to

attend, and who might want to attend (you can cc those people). If some key players are not able to make the requested time, set up another time that works best for everyone. You should create your own group contacts so you do not have to enter in everyone's name, if it is a meeting with more than just a few people. For example, you should have a Tier 1 contact list that contains only the Tier 1 technicians and their supervisor. Here are three items that should be on each meeting request:

- *State the purpose.* Put the reason for the meeting in the message heading. For example, "This meeting is to review the new product release." People want to be able to see at a glance just what the meeting is all about and why they should be there.

- *Prepare an agenda.* Don't just wing it. You need to put the topics you want to talk about in bullet point format. Make sure you thought each topic through, and have done the groundwork to determine the facts, issues, and the presentation possibilities. Make sure to have the topics and goals clearly written out so that the participants know what will be discussed, and are well prepared to review. You also need to be 100% ready to discuss any issues surrounding the meeting along with all the needed material.

- *Set a timeframe.* Most meetings should run from ½ hour to 1 hour. You might also want to set a timeframe around each item on the agenda.

2. **Send out any meeting material at least two days prior to the meeting**. This includes documents, PowerPoint's, charts, graphs, and any other reading material. This will give people a heads up on what will be reviewed, and give them time to be well prepared for the meeting. If possible, send out this material at the same time you send out the meeting request.

3. **Make copies for everyone.** You should print out enough copies of the agenda and meeting materials, and have them ready to pass out before the meeting even starts. Be sure to make use of this material. This should be the same material as what you previously sent out for pre-review.

4. **Begin the meeting on time**. Do not be late to your own meeting, and if you are waiting on participants, wait no longer than 5 minutes. They will get the point and be early for the next meeting. If you always wait for all participants, then there will always be delays.

5. **Set up the ground rules (also known as "Norms")**. One of the biggest problems in meetings is the use of laptops to check e-mail, getting calls on cell phones, conflict between employees when discussing a certain topic, people who want to take over the meeting, and people who just want to do the time and get out as soon as possible. Politely let everyone know that you will need their full-undivided attention, and that they should turn off all electronic gadgets. You should also state that you expect everyone to act professionally, and that you expect everyone to participate equally.

6. **Get to the point.** The purpose of the meeting is to achieve a result of some sort, whether it is informational, discussing new goals, or going over a new process, etc. After the usual two or three minute pleasantries, it's time to get down to business. Don't be embarrassed by stopping the chitchat and get straight to item one. You will show strong leadership skills if you use your time effectively. It will generate more enthusiasm and a feeling of accomplishment. Be an effective facilitator by keeping the participants on track to accomplish the goals of the meeting.

7. **Make sure you prioritize the meeting subjects.** If you have ten topics to discuss, do not put the most important ones at the bottom of the list.

8. **Follow the agenda and check off each item once discussed.** This will show everyone that you are serious about each topic, when it is time to move on, and that you are in full control.

9. **Take notes throughout the meeting.** Be sure you have a pen and notepad by your side and take plenty of notes. This will not only ensure you will cover all the important points, it shows others how serious you are, which will give them confidence that their points are well taken. If possible, try to have someone in the group take notes for you, especially if you are in more of a presentation type of mode.

10. **It's easy to get off topic.** Try to stay focused and stick to the meeting agenda. Sometimes it's all right to go off topic if it relates to the subject at hand, but in most cases, even though the topic being discussed is interesting, it does not relate to the meeting agenda. You should offer to set up another meeting to discuss the other topic if it is important, but turn everyone's attention back to your meeting as soon as possible. A common phrase to use when you want to steer the meeting back to the agenda is, "We can take that off-line if you would like to discuss further." If there are too many conversations going on at once, find the one that is the most important and ask them to share the information being discussed, it might be very interesting and everyone should be aware of the topic. You can also calmly let the people who are in other conversations to please rejoin the group discussion. You can say to the participants, "With too many conversations going at once, some very good ideas might be lost."

11. **Get the quiet people to talk more, and the dominant people to talk less.** More often than not, you will have one or two individuals who will continually share their views over each and every statement you make. Sometimes people are afraid to say a word because the dominant person, who might have more knowledge and certainly more confidence, intimidates them. You will always have the monopolizers, avid talkers, devil's advocates, cynics, yes men, chicken-little's, joker's, and angry people. Do your best to bring everyone into the conversation and keep it on an even playing field. Carefully interrupt the dominant person and ask someone else in the room for their opinion on the subject. The more you know the characters in your company, the better prepared you will be able to handle them.

12. **Get them to listen without saying a word.** Sometimes just the right look will get people to pay attention to you. Things like raising your

eyebrows, giving them a steady stare, or even just stop talking in mid sentence will help get their attention and focus back onto you. This usually happens when there are too many conversations going on at once.

13. **Look for signs of when you've talked long enough.** You will be able to tell when the group is starting to fidget, look at their watches or clock, or when it is obvious someone else wants to speak. You want to be known as a person who gives a good meeting, and not a meeting hog.

14. **Know when to end the meeting**. If the meeting topics end before the allotted time, and if there is nothing more to discuss on the matter, then go ahead and finish the meeting. If it is running late, try and wrap it up as soon as possible. Quite often people have other meetings scheduled, or will take their lunch between your meeting and the next meeting they have scheduled. So do your best to not go over the allotted time.

15. **Before you end the meeting, make sure you have covered the important points.** Make sure all of the important items have been discussed, go over the action items, and make sure no one leaves confused. Ask if anyone has any questions, and if so, repeat the question asked so that the person feels good that you understood what was being said, and that you shared it with everyone in case they did not hear it.

16. **Send out an overview after the meeting.** Depending on the importance of the meeting, it is a good idea to send out a brief review or "Minutes" soon after the meeting to not only the attendees, but to all you think might be interested. This should be done within a few hours of the meeting to keep up the enthusiasm. People will address action items better and faster when it is still fresh in their memory. The minutes should record who attended, what was discussed, any agreements that were reached, and any action items that were assigned. Distributing the minutes informs those not at the meeting of the progress that was made, and reminds everyone of their action items.

17. **Create an action list and schedule a follow up meeting**. You will find that it is quite common to set up a follow-up meeting. If so, set up the next meeting as soon as possible to keep up the enthusiasm. This also gives true purpose to the original meeting. This is why it is so important that everyone understood what the meeting was all about. There should be no confusion on their given tasks. Create a list of what is expected from either the group or individual, and send it out to the participants with the follow up meeting request, which is usually one week out. You should include:

   o The specific task.
   o The name of the person who committed to "owning" the task.
   o The due date of the task.
   o An agreement about what constitutes completion of the task.
   o True accountability for the task, and the expected deadline. You need to make sure that they know you expect this.

Meetings, when done right and deemed necessary, are keys to department and company success. A good idea is to have a regularly set meeting, even if they last only a few minutes. That way people will be use to the routine and it won't feel like all you do is set up meetings. Here are a couple of ideas for regularly set meetings:

- ✓ **Have a scheduled daily meeting**, preferably in the morning around 9:00am or 10:00am, with *key individuals* such as SME's, supervisors or leads of your department. Keep it to around 15 minutes. Set up a daily calendar event and send out an e-mail invite. There should be no agenda, just basic open conversation. These quick daily meetings help keep everyone on the same page. You can discuss progress on projects, review assigned tasks, make sure any outstanding problems are resolved or being worked on, and cover the events and happenings within the company. Your supervisors and/or leads can then relay pertinent information to the rest of the team. If you were only managing a few people, then you would want to meet with the whole staff.

- ✓ **Have a scheduled monthly meeting** with the *entire staff* of your department. Always adhere to the schedule or it will not be taken seriously. This would also be a perfect time to buy pizza, or sub sandwiches for the whole team. You can make it a "lunch and learn" if desired. Always stress the importance of communication and keep an open mind to all questions asked. If you do not know the answer, don't just make one up, let them know you will look into it and get back to them. The important thing however is that you do indeed get back to them as soon as possible. That builds respect and trust. It also builds character and lets them know you truly do listen and care, even if you give them an answer that they do not like.

- ✓ **Have people want to go to your meetings.** Start it off with a joke or some topical humor. Ask a non-work related question to get them relaxed and talking. Keep the small talk to no more than one or two minutes. This will help break the ice and create a comfortable atmosphere. Also, do not make your meetings boring and predictable. Break them up by sometimes using presentations or hand outs, sometimes just make it a verbal meeting, sometimes draw it up yourself on the whiteboard, sometimes have someone else run most of the meeting, sometimes change the location, sometimes bring in food, and sometimes bring in bottles of water or soda. The goal is to be known as a person who really knows how to give a good meeting in everyway.

Participating in a Meeting

If you are participating in a meeting, here are 7 fundamental techniques to follow:

1. **Show respect to the meeting holder.** Arrive on time; be well prepared with all meeting materials printed out, notes on the subject at hand, and a pen and notepad to take notes.

2. **Do not state your opinion on every single topic.** Don't share your opinions just for the sake of it. You should not feel you always are expected to say something just because you are now in management. Sometimes it is better to say nothing and show you are intrigued with the conversation by intently listening. When the time is right, state your opinion.

3. **Don't be quiet throughout the entire meeting**. Sometimes you might feel left out due to quick conversational points being discussed, and you are not able to get a word in edge-wise. What tends to happen is the longer you are quiet, the harder it will be to say something as the meeting progresses. The people around you will almost forget you're there. The meeting might end and you did not say anything because you lost confidence in yourself. You need to speak up early in the meeting to establish your presence. State at least one opinion, as long as it is relative to the subject, early on in the meeting. When there is something to say, be sure to say it. Don't hold back. If the conversation is going to fast for you to jump in, just raise your hand up with a smile on your face and when noticed, state your opinion. It will be a bit of a tension reliever...

4. **Don't rattle on**. State what you have to say in as few words as possible. If you go on for too long, the point might be lost. You don't want the reputation as being the person "when asked the time, he builds you a watch."

5. **Do not say anything negative about anyone.** This includes your staff members, co-workers, and customers. A slight joke might be all right, but never be slanderous or bad mouth anyone.

6. **Don't feel like you're in a competition with your fellow co-managers.** Sure you want to make sure your boss or upper-management knows how talented you are, but at the same time saying less is sometimes more. You will be seen as a mature leader if you do not squabble, play mind games, or obviously show you are trying too hard to get their attention. Be calm, professional, and don't let them see you sweat.

7. **Don't agree with someone just because you feel intimidated.** This includes your boss and upper management. If you hold back an opinion, it could hurt the company. You will kick yourself for not bringing it up in the first place. Even worse, if you state your opinion after the fact, you will be looked at as spineless. When you feel you should say something, even if your opinion is not taken into account, at least you gave your true thoughts on the subject. Who knows, maybe your boss or upper-management is purposely testing to separate the followers who fly under the radar, with the leaders who have the courage to speak up.

Preparing & Delivering a Presentation

The same meeting management principles as previously described still apply when setting up a meeting presentation. Giving a presentation, however, differs from moderating or leading a meeting. Meetings alone can be a nervous enough experience, but when you have to actually give a presentation, you are presenting yourself as well as the subject at hand. You do not want to come across as a dull and unimaginable person. Even though you might know what you are talking about, the impression and perception you leave with a poor presentation will question your managerial capabilities. It might not seem fair, but that is the way it is.

The good news is that with the right preparation, you will find that you will not only give a great presentation, but also truly impress your staff, boss, and upper management. You might still be nervous, but at least in control. The best defense against anxiety is knowledge, honesty, and full preparation. When you present well, you will gain respect and be seen more authoritative. Effective speaking and presentation capabilities can even lead to further promotion, as this is not a skill everyone possesses.

Here are 15 valuable tips to use when giving a presentation:

1. **Be thoroughly prepared.** You will impress your audience with obvious preparation. Know your subject well along with a message that is clearly stated. If you have any doubts, seek advice. There is nothing wrong with asking for some tips or help.

2. **Think about the flow of the presentation, but not word-for-word.** You want to be fully prepared and confident on the key discussion points, but you should not have a word-for-word speech memorized. If you rehearse your presentation too much, you will sound like a robot. You need to know what you are going to say, just make sure it flows naturally.

   - Have a strong opening and closing. You want an eye-opener to grab their attention, and a grand slam to leave them with a good impression.

   - Have an introduction that will consist on what is going to be talked about, and a conclusion to review what had been discussed.

   - Create a list of key points. If you are not using PowerPoint, be sure you have the main discussion points right in front of you so you do not forget any important topics.

   - Support your introduction with your slides or materials, and use the key points to transition from one point to the next. Be sure your points flow and connect logically.

   - Summarize by asking if they have any questions. This not only helps end the presentation, but also justifies the understanding on what has just been presented.

   - Now practice by visualizing yourself giving a great presentation. You will naturally be unique; there is only one you. Think about moments of possible applauding, your opening line, going through the slides or materials, questions that might be asked, how you will answer difficult questions, when to tell a joke along with hearing the laughter, and your closing comments.

- Perform a practice presentation, especially if using PowerPoint, by going through each topic or slide. Use your notes or laptop to recite the presentation. Look in the mirror or record yourself if you are unsure about your delivery. There are speech-training organizations such as "Toastmasters" that can help build your public speaking confidence. If you have time, it would be a good idea to look into a communication course of some sort.

3. **If using PowerPoint...** Keep the slides simple and don't put too many words on them. The object is for your audience to see, not read, the material. You want big graphics with just a few important words. This will make the presentation more interesting. Your job is to talk about the meaning of the visual graphics. It is strongly suggested to learn PowerPoint if you have not done so already. Here are six points to keep in mind when creating a PowerPoint presentation:

  - **"Title"** page – This should contain the Title presentation name, Organization name, Company logo, and date. You can add your name if you would like. Try to have your company graphic somewhere in the background, just make sure the slide does not look too crowded.

  - **"Agenda"** page – List a few bullet points which will go over the main points that will be discussed.

  - **"Objective"** page – Create a short statement which gives the desired outcome of this presentation.

  - **"Subject Body Matter"** - Create a slide with a keyword or statement to discuss the main point. Some ideas would be to state the problems, solutions, costs if applicable, and action items. Your talking points from your main point should be presented one at a time, in bullet point form, each time you hit the space bar. Keep your text simple. The text on a slide is primarily there for you to key off as speaker. Try to keep each bullet point to just one line, so that the text does not look too crowded. Less is more when it comes to visual presentations. Only use the extra features when necessary so you do not distract your audience from your main points. Unlike the title page, the background should consist of very little graphics. Be sure to use high contrast between background color and text color so people can clearly see the material. The amount of slides you should use depends on the nature of the presentation. If your presentation is to educate or sell, you should keep the number to around 5 or 6. You should spend no more than 1 minute on your main point. Try not to go over 2 or 3 minutes per additional bullet point. If your presentation requires a lot of statistical data, you might need around 20 to 25 slides. If this is the case, each main point and following bullet points should be no more than 1 or 2 minutes per slide. Keep the total time in mind when creating your presentation. You do not want to go too long or too short.

- **"Summary"** page – List the points of what was just discussed, along with the desired outcome.

- **"Questions?"** page – This simple page would be at the very end of the presentation. This is the time you ask the audience if they have any questions. This is also the indicator that the presentation is about to end.

4. **If you are using a projector...** If you have never used a projector before, you should practice setting up and taking down the projector and laptop at least 5 times before you give your first presentation. Your goal is to be able to do this with your eyes closed. Have the PowerPoint file on your laptop desktop for easy access. Pack up all equipment for easy set up and take down, and if possible have a spare projector lamp and cord.

5. **Always have a backup plan...** Projectors might break down, your laptop might not boot up, or some other complex equipment will inevitably go wrong at the worst possible moment. If this happens, most importantly keep calm. Don't lose your cool and be bumbling around trying to fix everything. If you can show grace under pressure, you will be seen as an emotionally controlled manager. Make sure to have a copy of the main talking points that you can discuss. Just start back up verbally, instead of visually, where you left off.

6. **Know your audience.** Think about what it will take to get them interested right from the beginning. If it is an audience who is not technical, do not blind them with science. If the audience is technically inclined, do not use meaningless eye candy graphics. A good-looking presentation that has irrelevant meaning to the audience will be a waste of time. A presentation to upper management would most likely be much different than a presentation to your front line staff. If it were a mix from low end to high-end personnel, then you would need to mix up the presentation just right.

7. **Know the true goal for the presentation.** You need to know exactly what it is you need to accomplish buy giving this presentation. It is imperative you get your point across on your expectations, and if applicable, what upper management expects from you.

8. **Look at the audience as a whole.** Don't just single out one or two people. Instead, try to make eye contact with numerous people throughout the room. If you just look at a one or two people, not only will you make them nervous, you won't be including the audience as a whole. They might loose attention and feel like they are unimportant to the mission at hand. A good tip is to find a couple of individuals on the right, center, and left that you can use as a target. Try to spot these people out before you start the presentation. They should also be located in the middle rows. This will help you keep from just looking at the people in the front row. While talking to them, swing your view from one person to the next casually and slowly. Pause for a longer period while looking straight ahead. Try not to stare. Don't feel like you have to always be looking around, just casually glance around the room. Try to make them feel comfortable.   If you are giving a presentation to just a few people, then just be sure to give each person at least a couple of glances.

9. **Show your personality, don't be stiff, and make them laugh**. Show your character and charisma when presenting. Be passionate about the subject. Move around a bit and show that you are relaxed. It should not feel like a boring school lecture either. Tell stories that relate to what you are talking about. Make them laugh to ease any tension. This also helps them re-adjust to the serious material.

10. **Talk with your audience, not down to them**. You want to hold the audiences interest, not yours. You need to interact by creating a conversation. Ask them questions and listen carefully when you're asked a question. Never cut them off, and make your answer brief.

11. **Be Flexible.** Stick to your main points, but be ready to adjust your presentation to the particular desires of your audience. Gloss over minor points for which your audience has no interest. Welcome questions and comments.

12. **Try not to use "uhm" or "ah" words**. It becomes a distraction and people even play games by counting the number of times these useless words are said, which distracts them to listen to the topic at hand.

13. **Don't be afraid to say, "I don't know."** If your unsure about a question, just take a note and let them know you will get back to them with an answer.

14. **Know when to end the presentation.** If you're running behind, start to wrap it up as fast as possible. Your employees and upper managements time is precious and you don't want them looking at their watches. If you feel like the meeting in not going the way you expected and you are getting sighs of boredom, you might want to skip the least important points and just focus on the remaining points.

15. **People want you to succeed**. Just remember that you're not giving a presentation to be judged for a score, it is to convey information. If you have fun with presenting, the audience will leave happy. You will get through it and will be admired for the ability to give such a presentation.

Communicating Change to your Employees

The saying, "The only constant is change," particularly holds true to business management. One of the key strengths of a great manager and leader is the ability to accept change and orders that come down from above, with enthusiasm and confidence, in which you then translate the directive with the same enthusiasm to your team. Even if you are not worried about the changes taking place, that does not mean your staff isn't concerned. They generally resist change because they do not know, or have a lack of knowledge, on what's coming ahead. It is also because of the way the change is communicated to them. Constant clear communication throughout the change process is the key. The change can be as major as a company takeover, or as simple as a small change in organizational structure. Whatever the change, it needs to be clearly communicated to your staff to relieve any possible anxiety.

You will most likely get some worrisome and sarcastic remarks from some of the team members, but that's natural so don't worry about it. Don't get angry about complaints, even though you may be angry about the change yourself. They may just need to blow off some steam, and the best thing you can do is show that you do care and understand their frustrations. You might want to share some of your own frustrations as well; as long as the main take away point is optimism for the future. Your main concern is to make sure the change or transition goes smoothly and everyone knows the new objective. Don't wait for someone else to tell you what you should do. Take the steps to prevent unwanted surprises, continually meet with your boss and staff to keep them updated, and don't make or implement major changes until you have consulted with your staff. If you show you are embracing the changes with optimism and leading by example, your staff will most likely follow with little to no reservations.

You need to determine:

- What is the reason for the change?
- Why is there change?
- What is the goal you or the company hopes to achieve?
- Will it make your department or company more efficient?
- Will there be a need for more resources?
- Where is the change coming from, you or upper management?
- Who will benefit from this change?
- Who can be negatively affected by this change?

Your goal is to have your staff understand the need for the upcoming change. Even if it is perceived as negative, it should still be perceived as a need for a change in direction, or even to keep the company afloat.

Here are 12 points to keep in mind when dealing with change:

1. The key to a successful implementation of change is to communicate consistently and frequently. Clearly communicate the vision, the mission, and the objectives. Help people understand how these changes will affect them personally, and the steps taken to make sure the change is as seamless as possible. The more information you give, the less uncertainty and anxiety there will be. The less you share, the more misconceptions, which will most likely be more negative than positive. Lack of communication is one of the biggest complaints employees have towards their manager. Be known as the manager who over-communicates, rather than under-communicates. This will also help build trust in you as a leader.

2. Communicate the reasons for the change so that everyone fully understands the need and purpose. No matter how senseless a change might seem, there are reasons behind it, and it is your job to convey those reasons to your staff. When they fully understand, they are more likely to make it work.

3. There may be times when you cannot, and should not, communicate any upcoming changes that are considered confidential. However, if the event is not confidential, be sure to communicate all that is known about the changes as quickly as the information is available.

4. You can either talk to everyone at the same time, or each individually. Here are some guidelines to follow:

   a. *Communicate to everyone at the same time if:*

      i. It is necessary for everyone to hear the news at the same time.
      ii. You want to get your employees involved to generate ideas and help in finding solutions to the change. This is also a good way to create teamwork within the group.
      iii. You want to briefly announce to everyone a major event and then immediately follow up with individual meetings.

   b. *Communicate to each person individually if:*

      i. You anticipate that it will cause a high degree of emotion, which can be counter-productive.
      ii. The subject matter is sensitive and can be consider private or embarrassing.
      iii. The changes involve actions that should remain confidential. It might be related to pay, classification, employment status, or downsizing.
      iv. If you know there will be troublemakers in a full group setting that might make matters worse.

5. You can either verbally share the change information or write it out. In most cases, it is a good idea to use both written and verbal communication. A good rule of thumb would be, the more emotional the issue, the more it should be verbal rather than written. You might also want to document the conversation with any expectations or concerns as a backup. Here are some guidelines to follow for both verbal and written communication regarding change:

   a. *Verbal communication is more appropriate when:*

      i. You know that they will not take the written message seriously, or will not fully understand its meaning.
      ii. You want to grab their attention immediately, and not take the chance that they will automatically check to see if a message is waiting for them in their inbox.
      iii. Emotions are just too high. Verbal communication provides chances for both you and the other person to let off steam and cool down. They will then have a better chance at understanding the reasoning behind the change.
      iv. You are looking for feedback visually and not by an e-mail response.
      v. You need to convince or persuade the team to accept the change. You will have a better chance at getting your point across verbally if it is asking for more of them to do.
      vi. The details of the change are too complicated, and cannot be well expressed written on paper or in e-mail format.

   b. *Written communication is appropriate if:*

      i. The change is general enough and does not necessarily affect your department.
     ii. You need documentation of the communication for future reference.
    iii. Your staff will be referring to details of the change at a later date.
    iv. After you gave a verbal statement, you are following up with updated information.

6. Let your staff ask questions and provide honest answers. If you do not know the answer, it is better to say, "I don't know, but I will find out as soon as possible." Be sure to always follow up. Also, listen and don't be defensive. In most cases the change will be out of your control so do not take complaints personally. Be sure you have said all what you have to say, and not end the conversation until you made the point perfectly clear. Do not just state the change as fact, and then quickly flee the scene.

7. After you have communicated the upcoming changes to your department, if you feel that the information is very important, ask upper management to stop by and briefly talk with your staff members. This should calm them down, and make them feel good, since upper management took the time to make sure everyone was on the same page.

8. Get involved and communicate right away before the rumor mill and grapevine starts to spread around. The longer you wait, the more exaggerated the suspected change can get.

9. Sometimes change, which resulted in the loss of fellow employees, processes, or organizational structure, is very sad. It should not be celebrated, and it is all right to mourn and recognize the loss. It will make you look more human than just a manager who thinks about the numbers. This will also help your staff accept and move on to a new adventure.

10. Don't forget that you will not only be giving facts about the change, but watched carefully on *how you act* towards the change. If you are *saying* one thing, but your *actions* are saying something else, your staff might come up with a different conclusion. You might of thought that you conveyed the changes clearly, but then came to find out that they understood something completely different. If you are too lackadaisical and show little concern, they will as well. If you come off as intense and worried, so will they. You need to act in a way that is relevant to the change. Keep this in mind whenever you are communicating with your staff.

11. Be sure to follow-up to make sure there are no problems related to the change. Old habits can easily start to creep back into their former state, so it's necessary to stay on top of the situation until you are 100% confident that the change has taken place with no ill effects.

12. Don't forget that change is stressful for everyone. Just because they complied with little resistance does not mean you should take them for granted. Make it a point to recognize employees for their effort and cooperation.

In every way, effective communication is your most important tool. If you follow the points just given, you will be looked at as an effective communicator of change. The only people who will not accept your statements will be those who are most likely unhappy with the present situation anyways. If there are those who do resist or retaliate against change, they need to be dealt with before they influence the attitude and performance of their peers. Do not permit any resistance to change or else you will be broadcasting the wrong message.   Use good judgment, be thoughtful and willing to listen to any of your employees concerns, but make sure they adapt to the change, as it is inevitable.

A short story about giving a presentation

John never gave a presentation before and was extremely nervous. Sure he had been involved in many meetings, but to actually talk to upper management while using a laptop and projector was nerve racking. When he gave the presentation, he was only halfway through the slides when the allotted time for the meeting was over. He was stiff in his presentation, the slides had too much text and were hard to read, and he did not cover all of the main points. John realized that he did not plan out the presentation as well as he should have. He learned the hard way that he needed to make sure he timed his presentation, use quick bullet points instead of long sentences, and to be more relaxed.

The next time John was to give a presentation, he made sure the slides were quick and to the point, and that there was enough time to cover all of the material. Unfortunately, John showed up to his own meeting just a few minutes before giving his presentation, and sure enough, this time the equipment was not working. He tried to fix it by checking the connection from the laptop to the projector, and confirmed there was power, but still no luck. He had some notes to go of off, but the presentation needed visuals and turned out to be ineffective. He was also stressed due to the malfunction.

From that point on John made it a point to arrive at least 15 minutes early to a presentation meeting, test all equipment, have short bullet points in the PowerPoint presentation in which to talk about, and just relax and be himself. He also made it a point to be fully comfortable with setting up and tearing down all of the equipment, and practiced speaking about the main points of his presentation while going through each slide. John is now considered a great presenter with excellent communication skills.

Epilogue: The moral of the story is you need to be fully prepared in order to relax and be yourself. If you approach the presentation as being too uptight, the presentation will come off as uneventful. If your approach is lackadaisical, you will not be prepared to handle any problems that might appear. By getting it just right, you will be able to have a successful presentation. The key is to be fully prepared by creating the right presentation for the occasion, practice speaking about the main points (but not word-for-word), making sure everything is working (have spares if possible), and always have a backup plan. Once all of this is in order, you can relax, be yourself, and present the meeting knowing you have everything under control, no matter what happens.

Quick Lesson Summary

- Business writing is an essential part of management. You will be creating processes and procedures as well as constantly creating and responding to e-mail. When it is an informal subject, most likely through e-mail, write like you are talking to the person. When it is a formal subject, like an important process, keep it formal. A good idea is to have someone who you trust and understands the tasks at hand to review the process before you send it out to everyone. Know what type of information you will convey, think about what you want them to hear, what you are going to say, who will be the recipients of the information, create the written form of communication, and finally proofread and edit before you send it out.

- The way you verbally communicate with your employees, co-managers, your boss, upper-management and customers, can make you or break you. This goes for face-to-face meetings, phone calls, and even hallway chats. How you handle yourself during these types of conversations is how you are looked at as a manager and leader. Being easily accessible and willing to talk to your employees about subjects related to work and home, with professionalism and compassion, is key.

- Part of being a manager is holding and participating in meetings. This is the best way you can get your point across and share visions and goals. You need to be fully prepared, or else it can be a waste of time. It is also important to determine if a meeting is really necessary. Sometimes a quick memo or conference call could suffice. Keep the meeting interesting and make sure you get them to listen to you. It is suggested that you have daily or weekly meetings with key staff members, and weekly or monthly meetings with your whole staff. Try not to go over the scheduled time and stick to the agenda.

- When giving presentations, you are presenting yourself as well as the subject at hand. Even though you might know what you are talking about, the impression and perception you leave with a poor presentation will question your managerial capabilities. Successful presenters are fully prepared and rehearse the main topics, but not word-for-word. Create the right flow, know how much time you have, and know when to end. Knowing PowerPoint and how to use a projector is strongly suggested.

- Change is inevitable, and the sooner you can accept and embrace the change, the sooner your employees will as well. People resist change because they do not know, or have a lack of knowledge, on what's coming ahead. If you have constant clear communication throughout the change process, you will relieve any anxiety amongst your employees. Know the times when you should talk to them verbally, in writing, or both. Also know when to talk to them as a group, individually, or both.

LESSON 8 – BUSINESS BASICS PART I – BUSINESS TYPES, ETHICS & LAW, ECONOMICS, FINANCE & ACCOUNTING

Introduction: How the money and the business flows...

Managing your own department is only part of the responsibilities in the world of management. Most companies have multiple departments to run the business. No matter what department you run, you should know how to interact and understand the functions of each department within a business organization. These next three lessons cover the fundamental basics of what is taught in an MBA course, including the parts of an organization that make up a business. If anyone of these particular departments are ones in which you currently work in, or would like to be a part of, you should find individualized training, which will go into more in depth detail regarding the subject matter. For continuity, we will use the point of view of how a "Customer Service Manager" might interact with the departments described in these next three lessons.

Managers spend time with other departments working on inter-department workflow processes, in daily or weekly management meetings, on conference calls, or meetings with the CEO. Your co-managers from different departments will be your allies and you want to keep them close. You should always have a cooperative relationship with your fellow management staff. This is why you need to understand, at least at a basic level, the functionalities of their departments. You want to be able to understand the basics of what they are talking about, especially when they are going over their performance goals. You also want to be able to understand what the CEO is talking about, much of which is usually financially based, and how you will be able to share the company's vision with your department.

You will be in a much stronger position if you understand the dynamics of finance and overall business theory. It's not merely for the sake of understanding another discipline, but in order to make sounder decisions likely to produce a greater return for your department. You can stand behind the logic, and not worry about the skills to challenge the assumption. By understanding the basic financial terms, economics, legal, ethics, sales figures, marketing strategies, customer service and operating functions, you will feel confident, and not blinded by science, when you are in management meetings. It will give you a chance to contribute more, and not be self-conscious about your lack of knowledge.

In this lesson we will be reviewing the different types of business along with an overview of ethics, economics, finance, accounting, budgets, and legal.

Business Types

A business in its most basic form sells a *product* such as shoes, cars, and burgers, or delivers a *service* such as telephone, cable TV, and auto repair. The goal is to make a profit. Businesses use some combination of labor, equipment, and materials to produce products or services.

Here are the most common forms to set up a business organization, with a brief explanation of each:

Sole Proprietorship – A business owned by one person who is self-employed and has the rights to profits and is responsible for debts. The upside is full control, can sell whenever desired, and fewer regulations. The main downside is the owner is personally liable for all business debts, and it is harder to raise capital from investors. Most small businesses are organized as a sole proprietorship and will usually incorporate when the business grows in size.

Partnership – A business owned by two or more individuals who contribute funds and shares the profits and debts. Common Partnerships are accounting, law, consulting, and architectural firms.

Corporation – A business in which legally the owners are not personally liable for the financial obligations of the business. They can only lose the money they invest in the corporation. The investment is when they contribute money, or if applicable, when they buy stock in the company. A share of stock represents a share in the ownership. If the company is a publicly held corporation, the general public can also own stocks. Owners are not personally liable and a corporation is often referred to as a "legal person." It can use the terms "Inc." "Incorporated," or "Company."

Limited Liability Company (LLC) - A business authorized by state law. Although exact characteristics vary by state, the most common characteristics of the limited liability company are that it has:

1. Limited liability, that is, the owners of the company are not liable for more than the capital they have invested in the business.
2. Managed by members or managers, owners can be members or managers.
3. Limitations on the transfer of ownership.

LLC's are becoming an increasingly popular way to start a business because LLC's are generally a less complicated business structure than a corporation, and provide a significant amount of protection.

Business Ethics and Law

Using the same moral guidelines you already follow yourself, knowing the difference between right and wrong, also goes for business. It will tell you what is right or wrong in any business situation. Sometimes, however, what might be best for the company might seem morally wrong personally. For example, buying cheaper goods from another country will help increase the company's profit margin, however, that country legally allows children to work for low wages. At the end of the day, businesses should be as ethically sound as they can when determining the "greater good" for all involved.

Companies that violate the more obvious ethical practices can result in huge consequences. Just look at what happened to Enron. Problems usually start off small, but build into bigger ones unless standards are truly set and followed. With the pressure to achieve the numbers, bad decisions can be made. This can be pressure on the customer service representative to wrongly fill an order, to senior management falsifying the financial health of the company.

Some business ethics, however, are much more easily recognizable as being obviously ethically wrong. To name a few:

- Money lost to Fraud
- Money lost to Embezzlement
- Accuracy of books, records, and expense reports
- Proper use of organizational assets
- Protecting proprietary information
- Discrimination
- Lying
- Over charging
- Charging for work that was not necessary
- Withholding needed information
- Abusive or intimidating behavior toward others
- Misreporting actual time or hours worked
- False insurance claims
- Kickbacks and bribery
- Proper exercise of authority
- Theft of business equipment and supplies
- Trading or accepting goods for unauthorized favors
- Moonlighting, which causes poorer work performance
- Knowingly ignoring the health and safety of employees
- Sexual harassment
- Evading someone's privacy

Using basic common sense, if you as manager always act with integrity, you will not violate business laws or be associated with bad work ethics. This not only prevents any problems for you personally and professionally, you will also be seen and known as a solid and trustworthy leader. Make it known that everyone is expected to adhere to the highest standards of business ethics and must understand that anything less is totally unacceptable.

Standards regarding ethical behavior need to be developed, set, and communicated throughout the entire company. For more information on ethical issues, go to www.ethics.org.

The legal department of a company takes charge of all legal matters of the company including labor laws, contracts, and legal representation. They are the team who will get involved with any legal troubles. You would have to take a course in business law to understand all of the ramifications associated with the legal department, however, we will give a brief explanation of some of the most known business laws faced by the legal department.

Basically, business law governs the rules of conduct of people and organizations in business, and is meant to enforce justice and obligation. The major areas of business law are:

Antitrust – which its laws ensure that competition remains fair by prohibiting companies from merging with one another, or acquiring one another, to form monopolies. A monopoly exists when there is only one supplier of some product or service, and can then charge whatever price it wants due to there is no longer any competition.

Bankruptcy – which laws let a company that is having financial problems seek protection from the demands of creditors. Chapter 11 of the bankruptcy code regulates liquidation, which means closing the company and selling its assets to creditors, and chapter 7 regulates reorganizations, which means a court supervised restructuring of a company while its creditors wait for payment.

Business organization – which are the laws that govern the formation of a business.

Consumer protection and product liability – which are regulations regarding products, services, and credit practices. Consumers should be able to assume that products will work and food is safe to eat, which is FDA regulated. Also a company cannot knowingly sell a product that it believes will be unsafe or harmful for its intended use.

Contracts – which are legally binding exchanges of promises or agreement between parties that the law will enforce.

Employment – which are laws that regulate the hours and conditions under which people work, such as child labor laws, sets minimum wage, and expands the rights of disabled people. You need to take all discriminatory laws associated with employment very seriously. The Equal Employment Opportunity Commission or the EEOC enforces these laws. The website is www.eeoc.gov.

Intellectual property – which laws protect copyrights, trademarks, and patents.

Securities regulation – which is governed by the Securities and Exchange Commission (SEC). It polices the financial markets regarding insider trading, stock price manipulation, improper financial reporting, and improper and illegal practices at brokerage firms.

As manager, if you encounter any type of legal issue that you are not 100% aware of, or not comfortable with, be sure to ask your boss or the legal department for help. This includes the signing of any legal documentation. Always be careful on what you say and how you act. If you do get into some trouble, contact an attorney right away. However, common sense should always prevail, and you will be all right as long as you are ethically sound whenever any possible legal issues, such as discrimination or consumer protection, occur.

Basic Economics overview

Although there are many interpretations, economics is basically "the study of what constitutes rational human behavior in the endeavor to fulfill needs and wants." In business, companies follow economic news to make decisions on what products to make or discontinue, when to hire or lay off employees, build or sell a factory, spend more or less on advertising, etc. Economics is a vastly huge subject and can go into a world of theories and complicated mathematical formulas. We will, however, cover some of the basics.

The foundation of economics is **Scarcity**, which refers to the tension between our limited resources and our unlimited wants and needs. Scarcity is the basic economic problem that arises because people have unlimited wants, but resources are limited. Because of scarcity, various economic decisions must be made to allocate resources efficiently. These decisions are made by giving up, or *trading off*, one want to satisfy another. For an individual, resources include time, money and skill. For a country, limited resources include national resources, capital, labor force, and technology. The most common phrase that you have probably heard regarding economics is, "Supply and Demand."

Supply is the *quantity* of a product produced and offered for sale. The more buyers are willing to pay, the more incentive to increase the supply. On the other hand, the less that buyers are willing to pay, the more incentive to lower the price to decrease the surplus. For example, if the quantity supplied of the product is 30, and the quantity demanded for the product is 20, there would be a surplus of 10 products (30-20=10). The sellers would have to lower the price in order to sell excess supply.

Demand is based on *price.* The law of demand is basically; the higher the price, the lower the quantity demanded, and the lower the price, the higher the quantity demanded. As the price for a product rises, demand for that product will fall. On the other hand, if the sellers lowered the price for the product too much, demand would increase beyond what is supplied, and there would be a shortage. The optimal is to have equilibrium where the price point for the quantity supplied is in balance with the quantity demanded.

When the price is just right with no surplus and no shortage, supply and demand is known to be in **Equilibrium**. This means that the quantity demanded equals the quantity supplied. This is what economists use to look at regarding supply and demand for a product. A product is in equilibrium when the market price is set just right. If the market price drops, demand will exceed supply, thus prices will rise. If the market price increases, supply will exceed demand and prices will drop.

Basic Supply and Demand graph – The cross point is where supply and demand are in balance, or equilibrium, based on price and quantity:

Two branches of economics are **Microeconomics** and **Macroeconomics**. Microeconomics is the study of the decisions of individuals, households, and businesses in specific markets, whereas macroeconomics is the study of the overall functioning of an economy such as basic economic growth, unemployment, recession, depression, or inflation.

Microeconomics focuses on supply and demand and other forces that determine the price levels seen in the economy. It analyzes the market behavior of individual consumers and firms in an attempt to understand the decision-making process of firms and households. It studies the shifts in demand based on income and other consumer factors. An increase in income normally leads to an increase in the amount people are willing to pay for goods, thus are more prone to buy more luxury items. There are also competing substitute products or services, which can lower the price of the original.

Macroeconomics focuses on the national economy as a whole and provides a basic knowledge of how things work in the business world, for example, the impacts of money supply, interest rates, unemployment, and government deficits.

The way we usually measure the size of an economy is by its **Gross Domestic Product** or **GDP**. GDP is the value of all the goods and services produced within our borders in one year. People who study macroeconomics would be able to interpret GDP figures and how they relate to our national economy. Basically, GDP measures the size of the national economy by the total value of all goods and services produced within a nations border. This is a key economic indicator for economic growth rate, which measures how much bigger or smaller an economy is one period, compared with the same period a year ago. The formula used, and a brief explanations of the components measured in GDP, is:

- GDP = C + I + G + (Ex – IM). C is for Consumption (household spending), I is for Investments (business spending), G is for government (federal, state and local spending). "Ex" is for Export (goods shipped out of the country that made them) and "Im" is for Import (goods shipped into the country that outside countries made). You can see that if any component increases, the total GDP increases. If any component decreases, the total GDP decreases. There is a never-ending business cycle, which is a long-run pattern of economic growth and recession, also known as boom and bust, because of fluctuations in demand. Recovery always follows recession, and vice-versa. A business cycle is like the domino effect: During a recovery, consumers buy more (C or Consumption), which then means businesses invest more in equipment and staff (I or investments), etc. During a recovery, the business cycle is on an upswing and GDP growth continues. During a recession, the exact opposite is true. This is important to know because as manager, you do not want to get stuck with excess inventory or hire un-needed additional staff because you didn't see the economic slowdown coming, or vice-versa because you do not have the goods to sell due to an increase in demand.

The **Federal Reserve**, also known as "the Fed," controls the U.S. money supply. It is the central banking system of the United States. It replaces old currency with new currency, guarantees bank deposits, and governs the banking system. The Fed affects the economy by moving interest rates, selling and buying government securities, and talking about the economy (known as "moral suasion"). The Fed manages two kinds of economic policy:

- *Fiscal policy*, which is the spending and taxation to stimulate or "cool" the economy by adjusting taxes and spending. It can raise or lower spending and raise or lower taxes. Using an increase in government spending to ignite a recovery is called *fiscal stimulus*. If the government spends more than it collects in taxes, it is deficit spending. The government can lower taxes as well to ignite a recovery instead of increasing spending. The government can do the exact opposite if it sees inflation heading upward to cool off the economy by raising taxes or reduce spending.

- *Monetary policy*, which uses interest rates, purchases, and sales of government securities to heat or cool the economy. The Fed sets the rate for short-term loans that banks make to one another, called the Fed funds rate, and the rate that the Fed makes with loans to banks, called the Discount rate. These tend to drive other interest rates. If interest rates are decreased, that makes for easier credit to start spending and increase demand, which also makes it easier to repay the loan. If it starts to overheat heading towards inflation, then the opposite is true to cool down the economy. The Fed can also sell government securities, which are bonds or government debt, to cool an economy. The government has the consumers and businesses money, which means there is less in circulation, thus less spending and less economic growth, which would result in reducing inflation. If the Feds want to heat up the economy, they buy back the securities, then cash will be back in the consumer and businesses hands to spend, etc.

At the end of the day, the government wants a sound currency, low unemployment, and sustained economic growth.

Here are some more economic terms, and key economic indicators or trends, which are commonly used:

- o **Bubble -** When the price of an asset rises far higher than can be explained by fundamentals.

- o **Business cycle -** The business cycle has four stages including expansion, peak, recession, and recovery. Lastly, recovery is what happens after security prices fall and eventually go back up.

- o **Capitalism –** Economic system based on private ownership, production, and distribution of goods. It is based on "Free Enterprise," which means the government should not interfere with the economy. It's about competition for profit.

- o **Consumer Confidence –** A psychological view from consumers on how they feel about the economy and their prospects in the current and future economy.

- o **Depreciation -** A fall in the value of an asset or a currency; the opposite of appreciation.

- o **Depression –** A bad, depressingly prolonged recession in economic activity. The textbook definition of a recession is two consecutive quarters of declining output. A slump is where output falls by at least 10%; a depression is an even deeper and more prolonged slump.

- o **Housing Starts –** The start of construction on new homes is an economic indicator. This is due to declining housing also means declining purchases that goes with a new home such as carpeting, appliances, drapes, electronic equipment, and labor such as painting and landscapers. There is a domino effect when housing sales are slow for both new homes and existing homes.

- o **Inflation -** Rising prices, across the board. Inflation basically means your dollar does not go as far as it used to as it erodes the purchasing power of a unit of currency. It is usually expressed as an annual percentage rate of change. If prices raise gradually, consumers can adjust. However, rapid inflation can destabilize the economy. Prices and inflation are key economic indicators.

- o **Pareto principle (also known as the 80-20 rule) –** This states that eighty percent of result is obtained due to 20 percent of actions. For example, 20% of the people own 80% of the wealth, or 20% of the sales force contributes to 80% of all revenue, etc. This rule can be used in just about any situation. For example, 80% of your better employees will only take 20% of your time to coach, thus the other 20% of your employees will take 80% of your time.

o **Prime Rate –** This is the rate on loans that a bank charges its most creditworthy corporate customers. This is set by several major New York banks. A *sub-prime* rate is for such companies or individuals that don't meet criteria of best market rates and have a history of deficient credit. Interest rates are a key economic indicator.

o **Recession** - A period of decline in a national economy over a period of time, usually two quarters of a financial year. Spending and demand decrease, making the economic climate more difficult.

o **Securities -** Financial contracts, such as:

Bonds, which is basically an IOU that states that if an investor lends money to the government or a corporation now, then they will pay your money back at a stated time in the future while making small interest payments to you along the way.

Shares, which is part ownership of a company.

Derivatives, which are financial assets that "derive" their value from other assets that grant the owner a stake in an asset. Such securities account for most of what is traded in the financial markets.

o **Stock market –** Basically, a high or raising stock market indicates a recovery is in progress and a failing market indicates recession. The Dow Jones Industrial Average (DJIA) is based upon 30 extremely large blue chip U.S. corporations, such as GE, Microsoft, and Coca Cola, and is used as a key economic indicator.

o **Unemployment rate** - The number of people of working age without a job is usually expressed as the unemployment rate, which is a percentage of the workforce. This is one of the key economic indicators. This rate generally rises and falls in step with the business cycle. The average goal is no lower than 4% and no higher than 8%. If it goes too much lower, then inflation usually occurs. If it goes too much higher, then the country could be headed towards a recession.

o **Venture Capital** (VC) – Private equity to help new companies grow. A valuable alternative source of finance for entrepreneurs, who might otherwise have to rely on a loan from a risk averse bank manager.

o **Yield –** The return on an investment expressed as a percentage of the cost of the investment.

Corporate Finance Overview

Corporate finance is the specific area of finance dealing with the financial decisions corporations make, and the tools and analysis used to make the decisions. Finance makes sure the company has the money it needs in order to operate. They are able to show external and internal parties financial data through financial statements, prepared by accountants, which are used to make decisions about the firm's financial condition, and to advise others about possible losses and profits. Finance analyzes the health and growth of a company, manages the company's cash, and deals with banks. Most mid to large size companies will have a CFO (Chief Financial Officer) who oversees the finance department, which normally consists of a controller, managerial accountant and/or general ledger accountant.

Finance is also involved with leasing property, equipment, purchasing raw materials, and pays employees. They provide helpful information in monitoring and evaluating management performance such as helping departments prepare their budgets and consolidate it into one company budget. They work with the Senior Management team (the CFO is part of this team) to set the company's sales and profit goals for the year. Senior Managers use accounting information in making investment decisions, investors use accounting information to value stock, and bankers rely on accounting information in determining any potential risks to lend money.

Besides what has been previously stated, some more detailed responsibilities of corporate finance are:

- Cash flow budgeting and working capital management, which is managing the relationship between a firm's short-term assets and its short-term liabilities. The goal of working capital management is to ensure that the firm is able to continue its operations, and that it has sufficient cash flow to satisfy both maturing short-term debt and upcoming operational expenses. Working capital is: "current assets minus current liabilities." Working capital measures how much in liquid assets a company has available to build its business.
- Comparing alternative proposals.
- Forecasting and risk analysis.
- Raise and manage its capital: Obtaining funds, debt or equity sources, long-term or short-term, and optimum capital structure.
- Allocations of funds to long-term capital investments vs. optimize short-term cash flow.
- Dividend policy.
- The risk-return framework and the identification of the asset appropriate discount rate.
- Valuation of assets. Discounting of relevant cash flows, relative valuation, and contingent claim valuation.
- The optimum allocation of funds. What to invest in? How much to invest? When to invest?
- How much money will be needed at various points in the future? How will it be funded?
- Identification of required expenditure of a public sector entity.
- Source of that entity's revenue.

We will not be able to go over each of the items just described, as you would need to take a full time financial course to fully understand it all. However, we will go over and discuss the items you might encounter whenever dealing with finance or upper management. We will present an overview of financial accounting and managerial accounting. We will discuss and have examples of two financial statements, the balance sheet and income statement. We will also discuss the cash flow statement. We'll cover terms like Assets, Liabilities, Equity, COGS, SG&A, EBIT, EBITDA, Margins, ROI, FIFO, LIFO and Capex. And, we will demonstrate some of the most common financial analysis ratios, present a basic overview of inventory accounting, go over basic accountant responsibilities, and finally ending up with how to set up a budget.

As a manager, you should understand the basic financial statements and the associated terms in order to know how your budgets, transactions, and decisions affect the company.

Financial Accounting and Managerial Accounting

Accounting provides the reliable and relevant financial information useful in making decisions. Monetary events are first identified such as the type of sales and expenses, then recorded by documenting and entering the data, and finally presented to external parties who are outside of the company, usually through financial statements, and internal parties who are the people inside the company, usually through various reports.

Financial Accounting provides information for external parties who are interested in the company's accounting information. Examples would be reports to investors and stockholders, creditors, taxing authorities or even customers, usually through financial statements. The two most common statements are the balance sheet and income statement. This summarized data is for the entire company as a whole, and is based on a historical performance by reporting on the past. Reliability is emphasized since information is used outside the company. Financial Accounting is driven by the rules of double entry accounting in which both sides of a transaction are entered – one debit and one credit. This keeps the books in balance. For example, the purchase of new equipment will be entered as an "increase to assets," and also entered as a "decrease to cash or increase to debt." Since accounting information is so important on making financial decisions, rules are established to ensure that people and organizations understand how accounting information is measured. In the USA, Generally Accepted Accounting Principles (GAAP) is the common standards that indicate how to report economic events. Following standardized rules also makes sure every asset and transaction is documented, each invoice and account is paid on time, nothing is paid more than once or left unpaid, keeps all financial matters under control, and reduces the chance of embezzlement. (Note: at least two employees should be involved anytime cash is expected to change hands).

The primary purpose for the financial accounting system is to be able to develop the needed financial statements, most commonly being the balance sheet and income statement, at the end of each month, quarter or year.

Managerial Accounting provides accounting information to internal parties for profit planning and budgeting, costs of an organizations products and services, and performance reports such as budget vs. actual results. These reports are for areas or departments of the organization and not the whole company. Analyzing the data from these reports are very useful for managers who direct, plan and control its day-to-day operations, to make decisions regarding the future. Managerial Accounting focuses on the future, rather than reporting on the past. Reporting on the past is the primary role of financial accounting. Because these reports are internal, and there are no regulations, it does not follow GAAP. The institute of Managerial Accounting sponsors the CMA (Certified Managerial Accountant) and developed the standards for ethical conduct, which are competence, confidentiality, integrity and objectivity.

Costing is also a major part of managerial accounting. Knowing the cost of goods to be sold is critical before planning for the future. Using a manufacturing company as an example, the elements that go into determining manufacturing costs are:

- *Direct materials or raw materials*, which include any materials that become an integral part of a finished product. It is a part of COGS as a direct cost of materials needed.

- *Direct Labor costs,* which are costs that can be physically traced to the actual production of the product. It is a part of COGS as a direct cost making the product.

- *Manufacturing overhead,* which encompasses all the costs that are not designated as direct material or direct labor such as the SG&A and indirect costs like the janitor who cleans the manufacturing warehouse, etc.

Numbers are the universal language of finance and are the raw materials of a balance sheet and income statement (or P&L – Profit and Loss - statement). We will discuss all of the major financial terms and their meanings within the balance sheet and income statement in the next two sections.

Financial Statements: The Balance Sheet

The balance sheet is often described as a "Snapshot" of the current company's financial condition on a certain date. It shows the "Assets" on the left, or top, of the balance sheet, and the "Liabilities and Owners Equity" on the right, or bottom. The Assets must balance out with the Liabilities and Owners Equity. Assets are what a company owns, such as equipment, buildings and inventory. Claims on assets include liabilities and owners' equity. Liabilities are what a company owes, such as notes payable, trade accounts payable and bonds. Owners' Equity represents the claims of owners against the business. The formula is Assets = Liabilities + Owners' Equity.

Example – The Balance Sheet. There are explanations for each item following the Balance Sheet:

Balance Sheet - Sample Corp. Fiscal Year (FY) 2007, 2008	12/31/2008	12/31/2007		12/31/2008	12/31/2007
ASSETS			**LIABILITIES and OWNERS' EQUITY**		
Current Assets			*Current Liabilities*		
Cash	$45,000	$40,000	Long-Term Debt – 1 Yr.	$12,000	$11,000
Marketable Securities	$65,000	$60,000	Notes Payable	$15,000	$14,000
Accounts Receivable	$85,000	$70,000	Accounts Payable	$13,000	$12,000
Notes Receivable	$45,000	$40,000	Taxes Payable	$11,000	$10,000
Inventories	$85,000	$80,000	Accrued Expenses	$21,000	$20,000
Total Current Assets	$325,000	$290,000	Other Current Liabilities	$10,000	$9,000
			Total Current Liabilities	$82,000	$76,000
Long-Term Assets					
Land	$85,000	$80,000	*Long-Term Liabilities*		
Buildings	$100,000	$90,000	Notes Payable	$30,000	$27,000
Machinery	$30,000	$25,000	Bonds Payable	$60,000	$52,000
–Accumulated Depreciation	($4,000)	($3,500)	Total Long-Term Liabilities	$90,000	$79,000
Net Tangible Assets	$211,000	$191,500	*Other Liabilities*		
Intangible Assets			Pension Obligations	$90,000	$82,000
Goodwill	$15,000	$5,000	Deferred Taxes	$70,000	$62,000
Patents	$20,000	$19,000	Minority Interest	$15,000	$12,000
Trademarks	$15,500	$13,400	Total Other Liabilities	$175,000	$156,000
Copyrights	$24,000	$22,900	Total Liabilities	$347,000	$311,000
Total Intangibles	$74,500	$60,300	**OWNERS' EQUITY**		
Other Assets			Preferred Stock	$60,000	$50,000
Investments	$25,000	$23,000	*Common Equity*		
Deferred Charges	$50,000	$45,000	Common Stock	$97,500	$89,000
Total Other Assets	$75,000	$68,000	Capital Surplus	$111,000	$99,000
Total Long-Term Assets	$360,500	$319,800	Retained Earnings	$120,000	$105,800
			–Treasury Stock	($50,000)	($45,000)
			Total Common Equity	$278,500	$248,800
			Total Owners' Equity	$338,500	$298,800
Total Assets	$685,500	$609,800	**Total Liabilities and Owners' Equity**	$685,500	$609,800

Here is a brief explanation of the type of Assets, Liabilities, and Owners' Equity associated with a common Balance Sheet:

Assets – which is everything the company owns. They are listed in order of their liquidity, which means how easily they can be converted into cash. Current assets are first, then non-current assets, and finally all other assets. Here are the most common types of assets:

❑ **Cash,** both in checking and savings along with petty cash.

❑ **Marketable Securities**, which are short-term investments, like U.S. Government securities or the commercial paper of other firms. These often earn higher interest than checking or savings accounts earn.

❑ **Accounts Receivable**, which is money owed to the company by its customers, usually within 10 to 60 days. There is usually also some bad debt, around 2%, that gets written off. For example, a customer who purchased your product but never paid.

❑ **Notes Receivable,** which is money due from debtors.

❑ **Inventory**, which is the goods for sale to customers, or goods in the manufacturing process.

  • The inventory for a *Manufacturer* would be the raw materials to make its products, the unfinished products still being made, and the finished goods that are awaiting sale.
  • The inventory for a *Retailer* would be just the finished goods. They would not deal with the raw materials or have a unfinished product.
  • The inventory for a *Service* company would have little to no inventory on their balance sheet due to the nature of the business.

❑ **Long-Term Assets or Tangibles,** also known as "Fixed Assets." The land, buildings, factories, and warehouses, including the machinery, furniture, computers, and fixtures that are owned by the company. These assets can depreciate, or lose value, on each year's balance sheet due to age, etc.

  • Accumulated depreciation is a way to allocate, which means assigning, the cost of a fixed asset with a life of over one year. The cost of the asset is charged against income over the life of the asset rather than all in one year. This is also known as a "contra account," which in essence carries a minus sign.

❑ **Intangible Assets**, which are non-physical products like *patents*, which are exclusive legal rights granted to an investor for a period of 17 years, *trademarks,* which are distinctive names or symbols granted for 28 years with option for renewal, *goodwill*, which is the amount of money paid for the asset above the value it was assigned by the previous owner, and *copyrights*, which is a form of intellectual property that gives the creator of an original work exclusive rights for a certain time period.

❑ **Investments, Prepayments and Deferred Charges**, which is monies already spent, that will yield benefits in upcoming years like insurance coverage, rent, etc.

Liabilities – which is everything the company owes, mostly to suppliers and creditors. Current liabilities are those payable within a year of the date of the balance sheet. Here are the most common types of liabilities:

- **Long-term debt**, which is the debt due after one year of the date of the balance sheet.

- **Notes Payable**, which are short-term borrowings that are payable within the year. It is a promissory note, which is basically a written promise to pay.

- **Accounts Payable**, which is the amount the company owes to suppliers.

- **Federal income taxes,** and when applicable city and state taxes.

- **Accrued Expenses Payable**, which is all other monies, owed at the time of creating the balance sheet including employees, contractors, utilities, etc.

- **Current portion of long-term debt**, which is the amount due within a year from the date of the balance sheet. This would be considered a current liability.

- **Notes Payable**, which are non-current (due after 12 months) borrowings. It is a promissory note, which is basically a written promise to pay.

- **Bonds payable**, which is the obligation due on maturity of bonds.

- **Pension obligations**, which is the liability for future pension benefits due to employees.

- **Deferred Taxes**, which are the longer-term tax obligations that have been deferred to some future period.

- **Minority interest**, which is the ownership of minority shareholders in the equity of consolidated subsidiaries.

Owners' Equity (also known as Stockholders' Equity - when applicable) – which is the amount left over for the company's owners after the liabilities are subtracted from the assets. The formula is "Assets – Liabilities = Owners Equity." This is also referred to as "Net Worth." If the company is incorporated, they can issue stock. Stocks represent ownership in a corporation. A share of stock is one unit of ownership. Investors buy stocks to share in the company's profits, where as the company issues stocks to raise money from the investors. If the company is not incorporated, such as a Sole Proprietor, they will not have accounts for stock, but will invest the money back into the company through "Retained Earnings." If this number is zero or negative, then the company is obviously in trouble and steps will need to be taken, or else there is the chance of bankruptcy.

- **Preferred Stock**, which is a type of stock that pays a dividend. It is a payment from profit made to stockholders out of the company's income at a specific rate, regardless on how the company performs. Owners of preferred stock do not have voting rights such as who should be on the Board of Directors or whether or not to sell the company. They only get dividends if the company has earnings to pay them. It is called preferred because the dividend must be paid before dividends are paid on the common stock.

- ❑ **Common Stock**, which the owners have voting rights, but do not receive dividends at a fixed price. The value of the stock can rise or fall.

- ❑ **Capital Surplus**, also known as "additional paid-in capital," is the amount paid to the company in excess of the par value. When a company issues a stock, the stock has a par value, a value assigned to a share of stock by the company. This value does not determine the selling price, or market value, of the stock. The selling price that the investor pays per share is determined in the market.

- ❑ **Retained Earnings**, which is money reinvested into the company and becomes part of the capital that finances the company.

- ❑ **Treasury stock**, which is stock in the company that has been repurchased and not retired.

As you can see, the "Total Assets" for each year equaled the "Total Liabilities Equity." It is called a "Balance Sheet" because it has to balance. Each dollar value was a "Snap-Shot" on the date of the financial statement. Assets are in order of their liquidity and how fast they can be converted into cash. Current assets are expected to be liquidated within one year of the date of the Balance Sheet. Liabilities and Equity are in order in which they are to be paid. Current Liabilities are payable within one year. Also, as you can see, there are two years of figures on the balance sheet for comparison and trending purposes.

Managers seeking to lead their department must learn to read between, above, and around the numbers to uncover two key indicators: proportion and direction.

Proportion: Your company's financial reports reveal interesting and important information on the proportion of physical assets (plant and equipment) versus cash flow. This is important because the speed at which a company turns over its assets reveals how capital-intensive (requires large amounts of money) that business is. If you turn over assets quickly, you can afford low margins (profit) per sale. If you turn over assets slowly, you must earn a steep margin per sale. The key point here is if you turn over assets slowly, and earn little profit per sale, you will not be adequately profitable. It's the proportion of cash flow versus physical assets on the balance sheet that tells you how hard you have to work those physical assets to make an adequate profit. The larger the investment in assets one has to make in a business in relation to sales, the greater the margin one needs to make on each sale.

Direction: A general sense of a company's direction can be assessed from its financial statements. Sometimes relationships between a company's resources and its sales growth get out of whack. If a company must invest a disproportionate amount of assets for each dollar of sales increase, then the company will be pouring extra money into its assets to such an extent that it will eventually run out of money. For example, if a company wants to grow by 20% on a sustainable basis, management must continue to add 20% to the retained earnings. This is reflected in the balance sheet in the shareholders equity. If shareholders equity grows by only 10% at a sustainable level, the company can grow by only 10% at a sustainable level. The only way to exceed 10% growth is to increase profitability or acquire additional debt (borrow more money). This is why it is so important to understand how to read the balance sheet so you can see a snapshot of the company's direction.

Financial Statements: The Income Statement

Income statements show the results of a company's operations, which are usually given quarterly or by fiscal year. It shows the sales, also known as revenue, and expenses. It also shows whether the company had a profit or loss during that period. The Income Statement is also known as the "Profit & Loss" statement or "P&L." Simply put, the formula is: "Revenue – Expenses = Income." The easiest and best scenario is, "The higher the sales and the lower the expenses, the greater the income." There are all types of expenses that are generated in a company and this statement sees how the company is spending its money, and how management is most and least effective.

As previously described, the Balance Sheet shows the value in the company's accounts at a certain period, whereas the Income Statement covers operations over an entire period.

The income statement gives you the "Net Income," also known as "The Bottom Line," after all costs and expenses have been subtracted from all possible income including total sales, interest earned on investments, and sale of a non-tangible item like a patent.

Example – Income Statement - There are explanations for each item following the Income Statement:

Income Statement Sample Corp. FY 2007, 2008 Figures USD	2008	2007
Sales (Revenue)	15,500,000	14,625,000
Less: Cost of Goods Sold (COGS)	(9,900,000)	(10,500,000)
Gross Income	5,600,000	4,125,000
Less: Selling, General, Administrative Costs (SG&A)	(3,300,000)	(2,350,000)
Operating Income Before Depreciation (EBITDA)	2,300,000	1,775,000
Less: Depreciation, Amortization, Depletion	(11,000)	(10,000)
Operating Income (EBIT)	2,289,000	1,765,000
Less: Interest Expense	(93,000)	(89,000)
Non-operating Income	2,196,000	1,676,000
Less: Non-operating Expenses	(42,000)	(40,000)
Pretax Accounting Income	2,154,000	1,636,000
Less: Income Taxes	(1,350,000)	(1,240,000)
Income Before Extraordinary Items	804,000	396,000
Less: Preferred Stock Dividends	(87,000)	(85,000)
Income Available for Common Stockholders	717,000	311,000
Less: Extraordinary Items	(18,000)	(15,000)
Less: Discontinued Operations	(400,000)	(100,000)
Adjusted Net Income	299,000	196,000
Earnings Per Share (200,000 shares of stock)	$1.50	$0.98

Here is a brief explanation of the type of accounts associated with a common Income Statement:

- **Revenues** – also called "Sales, "Sales Revenue," or "Sales of Goods or Services." It is also known as the "Top Line." It is the amount of money the company made, before any expenses, on its operations. This, however, would not pertain to any income made from selling plant equipment or interest on marketable securities, etc. When applicable, income other than what is considered revenue is shown in "Other Income or Interest Income."

- **Cost of Goods Sold – also known as, and pronounced, "COGS" or "Cost of Sales"** – These are direct costs or direct expenses because they are directly associated with making what the company sells (i.e. manufacturer), cost directly associated with the service the company supply's (i.e. Internet Service Provider), or what a company would pay for merchandise it sells in stores (i.e. retailer). For example:

- If the company were a *manufacturer*, the COGS would be the cost of materials and the wages for those making the product, along with the factory operational costs associated with the product like freight and transportation, rent, power, lights, maintenance, etc.
- If the company is a *service-related* business, COGS represents the cost of services rendered or cost of revenues.
- If the company were a *retailer* then the COGS would be the price paid to the suppliers for the merchandise it sells in the stores, including the transportation costs of getting the goods into the stores.

□ **Gross Income** – also called "Gross Profit." It is the money the company earns on its sales before SG&A.

□ **Selling, General, and Administrative Expense also known as "SG&A"** – It is the salary of the sales people and the commissions, sales expenses, marketing expenses, managers salaries and benefits, office expenses like the power, lights, rent, supplies, and everything else needed to run a company. This also includes the cost of the supporting departments like HR, IS, Finance, etc. Basically SG&A is all costs that are not directly producing the product, or after a retailer buys a product from a supplier, as described in COGS above.

□ **Operating Income Before Depreciation -** This is gross income or gross profit minus SG&A. This is also the EBITDA number. For more information on EBITDA, see the related ratio explanations later in this lesson.

□ **Depreciation Expense** – This is the amount of depreciation charged against sales during the period. This is not the same as accumulated depreciation on the balance sheet, as that is the total of all past depreciation. This depreciation expense will be on the income statement, and also added to the accumulated depreciation on the balance sheet at the beginning of the period.

□ **Operating Income** – Gross income minus SG&A gives you the operating income. This is also considered EBIT or operating profit. For more information on EBIT, see the related ratio explanations later in this lesson.

□ **Interest Expense** – This item reflects the costs of a company's borrowings.

□ **Non-operating Income** – An example of this would be money won from a lawsuit. Another example would be interest made on marketable securities. This is also called extraordinary or nonrecurring income.

□ **Non-operating Expenses** – This could be the cost of litigation or settlements paid in lawsuits, closing down a division, etc.

□ **Pre-Tax Accounting Income** – Also known as "Income Before Taxes." This is the income before taxes.

□ **Provision for Income Taxes** – Taxes that will be charged against the income in this period, even if they have not been paid in this period. This will be the income tax charged to income for the period.

□ **Income before Extraordinary Items** – This is the pre-tax minus income tax.

□ **Preferred Stock Dividends** - Each share of preferred stock is normally paid a guaranteed, relatively high dividend and has first dibs over common stock at the company's assets in the event of bankruptcy. In exchange for the higher income and safety, preferred shareholders miss out on large potential capital gains (or losses). Owners of preferred stock generally do not have voting privileges.

❑ **Net Income Available to Common Stockholders** - The net income applicable to common shares figure is the bottom-line profit the company reported. To get the basic earnings-per-share (Basic EPS) figure, analysts divide the net income applicable to common by the total number of shares outstanding.

❑ **Extraordinary items** - Are events that occur infrequently and are unusual. They can include acts of God as long as they rarely occur in the area where the business operates.

❑ **Discontinued operations** - Occur when a significant segment of a business has been identified for disposal. Once so identified, any gain or loss from operations of the segment while it is being disposed of and any gain or loss on the sale of the assets of the segment, are reported separately from the remaining, continuing operations.

❑ **Net Income (Loss)** – This is also known as, "The Bottom Line." Net income is what's left after subtracting the COGS, SG&A, and all the rest of the expenses and taxes on the income statement. Of course, if expenses exceed income, this account caption will read as a net loss. The dollar amount would be in parentheses and/or in red. For more information, see the related ratio explanations later in this lesson.

*Comprehensive Income is fairly new (1998) and takes into consideration the effect of such items as foreign currency translations adjustments, minimum pension liability adjustments, and unrealized gains/losses on certain investments in debt and equity.

❑ **Earnings Per Share (EPS) -** This is Net income remaining for stockholders ÷ Common shares outstanding, also considered part of the bottom line. In this example for 2008, $299,000 (Net income) ÷ 200,000 (200,000 shares of stock) = $ 1.50 per share.

Income statements are like a management report card. It lets you investigate where sales are rising or falling, whether costs are rising or falling faster or slower than sales, if interests expense is rising or falling year to year, of if there were any extraordinary changes, etc. For example:

- A manager of a department who produces a product can do their part by keeping control of COGS by always being aware, and trying to reduce, the cost of materials, parts, hardware, etc.

- A manager of customer service would be able to reduce their part in SG&A by reducing overtime, unnecessary office space expansion, supplies, etc.

- Also, you can do a basic calculation on revenue per employee (divide the revenues by the total number of employees), and calculate the net income per employee (divide the net income by the number of employees). If you see a downward trend, then it could mean that the company is not effectively managing its employees.

Financial Analysis Tools - Ratios

Statements alone will let you see dollar amounts; however, you also need to analyze these statements by relating the account values to one another. Financial ratios are the most common way to do this. A ratio is a calculation of just a simple division problem that shows the relationship between two values. Financial ratios are used to show the relationship of two financial statement accounts to measure a company's performance, and whether it is creditworthy. Here are a few of the most common ratios so you can get an idea on how it all works:

LIQUIDITY RATIOS

Liquidity ratios demonstrate a company's ability to pay its current obligations. Some of the best-known measures of a company's liquidity include:

Current ratio = Current Assets ÷ Current Liabilities: Also known as working capital ratio. It measures the ability of a company to pay its near-term obligations. The general rule of thumb is a current ratio of 2.0 or better. Using the balance sheet example shown earlier for the year 2008, the total current assets of $325,000 with $117,000 in current liabilities would have a 4.2 current ratio ($325,000 ÷ $82,000 = 4.2).

Quick ratio = Quick Assets (*cash + marketable securities + receivables*) ÷ **Current Liabilities:** Also known as an acid test. This is a stricter definition of the company's ability to make payments on current obligations. Ideally, this ratio should be 1.0 or better. Using the balance sheet example shown earlier for the year 2008, the cash plus the marketable securities plus the account receivables would equal $195,000 ($45,000 + $65,000 + 85,000) with $82,000 in current liabilities. The quick ratio is 2.4 ($195,000 ÷ $82,000 = 2.4).

Accounts Receivables Turnover = Net Sales ÷ Accounts Receivable: Also known as Sales to Receivables. It measures the annual turnover (the number of times the receivables went through a cycle of being created and collected, thus turned over, in a period) of accounts receivable. Essentially, Accounts Receivable Turnover is the average amount of time that it takes a given client or group of clients to pay outstanding invoices after they are generated and mailed to the customer. It is best to use average accounts receivable to avoid seasonality effects by adding the AR at the beginning of a period from the balance sheet to the AR at the end of a period, and divide the sum by two. A high number reflects a short lapse of time between sales and the collection of cash, while a low number means collections take longer. Using the income statement and balance sheet examples shown earlier for the year 2008, the Sales is $15,500,000 with $85,000 in accounts receivable (on the balance sheet). The Accounts Receivables Turnover = 182 times ($15,500,000 ÷ $85,000 = 182). See the Collection Period below to associate this turnover number with the average number of days it takes the company to collect its receivables.

Collection Period = 365 ÷ Accounts Receivables Turnover: This measures the average number of days the company's receivables are outstanding between the date of credit sale and collection of cash. For example, the turnover as described above is 182 times. The result would be 365 ÷ 182 = 2 average days to pay.

Whether this is good or bad depends on the industry norms and credit terms established.

Annual Inventory Turnover = COGS for the Year ÷ Average Inventory Balance: This shows how efficiently the company is managing its production, warehousing, and distribution of product considering its volume of sales. Higher ratios, over six or seven times per year, are generally thought to be better, although extremely high inventory turnover may indicate a narrow selection and possibly lost sales. A low inventory turnover rate, on the other hand, means that the company is paying to keep a large inventory, and may be overstocking or carrying obsolete items. For example, the COGS from the income statement are $9,900,000 and the Average inventory balance on the balance sheet is $85,000. The Annual Inventory Turnover = 116 ($9,900,000 ÷ $85,000 = 116). See the Inventory holding period below to associate this turnover number with the average number of days that elapse between finished goods production and sale of product.

Inventory holding period = 365 ÷ Annual Inventory Turnover: Also known as Days' Sales on Hand. This calculates the number of days, on average, that elapse between finished goods production and sale of product. For example, lets say that the turnover as described above is 116 times, then the result would be 365 ÷ 116 = 3.1 average days worth of sales in inventory. Whether this is good or bad is the comparison with the industry norms.

LEVERAGE RATIOS

Leverage Ratios are used to understand a company's ability to meet it long term financial obligations. These can also be considered as Solvency Ratios which measures the capability of a compnay to pay its bills on time.

Debt-to-Equity ratio = Total Liabilities ÷ Total Owners' Equity: This indicates what proportion of debt (trade credit, liabilities, and borrowings) and equity (shareholders purchased stock and earnings reinvested into the company rather than taken as dividends) that the company is using to finance its assets. A company is generally considered safer if it has a low debt to equity ratio. In general, debt should be 1.0 or less which means that half of the company's total financing, or less, comes from debt. Using the example from the above balance sheet for 2008, the Debt-to-equity ratio would be 1.0 ($347,000 ÷ $338,500 = 1.0).

Debt ratio = Long Term Debt ÷ Total Assets: This compares the company's long-term debt to the company's total financial resources. A debt ratio greater than 1.0 means the company has negative net worth, and is technically bankrupt. Using the example from the above balance sheet for 2008, the debt ratio would be 0.13 ($90,000 ÷ $685,500 = 0.13). This tells us 13% of the company's total financial resources are in the form of long-term debt. The lower the number the better, and if it starts to reach 50%, you want to be sure the company has a reliable earnings stream.

Earnings Before Interest and Taxes (or EBIT, pronounced e-bit) = Revenue - Operating Expenses or OPEX: This is not a ratio, however, it is important and needs to be explained before going on to other ratios (it is also a non-GAAP metric). EBIT is an indicator of a company's profitability, calculated as revenue minus expenses, *excluding tax and interest*. It is used quite frequently in business financial conversations with the goal to become EBIT positive. EBIT is also sometimes referred to as "operating earnings," "operating profit," and "operating income," which can be found on the income statement. Using the example income statement above for the year 2008, it would look like: $15,500,000 (Revenue) – $9,900,000 (COGS) - $3,300,000 (SG&A) - $11,000 (Depreciation) = $2,289,000

Earnings before interest, taxes, depreciation and amortization (or EBITDA pronounced E-bih-dah): The same as EBIT, however, it takes the process further by removing two non-cash items from the equation; depreciation (meaning the gradual reduction of the value of a tangible item) and amortization (meaning the gradual reduction of the value of a non-tangible item). EBITDA is used when evaluating a company's ability to earn a profit, and it is often used in stock analysis. Using the example income statement above for the year 2008, it would look like: $15,500,000 (Revenue) – $9,900,000 (COGS) - $3,300,000 (SG&A) = $2,300,000

Times Interest Earned (TIE) Ratio = Earnings Before Interest and Taxes (EBIT or Operating Income) ÷ Interest Expense: Also referred to as "interest coverage ratio" and "fixed-charged coverage." A metric used to measure the company's ability to pay the interest on long-term debt. You use EBIT because you want to measure the capability to pay the interest expense out of operating income before you deduct interest out of that income. You use income before taxes because interest is tax-deductible. In general, a higher interest coverage ratio means that the small business is able to take on additional debt. EBIT of at least three to four times interest earned is considered safe. Bankers and other creditors closely examine this ratio. Using the dollar amounts from the EBIT example above, and the interest earned from income statement for 2008, would look like: TIE = $2,289,000 ÷ $93,000 (which is 25 times).

PROFITABILITY RATIOS

Profitability Ratios are used to assess a business's ability to generate earnings as compared to its expenses and other relevant costs incurred during a specific period of time. For most of these ratios, having a higher value relative to a competitor's ratio, or the same ratio from a previous period, is indicative that the company is doing well.

Gross Margin = Gross Income ÷ Net Sales (Revenue): Also known as Gross profit. Gross margin is the gross income as a percentage of sales. This measures the margin on sales the company is achieving. It can be an indication of manufacturing efficiency or marketing effectiveness. You get the gross income by subtracting the COGS from the Sales on the income statement. Using the example income statement above for the year 2008 to get the gross margin, it would look like: $5,600,000 (gross income) ÷ $15,500,000 (revenue or sales) = 36% (which translates to 64% of its sales spent on COGS). The higher the gross margin the better. It depends on the value of the product. It could be charging more money for a high quality product while maintaining relatively steady COGS, or by offering something a customer values that can be made cheaply.

Operating Margin = Operating Income (aka EBIT) ÷ Net Sales (Revenue): Operating margin measures the operating income as a percentage of sales. If there is a good gross margin, but poor operating margin, most likely there is mismanagement that accounts for SG&A expense. Using the EBIT example and revenue from income statement above for the year 2008, to get the operating margin it would look like: $2,289,000 (EBIT or operating income) ÷ $15,500,000 (revenue or sales) = 15% operating margin. Again, the higher the profit margins the better.

Net Margin = Net Income ÷ Net Sales (Revenue): Also known as Net profitability. This measures the overall profitability of the company, or the bottom line, as a percentage of sales. A net margin range of around 5% is common, however, somewhere around 10% would be excellent. In general terms, net margin or profitability shows the effectiveness of management. Though the optimal level depends on the type of business, the ratios can be compared for firms in the same industry. The net income would be on the bottom of the income statement (this figure is the revenue minus all the production, operating, interest, taxes and other expenses). Using the income statement above for the year 2008, to get the net margin it would look like: $299,000 (net income) ÷ $15,500,000 (revenue or sales) = 2% net margin.

Asset Turnover = Net Sales (Revenue) ÷ Total Assets: Also known as Investment turnover. This measures a company's ability to use assets to generate sales. Although the ideal level for this ratio varies greatly, a very low figure may mean that the company maintains too many assets or has not deployed its assets well, whereas a high figure means that the assets have been used to produce good sales numbers. A ratio of 1.0 is the average, but it all really depends on the type of business. The lower the turnover usually means the higher the profit margin on the product, however the higher the turnover is to be expected on highly competitive retail stores. Using the balance sheet above for the year 2008, to get the asset turnover it would look like: $15,500,000 (revenue or sales) ÷ $685,500 (total assets) = 23 times.

Return on assets (ROA) = Net Income ÷ Total Assets: This indicates how effectively the company is deploying its assets. A very low ROA usually indicates inefficient management, whereas a high ROA means efficient management. However, depreciation or any unusual expenses can distort this ratio. It's a useful number for comparing competing companies in the same industry. Using the income sheet for net income, and the balance sheet for total assets for the year 2008, to get the ROA it would look like: $299,000 (net income) ÷ $685,500 (total assets) = 44% ROA.

Return on investment (ROI) = Net Income ÷ Owners' Equity: Also called Return on equity or ROE. This is a key measure of return for both shareholders and management. It indicates how well the company is utilizing its equity investment. Due to leverage, this measure will generally be higher than return on assets. ROI is considered to be one of the best indicators of profitability. It is also a good figure to compare against competitors or an industry average. Generally, companies usually need at least 10-14 percent ROI in order to fund future growth. If this ratio is too low, shareholders will sell their shares to invest in a company with a better return, and the Board of Directors (BOD) might have to replace management. On the other hand, a high ROI can mean that management is doing a good job, or that the firm is undercapitalized. Using the income sheet for net income, and the balance sheet for owners' equity for the year 2008, to get the ROI it would look like: $299,000 (net income) ÷ $338,500 (owners' or shareholders equity) = 88% ROI.

By calculating ratios, you can find patterns like is the company generating cash? Is the liquidity strong? Does the company have too much debt or too many assets? Is it growing the assets faster than sales? Are the margins weak or strong? How do the ratios compare to the last couple of years, etc? You can compare ratios using industry norms published in Standard & Poor's or Dun & Bradstreet.

It is imperative to calculate accurately on all financial statements, as these will tell you the company's performance and creditworthiness. All red flags, such as increasing earnings and declining cash flow, should be taken seriously. Again, the goal is to be EBIT positive and you should always do your part to help get to that point and stay there.

Some other ratios that investors look at are:

- **Earnings Per Share** (EPS) = Net income remaining for stockholders ÷ Common shares outstanding (also considered part of the bottom line). For example, $700 (Net income) ÷ 1,000 (1,000 shares of stock) = $ 0.70

- **Price Earning Ratio** (PE) = Market price ÷ Earnings per share

- **Dividend Payout Ratio** = Dividends per share ÷ Earnings per share

- **Dividend Yield Ratio** = Dividends per share ÷ Current market price

What is the Cash Flow Statement?

The cash flow statement is a measure of a company's financial health. The cash flow statement differs from these other financial statements because it acts as a kind of corporate checkbook that reconciles the balance sheet and income statement. The cash flow statement records the company's cash transactions, both the inflows and outflows, during the given period. While an income statement can tell you whether a company made a profit, a cash flow statement can tell you whether the company generated cash. It shows whether revenues booked on the income statement have actually been collected. At the same time, however, the cash flow does not necessarily show all the company's expenses. Not all expenses the company accrues have to be paid right away. So even though the company may have incurred liabilities it must eventually pay, expenses are not recorded as a cash outflow until they are paid.

The most commonly used format for the cash flow statement is broken down into three sections:

1. **Cash flows from operating activities**. These flows are related to your principal line of business and include the cash receipts from sales or for the performance of services, payroll and other payments to employees, payments to suppliers and contractors, rent payments, payments for utilities, and tax payments.

2. **Cash flows from investing activities.** These are capitalized as assets on the balance sheet. Investing activities also include investments that are not part of your normal line of business. These cash flows could also include purchases of property, plant and equipment, proceeds from the sale of property, plant and equipment, purchases of stock or other securities other than cash equivalents, and proceeds from the sale or redemption of investments.

3. **Cash flows from financing activities.** These flows relate to the businesses debt or equity financing. They include proceeds from loans, notes, and other debt instruments, installment payments on loans or other repayment of debts, cash received from the issuance of stock or equity in the business, and dividend payments, purchases of treasury stock, or returns of capital.

Cash for purposes of the cash flow statement normally includes cash and cash equivalents. Cash equivalents are short-term, temporary investments that can be readily converted into cash, such as marketable securities, short-term certificates of deposit, treasury bills, and commercial paper. The cash flow statement shows the opening balance in cash and cash equivalents for the reporting period, the net cash provided by or used in each one of the three categories just described, the net increase or decrease in cash and cash equivalents for the period, and the ending balance.

Accounting and the Accountant

Accounting keeps track of the flow of money by keeping financial records of sales, expenses, receipts, and disbursements of cash, including calculating the taxes the company owes. An accountant's primary function is to develop and provide data measuring the performance of the firm, assessing its financial position, and paying taxes. They are responsible for preparing financial statements such as the income statement, balance sheets, and cash flows. Some common responsibilities and controls of the accountant, also sometimes known as the controller, are:

- **Accounts Receivable,** which tracks the money the company is owed and paid.

- **Accounts Payable,** which tracks expenditures and authorizes checks to be cut to pay bills to suppliers.

- **Payroll,** which ensures employees get paid.

- **Credit,** decides just how much credit will be extended to a customer. This gives selected customers who are in good standing time to pay, whereas COD (cash on delivery) is for customers who are not in good standing due to late payments, etc.

Accountants or bookkeepers use journals or ledgers, sometimes referred to as "the books" or "the books of accounts," to keep track of all transactions. These ledgers used to be on specially ruled ledger paper, however, accounting computer software is now more commonly used. Ledger entries can be made on a daily, weekly, monthly, or quarterly basis. It is common to have at least three ledgers: cash inflow ledger, cash outflow ledger, and the general ledger. At the end of the accounting period, the various journals and sub-ledgers are posted into the general ledger. Some common sub-ledgers are for separate kinds of transactions. For example, sales transactions in the sales ledger, payroll checks in the payroll ledger, invoice in accounts receivable ledger, and bills received in the accounts payable ledger. The financial statements we discussed earlier are drawn up from the general ledger.

These journals and ledgers will use a double-entry system. The two entries will show one debit, which would be an entry on the left hand side of an account, and one credit, which would be an entry on the right hand side of an account. These two entries offset each other and keep the books in balance:

The debit represents:

1. An increase in an asset account.
2. A decrease in a liability account.
3. A decrease in a revenue account.
4. An increase in an expense account.

The credit represents:

1. A decrease in an asset account.
2. An increase in a liability or owners equity account.
3. An increase in a revenue account.
4. A decrease in an expense account.

Once all of the transactions have been recorded and posted to the general ledger, they are then entered into the balance sheet and income statement and summed up. These are the accounts total or "Net Balances."

The financial statements for publicly held companies require an opinion written by an independent auditor. The auditor is a CPA (certified public accountant, licensed by the state where they practice) who audited the company's books and financial statements. If the CPA's opinion is approved "without qualification," then the auditor found the company is in accordance with GAAP. If the accountant's opinion is "qualified," then there was a practice or transaction not in accordance with GAAP, or for another reason to believe the statements do not truly reflect the company's financial condition.

Accounting for Inventory and Depreciation

Inventory is defined as assets that are intended for sale, are in process of being produced for sale, or are to be used in producing goods. Counting inventory is done in two ways: The *Periodic method*, which is a physical count daily, weekly, monthly or yearly, and *Perpetual inventory method*, which adjusts inventory with each transaction through computerized software, such as Fishbowl inventory.

Because prices of specific items can continually change, it affects the way a manufacturer accounts for materials it buys, and how a retailer accounts for the goods it buys and then sells, which affects its cost of goods sold (COGS) and its reported income.

The following equation expresses how a company's inventory is determined:

Beginning Inventory + Net Purchases - Cost of Goods Sold (COGS) = Ending Inventory

In other words, you take what the company has in the beginning, add what they have purchased, subtract what they've sold and the result is what they have remaining.

By re-arranging the formula you can get the COGS:

Beginning Inventory + Net Purchases - Ending Inventory = Cost of Goods Sold

In other words, you take what the company has in the beginning, add what they have purchased, and subtract the inventory at the end of the period, which would then equal the amount of units sold.

FIFO, LIFO and Average Costing Method

These are three of the most common methods of accounting for inventories. Here is a brief explanation of each:

- **FIFO** (First in, First out. Pronounced fife-oh) - The company assumes that the first item making its way into inventory is the first sold. FIFO is used by businesses whose goods spoil quickly or frequently become obsolete. As prices go up, the FIFO method gives you the lower cost of goods sold because goods bought at the lower prices are the first to be used. This will give a better bottom line or net profit because the COGS is lower, thus gross sales is higher. With higher profits comes a higher tax bite, however, the higher income looks better to prospective investors and lenders. If prices are rising, FIFO gives a better indication of the value of ending inventory on the balance sheet. LIFO isn't a good indicator of ending inventory value, because the left over inventory might be extremely old and maybe obsolete. If prices are decreasing, which is not as common, the exact opposite of the above is true.

- **LIFO** (Last in, First out. Pronounced life-oh) - The company assumes that the last item making its way into inventory, or most recent, is assumed to be sold first. LIFO is used when inventory does not spoil or become obsolete. When the costs of goods rise, they first sell the more costly items. COGS will be higher, thus gross sales will be lower. Net profit will be lower, but so will the tax bite.

- **Average Costing Method** – This is used when COGS fluctuate frequently throughout the year. The peaks and valleys tend to even out and minimize the impact on the bottom line. It is the simplest method and doesn't track which items are sold, but just maintains a running average of cost per unit sold.

Whichever method is used, it is important to stick to just one and not switch due to possible tax implications, unless you ask the IRS for permission to change.

Accounting for depreciation deals with adjustments that are made to company profits once a month, or once a year, to account for expenses such as depreciation and amortization. The IRS has a depreciation table that specifies the life span for various types of business equipment. See www.irs.gov for more information. The most common methods used of accounting for depreciation are:

- **Straight-line depreciation** = Cost of asset ÷ asset's years of life.

- **Double declining balance** = Book value of the asset times twice the straight-line rate.

- **Sum of the year's digits** is a method of calculating depreciation of an asset that assumes higher depreciation charges and greater tax benefits in the early years of an asset's life.

- **MACRS (Modified Asset Cost Recovery System)** is the new accelerated cost recovery system, created after the release of the Tax Reform Act of 1986, which allows for greater accelerated depreciation over longer time periods. Faster acceleration allows individuals to deduct greater amounts during the first few years of an asset's life.

Methods of accelerated depreciation, such as double declining balance and sum of the year's digits, allocate more to the assets cost to the early years of its life, than straight-line depreciation. Accelerated depreciation yields lower income in those early years.

Setting up a budget for your department

You as manager need to fully understand your role in the budgetary process. It is the most basic financial planning and control tool. Every manager needs to know what costs are associated with their department, and how in relation are they doing to that budget. You might achieve your departmental goals, but if you go over budget in order to achieve those goals, you create financial problems for the company and jeopardize your own job performance review. In most cases, part of your performance appraisal will be based on whether or not you were within budget for the year.

Budgets need to be realistic. You can't just say at a whim you need 20 new people, just as upper management can't say you have only $10 for a years worth of training classes. Budgets are used to investigate variances, whether you went over or under budget, and address the reasons for the variances. You need to always look at ways to control those variances by controlling costs. By being on top of your budget, you might be able to make changes before it's too late and you end up having to reduce staff or eliminate a branch of your department.

Great managers always look at significant expenses they can reduce or eliminate, such as overtime, travel and entertainment. Also keep in mind, just because you created a budget for the year, it can change if sales are bad or below target. You might have the budget to hire someone, but it can be eliminated if sales do not improve, thus a hiring freeze. You might also have an employee who quits and you cannot replace them, which is known as attrition. You will during your managerial career have to deal with ways of cutting costs, including layoffs. On the other hand you might be able to increase your previously budgeted staff if sales are better than expected.

There are basically two types of budgets, a capital expenditure budget and operating budget:

1. **Capital expenditure** (also known as "Capex") relates to costs associated with plant and equipment. This is equipment that generally lasts for more than a year such as a copy machine.

2. **Operating budget**, which is related to the normal day-to-day operations and expenditures such as payroll, supplies, and miscellaneous. There are two types of budgets within an operating budget, sales budgets and expense budgets:

   • *Sales budget* is associated with comparison and variance of the actual revenue brought with the projected revenue.
   • *Expense budget* applies to all areas incurring operating expenses, including the sales department. This is the budget we will focus on.

Lets look at a budget as if you are the "Customer Service Manager" in which you would mostly work with finance on budgetary items like staffing (payroll), training expenses, software licenses needed, and general expenses. You would need to make sure that you have your staffing goals and needs figured out and stick to them as close as possible. You should really look over the budget carefully with finance; due to sometimes items might be in your bucket that you feel belong to another department. Finances job is to make sure everyone submits their required operational expenses and then compiles those numbers for upper management in a way that makes sense. Finance acts as a middleman between department heads and upper-management when it comes to budgets. It is not their job to decide on what you need. They have been given a monetary amount from upper management and should help you allocate to your needs.

Example - Operating expense budget for the Customer Service department.

Statement of Operations (example) - Sample Corp
for a period of: June 2008

Customer Service	Month Budget	Month Actual	Month Variance: B/(W)	YTD Budget	YTD Actual	YTD Variance: B/(W)
Payroll						
Payroll Expenses	120,000.00	115,000.00	5,000.00	720,000.00	710,000.00	10,000.00
Employee Bonus	1,000.00	1,000.00	0.00	6,000.00	5,000.00	1,000.00
Employee Overtime	1,500.00	5,000.00	(3,500.00)	9,000.00	28,500.00	(19,500.00)
Total Payroll	122,500.00	121,000.00	1,500.00	735,000.00	743,500.00	(8,500.00)
Fringe						
Fringe Benefits	300.00	350.00	(50.00)	1,800.00	1,500.00	300.00
Refreshments/Soda/etc.	50.00	70.00	(20.00)	300.00	150.00	150.00
Employee Appreciation	100.00	250.00	(150.00)	600.00	400.00	200.00
Total Fringes	450.00	670.00	(220.00)	2,700.00	2,050.00	650.00
Travel						
Meals	100.00	70.00	30.00	600.00	700.00	(100.00)
Hotel	250.00	200.00	50.00	1,500.00	1,400.00	100.00
Auto Rental	150.00	125.00	25.00	900.00	800.00	100.00
Airplane Tickets, , etc	500.00	750.00	(250.00)	3,000.00	7,200.00	(4,200.00)
Total Travel	1,000.00	1,145.00	(145.00)	6,000.00	10,100.00	(4,100.00)
Pro Service						
Recruiting Fees	750.00	800.00	(50.00)	4,500.00	4,700.00	(200.00)
Professional Fees	200.00	100.00	100.00	1,200.00	700.00	500.00
Legal Fees	75.00	0.00	75.00	450.00	100.00	350.00
Total Professional Fees	1,025.00	900.00	125.00	6,150.00	5,500.00	650.00
General						
Employee Training	400.00	500.00	(100.00)	2,400.00	3,000.00	(600.00)
Miscellaneous Expense	200.00	150.00	50.00	1,200.00	1,500.00	(300.00)
Project Materials	100.00	250.00	(150.00)	600.00	400.00	200.00
Equipment Rental	50.00	0.00	50.00	300.00	0.00	300.00
Postage and Delivery	50.00	45.00	5.00	300.00	270.00	30.00
Software License Fees	800.00	800.00	0.00	4,800.00	5,000.00	(200.00)
Outside Services - Other	100.00	50.00	50.00	600.00	500.00	100.00
Telephone	200.00	200.00	0.00	1,200.00	1,200.00	0.00
Cellphone	200.00	200.00	0.00	1,200.00	1,200.00	0.00
Utilities	300.00	300.00	0.00	1,800.00	1,800.00	0.00
Supplies	100.00	150.00	(50.00)	600.00	700.00	(100.00)
Total General	2,500.00	2,645.00	(145.00)	15,000.00	15,570.00	(570.00)
Total Operating Expenses	127,475.00	126,360.00	1,115.00	764,850.00	776,720.00	(11,870.00)

This example budget shows the different types of expenses, presented by finance, that have been determined by you and upper management along with the associated costs that your department has incurred. Generally, an operating expense budget will have the current months and year-to-date (YTD) budgeted and actual expenses along with the variance. The cells with parentheses means you went over budget. It is also highlighted in red. As you can see, this is an expense report for the month of June with YTD data, which in this case is six months worth of expenditures. Here is the breakdown:

- As far as *payroll*, you are under budget regarding the amount of staff you have allocated to your department, but you are way over on overtime. This has caused you to go over budget by $8,500 YTD. This clearly shows you better get on the ball and start hiring, or investigate on whether or not you have a process issue that is causing you to require so much overtime.

- As for *fringe benefits*, you went over for June, but still within your YTD budget, so there is not too much concern here.

- As for *travel*, you are over budget mostly because of higher than expected flight costs. You need to see if these trips are truly needed, and if so, try to book sooner to reduce costs.

- As for *professional services*, you are over on recruiting fees but under for legal or other professional fees. Chances are you do not need as much allocated to you for legal and you might want to adjust for next years budget.

- As for *general expenses*, you are over on training and should re-adjust to a more accurate cost for next years budget, due to the importance of training. You also need to re-adjust the needed software licenses for your hosted database solution. These both could have been mistakes at the time of creating the budget, which makes you look bad.

- Most other expenses are in check.

Overall for the month of June, you were under budget by a respectable amount, which is a good thing. However, YTD, you are over $11,870. This trend shows you will be at least $23,000 over budget by years end. This is not good. The two issues that stand out the most are overtime and flight costs. You would need to start reducing these costs right away. By also reducing the other not-so-significant costs, you might be able to get back to budget as every little bit counts. This is just an example, and hopefully you would not have ever let it get to this point. By looking at the monthly and YTD numbers, you will always know exactly where you stand.

It is your job to justify the needed requirements, such as the staff needed along with the different monetary levels associated with each staff member. However, you also need to work with upper management and understand where they are coming from if you cannot get what you requested. Sometimes, there is just not enough money in the budget to accommodate all of your requests.

The way you set up your department should help greatly in justifying certain requests, such as raises based on skill levels, materials to streamline process, and trending data that shows the need for more staff throughout the year. This will also help if you are asked to reduce head count in the new years budget. You will be able to make the most efficient cuts with the least harm to the department, while still being able to show the possible ramifications of the cuts such as less after hours coverage, which might reflect on customer survey reports and affect goals.

There is also the domino effect with a product related business where you can cut costs during projected slow sales. You should not have overtime due to fewer products, which in turn means less costs of materials, which in turn means less shipping and receiving costs, etc. For example, if you are overstocked, and costs are high while sales are low, as was anticipated, then you did not do your forecasting and cut production correctly. The bottom line is you need to be able to determine, and help adapt, to the priorities, trade-offs and needs to the business in order to make budget and stay profitable.

Quick Lesson Summary

- Four of the most common business types are: Sole Proprietorship, Partnership, Corporation, and LLC's.

- Always practice good business ethics and you should never get into any trouble. Understanding what is considered "non-ethical" will help in your future decisions.

- Knowing some of the most common economics terms, and economy basics, can help you understand the effect it can have on your company. You might be able to make sound hiring decisions based on economic news. It will also help you be able to participate in economic discussion with upper management, etc.

- There will be times when you are in an upper management meeting, or listening to a company wide CEO conference call, where many financial terms are used. You should know and understand the most commonly used terms and theory like EBIT, EBITDA, Margins, ROI and Bottom line. Most of the terms used are related to the Balance Sheet and Income Statement. Ratios are also used to determine percentages, which can be compared with industry standards.

- Know how finance and accounting practices are associated with your yearly budget. You need to know how the budget process works to not only talk the talk, but to make sure you are not cutting yourself too short, or looking bad asking for too much. Even though a lot of the information covered in this lesson may never pertain to you, the more you learn and understand, the more confident you will be whenever financial issues are discussed.

LESSON 9 - BUSINESS BASICS PART II – OPERATIONS MANAGEMENT, CUSTOMER SERVICE, IS & HR

Introduction: The engines of the organization

Operations Management has a wide scope of responsibility. It is the area of business that is concerned with the production of goods and services, and involves the responsibility of ensuring that business operations are efficient and effective. To name a few, it is the management of resources, the production and distribution of goods and services to customers, and the analysis of queue systems. It can be the engine to the back office of a bank, retail department store, a manufacturing plant, and even the process of making the food in a restaurant. For example, look at all of the operations management responsibilities of the store COSTCO:

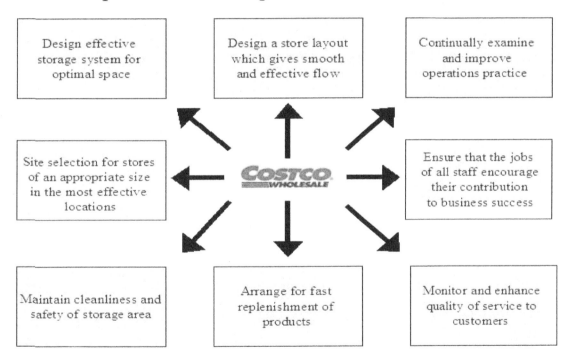

Some Operations Management Activities at COSTCO

Every day, you use a multitude of physical objects and a variety of services. Most of the physical objects have been manufactured, and people within organizations have provided most of the services. Every organization has an operations function, whether or not it is called "operations," such as the management of customer service functions like customer care and technical support.

In this lesson will give an overview of the basic functions within operations management. We will also go over Information Systems or IS, and Information Technology or IT. These two functions sometimes are combined into one group so we will discuss them as one unified group. There will be a discussion on disaster planning as well.

We will also discuss customer service and the duties of technical support, along with an overview of Human Resources or HR.

The day-to-day running of a company

Ultimately, the nature of how operations management is carried out in an organization depends greatly on the nature of products or services, for example, retail, service, manufacturing, wholesale, etc. Whatever the system or organization, the functions of operations management are always the same: (1) designing, (2) planning, (3) organizing, (4) directing, and (5) controlling. Management establishes the goals and objectives of the organization and plans how to attain them. Basically operations is about:

- Designing services, products and delivery systems.
- Managing and controlling the operations system.
- Continuously finding ways to improve its operations.

Every organization, be it a product or service organization, transforms certain inputs into outputs. The quality of these inputs is to be monitored regularly to get the desired output. The general model of operations management, which is a transformation process, would look like this transformation model:

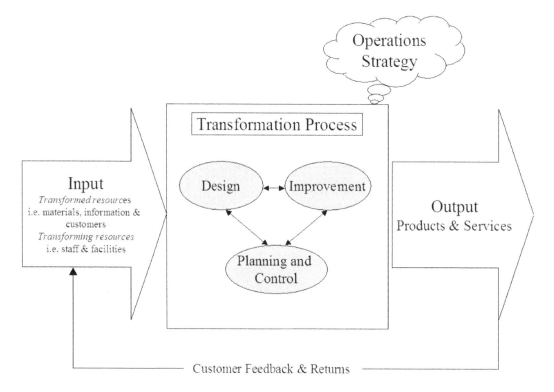

A transformation process is any activity or group of activities that takes one or more inputs, transforms and adds value to them, and provides outputs for customers or clients. Transformation processes include:

- Changes in the physical characteristics of materials or customers.
- Changes in the location of materials, information or customers.
- Changes in the ownership of materials or information.
- Storage or accommodation of materials, information or customers.
- Changes in the purpose or form of information.
- Changes in the physiological or psychological state of customers.

In many cases, all three types of transforming input resources, which are materials, information and customers, are transformed by the same organization. For example, withdrawing money from a bank account involves the account *information*, *materials* such as dollar bills and checks, and the *customer*.

A useful way of categorizing different types of transformation within operations management is into:

- *Manufacturing* – This is the producing of goods and physical creation of products, such as cars, and the running of the factory, which would include purchasing materials and supplies. There would also be inventory responsibilities.

- *Transport* – This is the movement of materials or customers, such as a taxi service or trucking fleet.

- *Supply* – This would be the change in ownership of goods, such as a retail store, supermarket, etc.

- *Service* – This could be considered the treatment of customers or the storage of materials, such as the back office duties of providing customer service in a call center, or warehouses to store goods.   Part of service would also be a possible output of customer feedback and return of goods.

Ensuring products are made; inventoried, shipped, received, repaired, and all the while managing the company's facilities, are considered part of operations management. In some cases, providing customer service functions like support or care, are considered part of operations, although sometimes customer service might be associated with sales, or even an entity unto itself.

Operations Management makes sure the business is running efficiently including employee productivity, delivery, cost control, and quality. The analyzing of processes using both mathematical and scientific data is crucial for optimal performance. With process analysis, you can identify improvements, that will turn into cost savings, which can then be passed on to the customer, streamline the company's infrastructure, and streamline inventory and supply chain issues. Some typical operating decisions would be:

- How much should you invest in developing new products?
- How much staff and space is needed?
- How do you determine the best buys on expensive items and equipment?
- What are the hours of operation?

- How long should a project take to complete?
- How much inventory is needed?
- How will the products be shipped?
- How will customer satisfaction be measured?
- How will the operating systems, workstations, and physical plant be designed?
- What are the processes and procedures used to ensure smooth operations?
- How to ensure quality and needed quantity of goods or services?

The examples just covered are only a few of the types of decisions an operations manager needs to make. Fortunately, there are many tools like flow charts, project task sheets, and cost/expense tools to help with making these types of decisions in all areas involved within operations management.

Operations managers are usually stereotyped as a plant manager in charge of a factory, however, there are also quality managers, production and inventory control managers, and line supervisors. In service industries, managers in hotels, restaurants, hospitals, banks and stores are operations managers as well. In the not-for-profit sector, the manager of a charity store, nursing home, and day center for older people, are all also considered operations managers.

Basic Decision Making Tools

Cost-benefit analysis is used to see if an investment is worth pursuing. You are measuring the benefits expected from a decision, measuring the costs associated with this decision, and then see if the benefits outweigh the costs. Most businesses have both fixed costs and variable costs. *Fixed costs* remain the same no matter how much the company makes or sells. Some examples would be the rent on a building, the insurance, exempt salaries, or the lease of a copy machine. *Variable costs* change with the company's production and sales volume of a unit. Some examples would be the cost of materials, delivery costs, compensation of the sales team, salaries of non-exempt workers, or the cost of paper and ink of a copy machine. If the benefits outweigh the costs based on analytical data, then you could go ahead with the planned course of action. A good tool to use would be:

o *Break-even analysis*. It lets you find when you first start making profit. If we were to base this on a product being sold, the formula would be: units sold = the fixed costs ÷ (the selling price minus the variable cost per unit).

A simple example would be if a copy machine is leased for $8,000 per year (which is the fixed cost) and you sell the copy for 10¢ (Selling price) but it costs 3¢ for the paper and ink per copy (the variable cost), the result would be:

$8,000 ÷ ($0.10 - $0.03) or $8,000 ÷ $0.07 which would equal 114,285 copies needed to be sold to break-even. That would be the point in which the machine paid for itself, the break-even point, and from that point on is when you would see profit.

If you are looking at two comparable pieces of equipment, you can use:

- *Crossover Analysis.* This lets you identify the point where you should switch from one product or service to another one that has similar benefits, but different fixed and variable costs. Using the same copy machine example, which we will call machine 1, and machine 2 that costs $4,000 with variable costs of 5¢ a copy, the formula would be: Crossover units = (machine 2's fixed cost – machine 1's fixed cost) ÷ (machine 1's variable cost – machine 2's fixed cost). The result would be:

  Crossover units = (4,000 - 8,000) ÷ (.03 - .05) or (-4,000) ÷ (-0.02) which would equal 200,000. This means that at 200,000 copies, the total cost of each of the two machines is equal. If you expect to sell more than 200,000 copies then machine 1 would be the best choice. If you expect to sell less than 200,000 copies then machine 2 would be the best choice.

Another example of cost-benefit analysis:

The customer operations manager is deciding whether to implement a new online training program that would cover approximately 33% of the current live based training. There is no budget to hire someone for this job specifically, so a decision needs to be made whether it is worth using an existing staff member to work on this project. A new more robust computer and training software will need to be purchased. Sales and Support will need to be trained as well as the existing customer base. Some production work will be lost due to pulling one person off of their normal duties to work on this project. Some of the work will also be outsourced.

Here is the cost-benefit analysis used to determine if the project is worth pursuing:

Costs:

Online training setup:

- Software for interactive training is $1,000
- 1 new PC dedicated to project is $2,000
- Web page and hosting setup (outsourced) is $10,000

Internal Training costs:

- Training introduction to sales and support of 10 people is $500 each for a total of $5,000
- Training introduction to the customer base of 4 people is $500 each for a total of $2,000

Other costs:

- Lost time: 1 Person for 6 months is $30,000
- Lost production through disruption: estimated $50,000
- Lost time for weekly meetings with key staff throughout project: estimated $10,000

Total cost: $110,000

Benefits:

- Reducing one day of live based training (hotel, training room, etc): estimated $25,000 per year
- Improved training efficiency, resulting in fewer support calls, thus eliminating need to hire additional support staff: estimated $80,000 per year
- Improved retention based on further understanding of product: estimated $40,000 per year

Total Benefit: $145,000 per year

The Break-even point would be $110,000 ÷ $145,000 = 0.76 of a year or approximately 9 months.

With this analysis, a decision based on facts, not just speculation, can be made. If needed, this cost-benefit analysis can be given to upper management to evaluate.

Critical Path Method (CPM) will help you plan and coordinate the tasks and activities in a project. CPM analysis requires that you first determine all of the steps necessary to complete the project. You then prioritize based on the steps that are dependant on others steps being completed first, as well as those that can run parallel to other tasks. It is one of the basic tools to use in Project Management. Project Management is the planning, organizing and managing of allocated resources to bring about the successful completion of a specific project.

Lets say you are planning on opening a telephone installation business and already know the main tasks needed to get started. You would assign a code based on each task and put them in order. The order would consist of the task that needs to be done before you can do the next one (predecessor), and how long you think each task will take.

Example – Project Task Sheet

Task Code	Task Description	Predecessors	Time (Weeks)
A	Find a location	none	5
B	Negotiate lease	A	1
C	Renovate office	A,B	9
D	Hire telephone business consultant	none	9
E	Purchase office equipment	A,B	1
F	Plan products to sell	D	2
G	Hire and train all staff,	D,F	7
H	Have product to sell and store	A,B and F	3
I	Conduct a test product installation	all	2
	Total time		**39**

Once you have created the task sheet, you would make a chart that visibly shows each task in relationship to each other, and in order. In this case you would separate what would be *facilities* related, which is getting the office space ready, and what would be *product* related, which is getting the phones, staff and training.

Example – Basic CPM chart

[Start] A = 5 weeks -- B = 1 week -- C = 9 weeks -- E = 1 week

H = 4 weeks -- I = 1 week [End]

D = 9 weeks -- G = 7 weeks

F = 2 weeks

The longest path through the project is called the critical path. In the example given, that would be from point A to point I. You can see by this chart that you can do certain tasks concurrently. Since you can do certain tasks concurrently, the total elapsed time would be 21 weeks; even though the total project time is 39 weeks.

PERT (Program Evaluation and Review Technique) is like CRM but the major difference is PERT enables you to make an optimistic, pessimistic and best guess estimate of the time it will take to complete each task of the project. A PERT chart is a project diagram consisting of numbered circles or rectangles representing events, or milestones in the project linked by directional lines representing tasks in the project. The direction of the arrows on the lines indicates the sequence of tasks.

Gantt Chart is used in project management to plan and track the progress of a project. Time is indicated as columns across the chart, with individual tasks represented as bars. The length and position of the bars shows the start date, completed days, and remaining number of days associated with the tasks.

Example – Basic Gantt chart

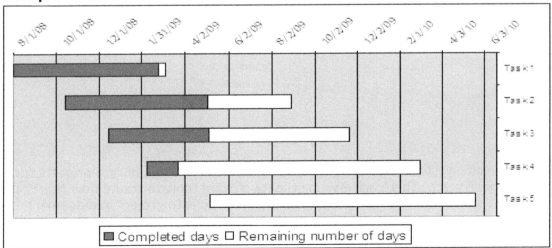

Decision tree is another visual flow chart tool. It is like PERT, however, it lets you consider choices and risk. It can help when deciding between different options by projecting possible outcomes. It gives the decision maker an overview of the multiple stages that will follow each possible decision. Each branch shows the probability of the outcome. The project, question or event is represented with a square. The decision is represented with a circle. Branches are represented by the choices that you have to make. The probability of each option is shown above each branch. The two or more branches that sprout from the same node must all add up to 100%. For example, if one decision circle has two options with one branch with a probability of 30 percent, then the other branch probability must be 70 percent. The probability percent is based on facts that you have determined, or have been given. You need to have sufficient data to best utilize the probability part of this tool.

Example – Decision tree. A simple analogy based on the decision on whether to invest in an online training program:

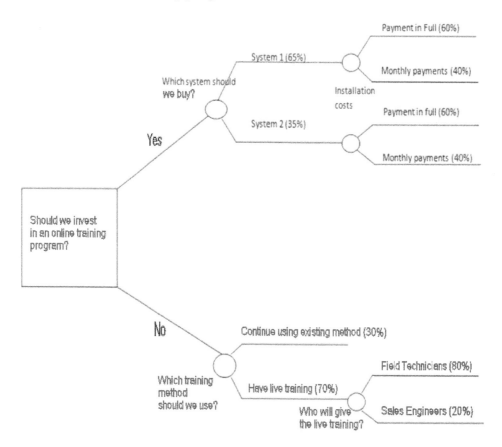

There are software tools that are excellent for planning and scheduling projects such as Microsoft Project. There are also excellent software tools to create flow charts like Microsoft Visio. If you are going to be heavily involved with project management duties and/or process documentation, these two tools are a must. It is also suggested that you take a separate project management course.

Quality Management

Quality Management is a method for ensuring that all the activities necessary to design, develop and implement a product or service are effective and efficient. All to often, quality is viewed as simplistic with the simple attitude of putting some quality standards in place and assign people to make sure they're observed. This is the wrong attitude, as quality, in any aspect of business, should be considered critically important. The attitude within the entire company should be that of accepting nothing but superior quality. Customer loyalty and superior quality go hand-in-hand. Loyalty is a direct result of customer satisfaction. Value is created for the customer, which also results in employee satisfaction. Customers will be less price sensitive and are more likely to recommend your company's products or services. Most of all, with customer loyalty due to superior quality comes higher profit and growth for the company.

Quality management can be considered to have three main components:

1. **Quality control** - also known as QC and IQC (incoming quality control) which is designed to meet or exceed customer requirements. An example would be a goal of no more than a 2% failure rate, based on random inspection, on the cosmetic look of a phone. The goal is to find ways to lower that percentage without increasing costs.

2. **Quality assurance** - also known as QA, which refers to planned and systematic production and testing processes to ensure proper performance of the product, to minimize defects, and ensure a high degree of quality. An example of a QA goal based on a software release would be a less than 2% trouble ticket rate based on a bug associated with the release.

3. **Quality improvement** - there are many methods and organizations for quality improvement. The bottom line is that they all strive for continuous quality improvement. Three basic rules for managing quality are:

   - Upper management must be completely involved and committed to excellence, not just supporting it. They should be willing to allow for independent assessment, accept the findings, and act on them.
   - The quality focus must be incorporated throughout the entire company, not just a group or two.
   - Quality improvement must be measured both on quality specific terms and the impact it has towards business goals.

Here are six of the most common quality methods and organizations used towards quality improvement:

   - Six Sigma - identifies and removes the causes of defects and errors in manufacturing and business processes. It uses a set of quality management methods, including statistical methods, and creates a special infrastructure of people within the organization who are experts in these methods. These experts are considered Green Belts & Black Belts. Six Sigma has two key methods:

     DMAIC - which is used to improve an existing business process:

- **D**efine process improvement goals that are consistent with customer demands and the enterprise strategy.
- **M**easure key aspects of the current process and collect relevant data.
- **A**nalyze the data to verify cause-and-effect relationships. Determine what the relationships are, and attempt to ensure that all factors have been considered.
- **I**mprove or optimize the process based upon data analysis using techniques like "Design of experiments."
- **C**ontrol to ensure that any deviations from the target are corrected before they result in defects. Set up pilot runs to establish process capability, move on to production, set up control mechanisms, and continuously monitor the process.

DMADV is used to create new product or process designs:

- **D**efine design goals that are consistent with customer demands and the enterprise strategy.
- **M**easure and identify CTQ's (characteristics that are "Critical To Quality"), product capabilities, production process capability, and risks.
- **A**nalyze to develop and design alternatives, create a high-level design, and evaluate design capability to select the best design.
- **D**esign details, optimize the design, and plan for design verification. This phase may require simulations.
- **V**erify the design, set up pilot runs, implement the production process, and hand it over to the process owners.

o   ISO 9000 - is a family of standards for quality management systems. ISO 9000 is maintained by ISO, the International Organization for Standardization and is administered by accreditation and certification bodies. There are eight ISO 9000 2000 quality management principles:

1. Focus on your customers
2. Provide Leadership
3. Involve your people
4. Use a process approach
5. Take a systems approach
6. Encourage continual improvement
7. Get the facts before making decisions
8. Work with your suppliers

o   TQM – Total Quality Management is a management approach to long-term success through customer satisfaction. All members of an organization participate in improving processes, products, services and the culture in which they work.

o   Kaizen – looks at eliminating waste from the business and production process, thus improving production and reducing costs without much of a monetary investment.

o   Benchmarking - is the process of measuring an organization's internal processes, then identifying, understanding, and adapting outstanding practices from other organizations considered to be best-in-class.

o Quality, Cost, Delivery (QCD) – offers a straightforward method of measuring processes while being applicable to both simple and complicated business processes. It also represents a basis for comparing businesses. QCD, as used in lean manufacturing, measures a businesses activity and develops key performance indicators. QCD analysis often forms a part of continuous improvement programs.

Supply Chain Management (SCM)

Supply Chain Management involves the flow of materials, information, and finances as they move in a level process from supplier, to manufacturer, to wholesaler, to retailer, and finally to the consumer. SCM involves coordinating and integrating these flows among all companies involved. Each level of the supply chain is described as a "tier." There can be several tiers beneath the final supplier.

Example - Supply Chain Management flow chart

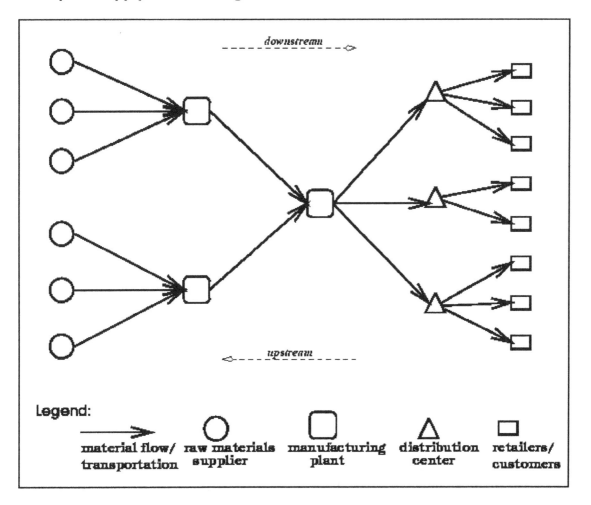

In the example given, materials flow downstream through a manufacturing level (tier) transforming the raw materials, which are the components or parts. These are assembled on the next level to form products. The products are shipped to distribution centers, and from there on to retailers and customers.

Logistics Management is the part of SCM that efficiently plans, implements, and controls the delivery and storage of goods and services.
Supply chain management flows can be divided into three main flows:

1. **Product flow** - which is the movement of goods from a supplier to a customer, as well as any customer returns or service needs.

2. **Information flow** - which involves transmitting orders and updating the status of delivery.

3. **Finances flow** - which consists of credit terms, payment schedules, and consignment and title ownership arrangements.

There are three levels of decisions associated with SCM:

1. **Strategic** - Long-term decisions related to location, production, inventory, and transportation.

2. **Tactical** - Medium-term decisions such as weekly demand forecasts, distribution and transportation planning, production planning, and materials requirement planning.

3. **Operational** - Day-to-Day decisions as part of normal managerial duties.

The following five steps are typical purchase procedures:

1. Specify the amount needed.

2. Determine the supplier based on pricing comparisons.

3. Negotiate the price as well as payment terms, warranty, and timed cost reductions. Dealing with supplies or commodities depends on their availability, price and quality.

4. Purchase the supplies.

5. Delivery and inspection of the supplies.

Focusing on certain areas within the supply chain can reduce costs. There might be times when buying in bulk is cost effective. JIT, FIFO and LIFO will be discussed in the following Inventory Management section of this lesson.

Manufacturing Resource Planning (MRP) as part of SCM can help plan and determine the supply needs and timelines for new manufacturing processes in order to predict product delivery schedules, and respond to changes in the market or product. It is a software based production planning and inventory control system used to manage manufacturing processes. The three major objectives of MRP are:

1. Ensure materials and products are available for production and delivery to customers.

2. Maintain the lowest possible level of inventory.

3. Plan manufacturing activities, delivery schedules, and purchasing activities.

Sophisticated software systems with Web interfaces are competing with Web-based Application Service Providers (ASP) who provide SCM service for companies who rent their service. A number of major Web sites offer e-procurement marketplaces, which is the business-to-business purchase and sale of supplies and services over the Internet. Manufacturers can trade and even make auction bids with suppliers.

The five basic Supply Chain Management steps are:

1. **Plan** – Strategic planning by developing a set of metrics to monitor the supply chain so that it is efficient, costs less, and delivers high quality and value to customers.

2. **Source** – Choose the suppliers that will deliver the goods and services you need to create your product including pricing, delivery and payment. Also managing the inventory of goods and services you receive from suppliers, including receiving shipments, verifying them, transferring them to your manufacturing facilities, and authorizing supplier payments. This is all done while at the same time continuously monitoring the metrics for possible improvement.

3. **Make** – Manufacture your product. Schedule the activities necessary for production, testing, packaging and preparation for delivery. Always measure quality levels, production output, and worker productivity.

4. **Deliver** – Also known as logistics. Coordinate the receipt of orders from customers, develop a network of warehouses, pick carriers to get products to customers, and set up an invoicing system to receive payments. Shipping options can include:

    - FOB (Free On Board) Factory Pricing where the buyer bears the shipping cost.
    - Freight Absorption Pricing in which paying some of the transportation costs are in line with competitors.
    - Uniformed Delivery Pricing in which a standard price is set no matter the location.
    - Zone Pricing in which you charge different prices for different geographical locations.

5. **Return** – Also known as RMA or Return Merchandise Authorization. A system for receiving defective and excess products back from customers, and supporting customers who have problems with delivered products.

Inventory Management

Inventory Management keeps track of goods and materials held available in stock. It allows the management of sales, purchases and payments. Inventory management software, such as Fishbowl, helps create invoices, purchase orders, receiving lists, payment receipts, and can print bar-code labels. An inventory management software system configured to a warehouse, retail, or product line, will help create revenue for the company and control operating costs. Here are five common inventory phrases:

1. **SKU** – Stock-Keeping Unit (pronounced Skew) is a unique combination of all the components that are assembled into the purchasable item. Therefore, any change in the packaging or product is a new SKU. This level of detailed specification assists in managing inventory.

2. **BOM** - Bill of Materials (pronounced bomb) is the term used to describe the raw materials, parts, sub-components, and components needed to manufacture a finished product. A BOM can define:

    • Products as they are designed, which is an *engineering* BOM.
    • As they are ordered, which is a *sales* BOM.
    • As they are built, which is a *manufacturing* BOM.
    • As they are maintained, which is a *service* BOM.

3. **JIT** – Just-in-Time – JIT is the practice of keeping very low levels of inventory and using sophisticated ordering and manufacturing methods to get the product into inventory *just in time* to be shipped. The goal is to maximize inventory turnover, and minimize the money tied up in inventory.

4. **FIFO** – First in First out (pronounced Fife-oh) - FIFO is pushing the old items up front to make room for new items in the back that are of the same kind. Items that are perishable and have a sell by date such as milk and eggs, or if you have a product that has periodic software upgrades, would use the FIFO method. You would want to use FIFO to reduce old stock in order to make way for the new stock.

5. **LIFO** – Last in First out (Pronounced Life-oh) – LIFO is pushing the old items back to make room for new items in the front that are of the same kind. The last items stocked will be the first items sold. This would be a typical stocking method for items that have no "sell-by" date associated with them, or at least one that is in the distant future, such as canned goods or a product that has no upgrade scheduled for awhile, etc.

COGS, LIFO and FIFO as pertained to accounting is discussed in Lesson 8.

Disaster Planning and Recovery

Although this might not be considered an operations responsibility, it still needs to be discussed. Disaster planning and recovery needs to be fully investigated on just how the company would react to disasters such as hurricanes, fires, major power outages, and even terrorism. Disaster planning and recovery should not only be planned for emergencies that would require evacuation or first aid, but also for recovering important company information.

First off the goal should be prevention. This especially holds true for potential internal disasters, as you have more control to prevent disasters from happening.

If disaster strikes, however, you need to be prepared. At least a couple of company personnel should have CPR training. There should be clear and precise directions posted everywhere regarding evacuation procedures. Management protocols need to be determined on how to make sure everyone has been accounted for, and for any additional steps that need to be taken. There also needs to be first aid kits and fire extinguishers located throughout the premise.

One example of planning ahead to recover from an internal company disaster would be by regularly backing up all data externally through an online backup service. You might even work in an organization, such as a telephone service provider, who should have a backup plan in order to continue to provide service to its customers during a major disaster.

Here is a list of organizations that can help with disaster preparation strategies:

FEMA (Federal Emergency Management Agency)
American Red Cross Disaster Services
The National Hurricane Center
The National Fire Plan
Center for Disease Control and Prevention

Make it a point to make sure your company has preventive measures in place, and is able to react to the best of its abilities to any possible emergencies or disasters.

Customer Service – Customer Care and Technical Support

Customer Service covers a vast array of support functions. It can be associated with technically supporting the customer, taking orders, collecting payments, booking flights, etc. Customer Service provides support to customers before, during, and after the purchase of a product or service. The rapid resolution of customer complaints about quality, defects, and delivery is essential. Customer service can either save or lose the account based on how the situation is handled. They also know the everyday problems customers face and learn more about product strengths and weaknesses than anyone else in the company. They will then be able to provide input to the design engineers, who can then make future products easier to use. In fact, customer service trends should be the first item discussed during management meetings.

On the other hand, word of mouth about bad customer service spreads just as it does about a good product. A potential future customer might not buy the product or service based on just a few negative comments, blogs, etc. Poor sales and possible churn (losing customers) can have nothing to do with the quality of the product or the sales-force selling the product, but poor customer service. Good customer service, however, can lead to better sales and retaining customer loyalty, thus increasing company longevity. Customer service is more than just supporting a customer, it can be a tool to improve sales or be the culprit of financial loss.

Even though customer service might fall under sales or marketing's responsibility, it can also be considered part of the back office operations group. For that reason we will discuss customer service in this lesson. You can also relate customer service to marketing and sales, which will be discussed in lesson 10.

First, lets determine what is a customer and who are they? In its most basic terms, a customer is an individual or organization that will benefit from the products and/or services the company offers. Customers may fall into one of three customer groups:

1. *Existing Customers* who have purchased or used the company's products and/or services within a designated period of time. For some organizations the timeframe may be short, for instance, a restaurant may only consider someone to be an existing customer if they have purchased within the last couple of months. Other companies may view a customer as an existing customer even though if they have not purchased anything in the last few years, for example, a computer manufacturer. Existing customers are extremely important since they have a current relationship with the company, and they give the company a reason to remain in contact with them. They represent the best market for future sales, especially if they are satisfied with the relationship they presently have with the company. Getting these existing customers to purchase more is significantly less expensive and time consuming than finding new customers, mainly because they are satisfied with the company. They should be easy to reach with promotional appeals such as discounts for a new product.

2. *Former Customers* who previously purchased from your company, however, they are not considered and *Existing Customer* anymore because they have not purchased within a certain timeframe. In most cases it is due to competition or because they did not receive good customer service.

3. *Potential Customers* who have yet to purchase, but have the requirements to eventually become *Existing Customers*. They have a need for a product, possess the financial means to buy it, and have the authority to make a buying decision. Targeting markets to find these potential customers will be discussed in lesson 10.

By understanding the different customer types, it is clear to see that it is not only marketing or sales that should be concerned, it should also be customer service. An *Existing Customer* might turn into a *Former Customer* if they receive poor customer service. A former customer will most likely never come back due to poor customer service. A *Potential Customer* might be put off if they read any negative blogs or hear bad comments. Bad word of mouth can potentially kill new customers.

Quite often the customer will complain directly to the sales person, who will then try to resolve the issue the best they can. This should not be the case. The customer should have high confidence in the customer service department and not even have to bother the sales person. Besides, sales should be selling, not supporting. One issue regarding sales, however, is when a sales person promises something that can't be delivered, or that they do not fully understand just what it is they are selling.

It is so important that the constant drive to satisfy customers is a priority for the customer service manager. Customer service must appreciate the role customers play in helping the company meet its goals. Customers are the reason a company is in business. Without customers, or the potential to attract customers, a company is not viable. The more customer service realizes this fact, the better the customer service will be given.

The most common form of customer service is the support of a service in a call center environment. Queue theory is used to determine how many agents are needed to minimize wait time, thus increasing value and providing a better customer experience. For example, if a customer has to wait on hold for longer than 30 seconds, there is loss in value. Queue theory can be used for any type of service related situations, for example, how many checkout counters are needed at a store, etc. Basically, when people have to wait there is loss in value. However, if there are too many employees in too many checkout stands, there is higher cost associated with the service provided. The goal of queuing theory is to find the perfect balance where the wait time does not lose too much value, and the costs are not too high. There are many software programs, such as Blue Pumpkin, that analyze these types of formulas and algorithms.

The most important aspect of customer service is the high level of customer satisfaction based on the customer's expectations, as described in the examples used in lesson 2. No matter the type of a customer service organization, the goals of service excellence are the same:

1. *Customer friendly attitude.* This includes creating a positive experience by being happy and willing to help, respectful, communicating with the individual as a person, relating to the situation with empathy and understanding, developing a personal connection, going the extra mile, following it to the end, and having grace under pressure. A communication style that builds a bridge instead of a wall is key.

2. *Technically proficient.* Being a customer friendly representative is important, but if the representative does not know what they are doing, it will create a bad customer experience. Proper training, providing the right materials, and using the right tools, is essential in providing excellent customer service.

3. *Understands the expectations, values and goals for the self and company.* Representatives might be friendly and technically proficient, however, they also need to know what is expected of them, and what their company is all about. Clearly defined goals, clear expectations, knowing just who their customers are (internal and/or external), and understanding the company's values provides the awareness needed to understand the employee's role in

the company. The more motivated the employee, the higher standard of customer service will be given.

Customer satisfaction surveys should be given to measure the success of the customer service department. Data should be gathered in an objective and consistent fashion. The data should never be manipulated, and to ensure objectivity, be given by a third party outside observer.

An interesting paradox regarding customer service surveys is the hidden traps between a "completely satisfied customer" and a "satisfied customer." A completely satisfied customer will be very loyal, whereas the satisfied customer is easily swayed to switch to a competitor. Although the overall results of the survey will still look positive, you should still be concerned of the "satisfied" or "average" results.

Customers are used to outstanding, low cost, quality based products and services. They now expect outstanding customer support. This is where many companies fail. Many times customers will not even state the reason why they stopped doing business with a company. However, in many cases, research shows it was due to previous trouble reports, which then pointed to poor customer service. When customers have to deal with customer service, they want, in this order:

1. Knowledgeable employees who can identify the customers' true needs.
2. First call resolution (no repeat issues).
3. To be treated with respect and that they are truly valued.
4. An employee who is truly trying to meet their needs.
5. To be taken care of as quickly as possible.

These five attributes, in conjunction with the three service excellence goals as previously stated, are the core basics in providing an excellent customer experience. Structuring the department to its optimum and building a strong motivated team will increase the possibilities in providing service excellence.

Even when excellent customer service is provided, there will still always be an upset customer. Whether it is a customer service representative, or even a member of upper management, the next 5 steps are very useful when dealing with an upset customer:

1. **First, just listen**. Let the upset customer get it out of their system. In time they will start to calm down. If they start being abusive, just calmly state, "I understand you are frustrated, and I want to help you, but let's please remain professional."

2. **Be sympathetic and empathetic**. Make sure the customer knows that you understand their frustration. Recognize how it must have felt to be the customer in this situation.   Reiterate the customer's complaint so that they know you are truly listening, understand, and care about the situation. Let the customer know you are sorry they have had such a tough time. Even if it's not the company's fault, many times an irate customer just wants to know someone cares that they are inconvenienced. A simple, "I'm so sorry this happened," will normally do. If you find that your company is at fault, definitely apologize again. Be sure to be sincere.

3. **Let them know that you want to fix the problem and make them happy**. A good rule of thumb is to put yourself into their shoes, and between the two of you come up with a solution. The customer will feel that they were heard. Once everything has been stated, it is a good idea to recap the agreed upon solution. Thank them for taking the time to speak with you. It is all right to say you're sorry, even if the problem was not related to you or the company.

4. **Document everything.** This will let the next representative who might interact with the customer know what the customer has previously experienced. It could be a touchy credit request or repeat issue in which they will not want to have to explain everything all over again. It can also be used to track for possible trends if the problem happens to other customers. Excellent documentation cannot be stressed enough...

5. **Follow up with the customer.** Let the customer know they can get a follow up call or e-mail to make sure all is resolved. If you have the resources, you can follow up on every customer issue, whether requested or not.

A positive approach is especially needed in customer service. A representative should not say, "I don't know," but should say, "I'll find out." They should not say, "No," but should say, "What I can do is..." Customer service should be thought of as a the group that provides the expected service from the customers point of view, makes an unhappy customer happy, provides the answer to a confused customer, be the calming shoulder to the upset customer, and all the while making the customer feel like gold and somewhat enlightened.

It is an art to turn an angry customer into a loyal patron. It is the art of service recovery. If you respond rapidly and creatively to address a precarious customer service situation, you can often stabilize that relationship and turn the individual who might have become your worst enemy, into your best friend. Go the extra mile and take the blame, even if unwarranted.

Companies need to take a systematic approach to develop a customer experience strategy as described in lesson 2. Although customers prefer speaking directly with a customer service representative, options should be given to the customer like a web based knowledgebase, FAQ page, e-mail interaction, chat, and IVR (Interactive Voice Response) with automated phone keypad or speech activated menu systems.

Here are some proven phone techniques that will help to make your phone conversations more effective. These basic soft skills should be used during every customer interaction:

- DO speak clearly and slowly; also lower your voice if you normally speak loud.
- DO use the customer's name.
- DO listen clearly and limit distractions. Concentrate on the customer, not any non-job related activities.
- DO always ask permission when placing a customer on hold. Two examples are: "Would you mind holding while I get your information?" and "Can you hold briefly while I see if (persons name) is available?"....
- DO always thank the customer for holding. Keep in touch with the customer during long holds, even if it is just to say you are still working on the issue.

- DO keep all conversations professional and not personal, unless the customer initiated the personal conversation.
- DON'T talk with anything in your mouth.

Quite often, the manager or a trainer will listen in on customer service calls. They also randomly record these calls. The form that follows shows some examples on what to look for regarding soft skill performance:

Example – Phone Monitoring Form

Sample Corp - Customer Service Phone Monitoring Form

Name:		Yes responses =	0
Call Date/Time:		No responses =	0
Account #/TN:		Automatic Fail =	0
Call Type:			
Call Number:		Monitor Percentage =	

Yes	No	N/A		
Greeting				Comments:
			Used correct greeting	
			Asked for customer's account number or TN#	
			Verified the authorized user (if applicable)	
Customer Name				Comments:
			Used the customer's name at least once during the call	
Listening				Comments:
			Used listening skills (doesn't interrupt, remembers info, etc)	
Courtesy				Comments:
			Used "please" when appropriate	
			Used "thank you" when appropriate	
			Showed interest and willingness to assist the customer	
			Showed empathy when appropriate	
			Apologized when appropriate (Business mistakes)	
Equipment Use				Comments:
			Noted account properly	
			Did not use mute button	
Soft Skills				Comments:
			Voice reflected energy and enthusiasm	
			Avoided long silence (more than 1 minute)	
			Used polite/appropriate tone	
			Used proper grammar and business language	
			Refrained from using company terms and jargon	
			Used positive words (I know, I'm certain,)	
Using Hold				Comments:
			Informed the Customer before placing them on hold	
			Kept in touch during long hold	
			Thanked the customer for holding	
Connecting Calls				Comments:
			Connected to the correct department/Queue	
			Informed customer where & why they were connected	
Closing				Comments:
X			Used proper closing - "Thank you for calling Company Name"	
Automatic Fail				Comments:
			Placed/Received Personal Topline Call	
			Disconnected call without sufficient reason	
			Failure to answer call	
			Failed to verify authorized user when required	
			Failed to access customer account	
			Failed to assist caller and transferred back into same Queue	
			Other	

Agent Signature:

Supervisor Signature:

Monitored By:

For Customer Service Supervisor:
Problem Solving
Yes/No - Understood request or problem
Yes/No - Probed for addt'l information to provide the best solution
Yes/No - Appropriate advice was given or action was taken

Additional Comments:

IS and IT – Information Systems and Information Technology

In this day and age, "IS" (Information Systems) is more important than ever. Basically, corporate "IS" is the area that includes the company's computers, specialized software programming, and data communications regarding the company's networking needs.

Systems analysts design and meet the hardware needs, while programmer's design and implement software packages such as a database management system (DBMS). Programmers use several programming languages to build programs such as *transaction processing,* which provides inventory and sales transactions, *Management information systems (MIS),* which gives management reporting tools used for organizing, evaluating, and efficiently running their departments, and *decision support systems (DSS),* which helps managers make difficult decisions and solve problems based on compiled data, documents, personal knowledge, or business models.

The "IT" department (Information Technology) is also sometimes known as "IS." In most companies, however, when talking about "IT," you are referring to the responsibility for implementing, installing, and maintaining the information infrastructure. They will install and/or repair the computer hardware such as the PC itself, the monitor, keyboard, or mouse. They will also load the computer software, which drives the computer hardware to perform the tasks like MS Excel, MS Word, or any other applications. These applications can be anything from inventory tracking to customer record keeping.

"IT" or "IS" also deals with networking, which basically means they make sure information flows from one computer to the next. The computers can be in the same office, or connected anywhere throughout the world. The means of communicating information from one place to the next is through data communications media such as CAT 5 cables, fiber-optic cables, microwave transmission, and satellite transmission. Local Area Networks (LAN) provide access for everyone in the same building through hubs and switches, which in most cases is connected together using CAT 5 cables. There are also VLAN's (Virtual LAN), in which people can connect to the company's network away from the office. For example, a person using their home computer can connect to the company's network securely to form a LAN. Even though they may be hundreds, if not thousands of miles away, they will still be part of the same network as everyone else in the office. Wide Area Networks (WAN) provides access to the outside world through routers, thus enabling organizations to gain access to global markets. The Internet makes it possible to connect any computer to virtually any other computer in any part of the world.

By strategically planning and implementing information systems that optimize the inherent benefits of information technology, the organizations performance is greatly enhanced. This requires effective leadership and vision, as well as knowledge of both information technology and the organization's business environment.

HR – Human Resources

HR, or Human Resources, deals with the human needs of employees. Individuals who work in HR really need to be a people person with a pleasant demeanor. HR has so many responsibilities that it is sometimes misunderstood. One thing that is certain, it is one of the most necessary departments in a corporate company environment. They have to be able to handle a crisis in a smooth, discreet manner. It can be related to health care issues, sexual harassment, or employee disputes. They must also be trusted to keep an employee's personal details to themselves. HR also tries to make sure that all employees are comfortable with their surroundings, and are working in a non-hostile environment.

Some of the responsibilities of HR are:

- Securing, offering and explaining benefits, like health insurance or 401k's.
- Managing on-the-job health and safety issues.
- Offering information or advice on special work programs like reimbursement for continuing education.
- Advertising available jobs, screening applicants, setting up interviews and potentially hiring applicants.
- Handling all paperwork related to the hiring or firing of employees.
- Distributing paychecks and bonuses, although paycheck disbursement may be outsourced to another company.
- Helping workers apply for family leave, maternity leaves, sabbaticals or disability payments.
- Possibly participating in motivational company wide events.
- Approving performance reviews and assessing raises or promotions.
- Handling complaints about employer abuses, sexual harassment, discrimination or hostile work environment charges.

Supervisors or managers from other departments may be responsible for hiring or firing employees, however, it usually has to be cleared by HR and go through the HR process. As a manager, always keep yourself on the good side of HR and keep them close to you at all times. In times of need or distress, they truly are your best friends...

Quick Lesson Summary

- Operations Management can cover a wide list of responsibilities. It controls the day-to-day functions of a company. It is a transformation process regarding any activity or group of activities that takes one or more inputs, transforms and adds value to them, and provides outputs for customers or clients.

- Whether your company is product based or service based, or both, the functions of Operations Management are always the same: (1) designing, (2) planning, (3) organizing, (4) directing, and (5) controlling.

- Cost-benefit analysis is a tool used to see if an investment is worth pursuing. Break-even analysis lets you find when you first start making profit, and Crossover Analysis lets you identify the point where you should switch from one type of product to another one that has similar benefits, but different fixed and variable costs.

- Critical Path Method (CPM) is a tool that helps plan and coordinate tasks and activities in a project. Gantt Charts, PERT and Decision Tree methods are also used. Microsoft Project is a great tool to use for Project Management.

- Supply Chain Management involves the flow of materials, information, and finances as they move in a process from supplier, to manufacturer, to wholesaler, to retailer, to consumer. Three levels of decisions associated with SCM are: Strategic, Tactical, and Operational. The five basic steps are: Plan, Source, Make, Deliver and Return.

- Quality Management ensures a product or service is effective and efficient, and is based on three main components: Quality control, Quality Assurance, and Quality Improvement.

- Inventory Management keeps track of goods and materials held available in stock. Sophisticated software not only keeps track of the goods and materials, but also creates invoices, purchase orders, and bar codes.

- Customer Service provides support to customers before, during and after the purchase of a product or service. Three steps that are essential in providing great customer service are: Having a customer friendly attitude, being technically proficient, and knowing the expectations, values and goals for the self and company. Use of surveys should be used to measure satisfaction levels. Surveys show that customers want:

  o Knowledgeable employees who can identify the customers' true needs.
  o First call resolution (no repeat issues).
  o To be treated with respect and that they are truly valued.
  o An employee who is truly trying to meet their needs.
  o To be taken care of as quickly as possible.

- "IS" is the area that includes the company's computers, specialized software programming, and data communications regarding the company's networking needs, whereas "IT" has the responsibility for implementing, installing, and maintaining the information infrastructure. They are sometimes both intertwined as one group.

- HR is one of the most necessary departments in a corporate company environment. They have to be able to handle a crisis in a smooth, discreet manner, whether it is a health care issue, sexual harassment, or employee disputes. They must also be trusted to keep an employee's personal details to themselves.

LESSON 10 – BUSINESS BASICS PART III – MARKETING & SALES

Introduction: Create it, Get the word out, and Sell it

A company's financial health starts with sales. A company must sell its products or services in order to pay the bills and earn a profit. R&D (Research and Development) first develops the product or creates a service, marketing then lets individuals or organizations know the company exists and what they are all about, and finally sales does the selling that brings in the money.

In this lesson we will go over the basic concepts of marketing and sales. This will include market strategies, market research, the 4 P's of marketing, sales tactics, type of sales, the sales force and the keys to developing successful products.

What is a Market and the Marketing Department?

A Market is a group of customers or potential customers. Companies focus on its particular market by getting practical information the company can use for sales, marketing, and product development. The market starts with the total population, then *Potential* markets that have an interest, then *Available* markets that have the money, then *Target* markets that are the customers the company has determined to serve (the served market), then finally the *Penetrated* markets who have already bought your products and/or services.

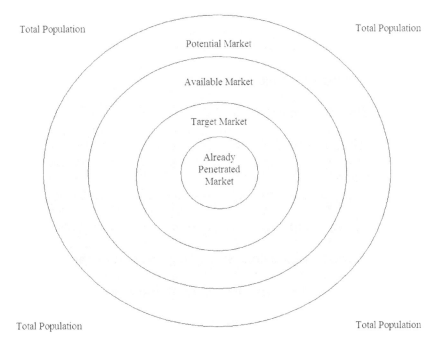

The market can then be broken up into segments and analyzed even further. We will review market segments later in this lesson.

The Marketing Department's key responsibilities is to determine the needs, wants, and demands of the consumer and finds ways to satisfy those needs within its product base. *Needs* represents items such as food, housing, and clothing, whereas *wants* represents cultural based items such as makeup or vacations. Demands are simply the wants of a consumer who has the ability to pay for what they want.

Marketing deals with goods (which are tangible), services (an intangible benefit to customer's), and ideas (concepts, images, etc). Quite often, as in this lesson, the word product can also refer to goods, services, or ideas.

Once the market has been establish, the marketing department looks at ways to best market the company's product. Marketing does more than just promotion, they dig deep to find, or even try to create, consumer trends related to what their company is all about. Marketing needs to know and understand the customer to the point where selling is almost non-essential, and the product or service can sell itself.

Marketers need to be creative people as there is a lot of competition out there. Due to this continuous competition, the cycle of creating something new never ends. A key objective of marketing is to provide products and services that customers really want. They need to make customers feel they have a good relationship with the company. In this way the customer feels more like a partner, not just a source of revenue for the company. Marketing is always trying to develop satisfying relationships with customers that benefit both the customer and the organization.

Marketing needs to know how their decisions could lead to problems for other departments within the company. For example, making a decision to incorporate advertising statements that are too generic can increase the amount of calls to customer support.

Just as there is a split in economics (microeconomics and macroeconomics), the same holds true for marketing. The marketing environment has similar components:

- **Microenvironment** deals with internal factors that can influence the company directly. The marketing department is always looking at new strategies and market approaches. They need to then get the rest of the company to follow their lead. The problem is most other departments are more resistance to change. Finance will be concerned about the cost, customer service will be concerned with the change in direction and the training needed, and R&D might have to look at a new development approach. The process of internal marketing is focused toward overcoming this resistance to change. The internal decision makers within the company need to look at the manpower, money, machinery, materials, and markets that are all part of the internal environment. Distribution channels such as suppliers, vendors, warehousing, and transportation of the product, are also part of the internal environment and will be affected by marketing planning and decisions. The same goes for outside marketing service agencies.

- **Macroenvironment** deals with the external factors outside of your company's direct control. *Demographic* and *Social* trends, *Economic* issues which impacts what people can afford to buy, *Environmental* factors such as the availability and cost of raw materials, the cost of energy and levels of pollution, *Technological* rate of change, and *Political* pressures such as legislation and effects from agencies like the FDA, FCC, or EPA that can stop certain marketing moves.

Marketers must also understand emerging technology and applications in order to truly understand what the customer expects technically.   It will also help spot potential business opportunities as well as potential threats.

Some considerations of a company's marketing program are *consumption* that seeks to get people to purchase more and more, *customer satisfaction* that's more concerned with happy customers than pushing a product people may not like, *choice* that gives many products to choose from (however may be costly to the company), and *lifestyle* that focuses on improving a person's quality of life.

Whether the company operates as a for-profit, or as a not-for-profit, customers may believe a company is dynamic and creative based on its advertising message. Marketing must also concentrate their efforts on the market associated with their products. In order to put marketing efforts into play, marketing needs to develop a marketing strategy, design a marketing plan, and then implement the marketing plan. These subjects will be taught throughout this lesson.

What are the Five Marketing Philosophies?

The Five Marketing Philosophies help determine the management of marketing. Companies approach and conduct business in different ways in order to achieve their organizational goals. The five competing concepts by which companies are guided in their marketing efforts are:

1. **Production concept**, which is based on the fact that consumers favor products that are available and affordable. Concentration on production efficiency and effective distribution networks outweigh the customer's actual needs and wants. This is used primarily when demand exceeds supply and the focus is on finding production methods that can bring the price down to attract more customers.

2. **Product concept**, which is based on ways to improve the quality, performance, and features to attract buyers. This philosophy tends to spend too much time adding features to their products, rather than thinking about what people actually need and want.

3. **Selling concept**, which places the focus on sales rather than what people actually need or want. Most of the time the product is misrepresented which results in high customer dissatisfaction.

4. **Marketing concept**, which focuses on what people need and want more than the needs of the seller. This concept is about the importance of satisfying the customer's needs to achieve company success. Products are developed around those needs and wants.

5. **Societal marketing concept,** which not only uses the same philosophy as the marketing concept, but also focuses around the products benefit to the betterment of society as a whole. Greater emphasis is put on environmental impacts, population growth, resource shortages, and social services.

The marketing concept relies upon marketing research to define market segments, their size, and their needs. The marketing department makes the appropriate decisions to satisfy those needs.

Market Research

Market Research helps companies understand and analyze their customers. Market research mostly focuses on the following four types of information:

1. *Demographic characteristics.* Research in consumer markets would include the age, race, sex, education, marital status, housing, income, and number of children. Research in business markets would include the type of industry, annual sales, number of employees and locations, and years in business.

2. *Buying behaviors.* Research is done to see how customers buy products such as in a retail store or online. Also, the frequency of purchases and the type of advertising or influence that motivated them to buy.

3. *Lifestyle or psychographics.* Research on the type of hobbies, sports, and vacations, TV shows, magazines, religion, frequency of fine dining, frequency of fast food, and even personality traits and sexual orientation.

4. *Customer Satisfaction.* Research through surveys on the perceived value for the price, ease of use, useful features, what they would like to see in the future, and whether they are likely to purchase more product.

Most often, it is the larger companies who invest in market research. Small companies feel they already know their customer base pretty well. Companies that sell *commodity products* such as gold, coal, grain, oil, rice and paper do not really need much market research as these products have characteristics that are indistinguishable across the companies that sell it. With *commodities*, customers are mostly concerned about low prices and fast service. Companies, like a phone manufacturer that only sells to one type of customer, is considered to be in a *homogenous market*. These customers share most characteristics. However, with a focus on *product differentiation*, companies can emphasize the quality of their products such as, "their coal burns longer," or "their phones sound better," than that of their competitors.

There are basically two types of market research; *primary market research*, which involves asking questions through a survey, an observational approach, or experimental approach, and *secondary market research*, which involves checking articles in newspapers, magazines, and books. Good secondary sources to help research your industry are NAICS / www.census.gov/eos/www/naics/, Hoovers / www.hoovers.com/free/, and Standard & Poor's / www.standardandpoors.com.

Secondary research is less expensive and quickest to perform, however, you get much more detail with a primary market research customer survey. For example, with primary research you can get a good feel from prospects on the value of a potential product release, and whether or not they would buy it. It can then be narrowed down to the type of prospect who would buy the product based on items such as age, location, and gender.

It is important to make sure the primary research survey questionnaire gives you the exact data you need or else you will be wasting everyone's time. By following these 7 steps, you should have all areas covered:

1. *What are the goals of the survey?* Think about exactly what it is you want to understand from your customers.

2. *Who will you survey?* You want to make sure you are surveying the right clientele. For example, if your company has two distinct areas with two distinct customers, you would not want to survey the wrong customers on a particular product release. You also might just want to ask a sample of your customer base to get an approximate value.

3. *How will you perform the survey?* Will this be done via a web site, through an e-mail blast, over the phone, or in person? Also, will you or someone within the company perform these surveys, or will you get an unobjectionable outside source? People tend to be more honest with an outside source rather than someone within your company. There are pros and cons to all of these methods. For example, an e-mail blast is quick and easy, but people tend to ignore them or might be too dissatisfied to even want to participate. The telephone requires more time and effort, and sometimes people hate answering these types of calls, however, you can get a personal verbal response. You need to determine what method your customers are most willing to participate in, and if the costs outweigh the benefits.

4. *Create the questionnaire.* Be sure to brainstorm with people within your organization to create the most effective and pertinent questions. Keep the survey as short as possible and test it out before you give it to your customers. The questions can be developed with a quantitative or qualitative response:

   - *Quantitative information* involves questions that have a numerical answer, which can then give you a percentage base. For example, you can have a question that has an answer of "yes" or "no" which you can then express data like, "76% of all females are likely to buy the product." These are considered closed-ended questions, which are easy to compile and compare. Ratings such as 1 – 5 or excellent, good, average, poor, and very poor are great to use for customer satisfaction surveys. You should be concerned with a rating of 3 or average as in most cases, it is a customer who is truly dissatisfied, however, does not want to come off too cruel. Poor and very poor are obviously big alarms that need immediate attention.

   - *Qualitative information* involves a verbal statement which can be used to study suggestions or comments, not just "yes" or "no" type of answers. These are considered open-ended questions that truly capture the customer's attitude and opinion. You should allow at least one open-ended question on the customer satisfaction survey.

5. *Present the survey.* If you followed steps 1 through 4 properly, getting the survey out to the customers should be straightforward. Make sure you have up-to-date contact information. If you run into snags, just make the necessary adjustments and carry on until your targeted numbers of surveys are completed.

6. *Analyze the data.* This is the anxious part of the project. Be careful not to analyze the surveys until all of the data is compiled, or else you might get a false sense of success or failure. Your heart wants a desired outcome and you might tend to analyze the data in an unobjective way. Be as objective as possible and look for trends, both positive and negative. This is an important aspect of being a strong manager and leader. This goes for any type of survey including customer satisfaction. There might be some surveys that are questionable that need attention, however, do not pertain to the questions asked. For example, you might want to know if a product is easy to use, however, the customer is upset at a salesperson for not returning a call and thus gives all "very poor" answers or a vulgar opinion. Make sure you keep the data in simple terms so that everyone can fully understand the results and what actions need to be taken. Report on the most important and major findings, and do not clutter the data with too much unimportant statistical analysis.

7. *Act on the results.* The most important aspect of the completed survey is what you do with the information given. Decide on the recommendations or evaluations and then determine what action needs to be taken. If, for example, improvements need to be made, address those issues immediately and after a period of a few months, send out a follow up survey with the pertinent questions to be sure all has been corrected. If the research was done to support a decision on a new product release, immediately start the process on determining the production, cost, and release dates.

Example – Basic individual Primary Market Research Questionnaire

1. Are you:
❑ Male   ❑ Female

2. What is your age?
❑ 18-24   ❑ 25-34
❑ 35-44   ❑ 45-54
❑ 55-64   ❑ 65 or over

3. What is the highest level of formal education you have completed? (Please check only one.)
❑ Attended High School   ❑ Graduated High School
❑ Attended College   ❑ Graduated College
❑ Post-Graduate Study Without Degree   ❑ Post-Graduate Degree

4. What is your marital status?
❑ Married   ❑ Single, Never Married
❑ Separated or Divorced   ❑ Widowed

5. How many children under the age of 18 live in your household? _____

6. What is your total annual personal income? (Include income from all sources— salary, bonuses, investment income, rents, royalties, etc. Please check only one.)
❑ Less than $30,000   ❑ $30,000 - $39,999
❑ $40,000 - $49,999   ❑ $50,000 - $59,999
❑ $60,000 - $74,999   ❑ $75,000 - $99,999
❑ $100,000 - $149,999   ❑ $150,000 - $249,999
❑ $250,000 - $499,999   ❑ $500,000 - $999,999
❑ $1 million or more

7. In which state and ZIP code area is your main residence?
State: _____   ZIP code: _____

8. What is your total annual household income? (Include income for all family members and include all sources—salary, bonuses, investment income, rents, royalties, etc. Please check only one.)
❑ Less than $30,000   ❑ $30,000 - $39,999
❑ $40,000 - $49,999   ❑ $50,000 - $59,999
❑ $60,000 - $74,999   ❑ $75,000 - $99,999
❑ $100,000 - $149,999   ❑ $150,000 - $249,999
❑ $250,000 - $499,999   ❑ $500,000 - $999,999
❑ $1 million or more

9a. Do you own a home, condominium or co-op as your primary residence?
❑ Yes   ❑ No

9b. If "Yes," what is the present market value of your primary residence?
❑ Under $100,000   ❑ $100,000 - $199,999
❑ $200,000 - $299,999   ❑ $300,000 - $499,999
❑ $500,000 - $749,999   ❑ $750,000 - $999,999
❑ $1 million - $1.9 million   ❑ $2 million or more
If $2 million or more, please estimate value: _____ (please specify)

10. Do you own a second home, condominium or co-op?
❑ Yes   ❑ No

11. What is the total net worth of yourself and all members of your household? Include the estimated market value of your business if you own one, all real estate, including primary residence, car, household possessions, bank accounts, stocks, bonds and other investments and assets.
❑ Less than $50,000   ❑ $50,000-$99,999
❑ $100,000-$249,999   ❑ $250,000-$499,999
❑ $500,000-$749,999   ❑ $750,000-$999,999
❑ $1 million -$1.4 million   ❑ $1.5 million -$1.9 million
❑ $2 million -$4.9 million   ❑ $5 million -$9.9 million
❑ $10 million and over

Analyzing your Customers and Competitive Market Strategies

Analyzing your customer base is needed before you can create a strategic marketing plan. You need to determine which customer market your company will be operating in:

- *Consumer market,* that buys your goods for individual or family use.

- *Industrial market,* such as manufacturers, who buy your goods for use in the production of other goods that are then sold to others.

- *Reseller market,* that buys your goods, usually through a distributor, in order to resell or rent to their customers.

- *Government market,* that purchase your goods to carry out governmental functions.

- *International market,* who buys your goods globally.

Competitively marketing your product is important as it plays a big part on how you are going to target your market.   Four strategies marketers use as a competitive edge, is to best determine if they are:

1. *Market leaders,* who are looking to dominate the industry. They look to protect their market share like developing new product ideas, and expand their market such as finding new users and uses for their product. Companies like Microsoft would fall into this category.

2. *Market Challengers,* who are looking to challenge the market leaders. Pepsi challenging Coke would be a good example of a market challenger strategy.

3. *Market Followers,* who are happy to stay at their current position. They wait to see what the market leaders are doing to gain market share, and follow the leader without having to worry about the risks and costs of any development research.

4. *Market Nichers,* who are looking at just a few target markets and not trying to compete with the overall market. They just look to gain a large enough share of its specialty market in order to maintain its profit margin. Many new businesses choose to be a market nicher.

Market Segments and Targeting your Market

Market Segments are parts of a market that are different from one another. They should be identifiable, accessible, substantial, unique, and durable. Six common segmentation strategies are:

1. *Geographic segmentations*, which divides the broad market into regional or local markets.

2. *Demographic segmentation*, which classifies the broad market such as age, gender, income, and race with different advertising campaigns that can be used to target specific segments like males 18 to 34 years old or working mothers.

3. *Psychographic segmentation*, which is social class from upper to lower, lifestyle, and personality.

4. *Behavioristic segmentation,* which is loyalty status, user rate, type of occasion, or benefits sought such as quality, service, or price.

5. *Product segmentation*, which divides the broad market by products like health food or junk food.

6. *Sales channel segmentation*, which divides the way a product is sold such as a can of Coke in a grocery store, restaurant, or vending machine.

Most often, market segments are combined. An example would be combining the product segment, such as a health food, in the demographic segment like the state of California. By segmenting markets, targeting certain factors, behaviors, and needs, and developing specific advertising, products, or services for specific markets, is extremely effective.

In contrast to consumer markets, industrial markets have customers who are fewer in numbers, but purchase larger quantities. Most of the segmentation strategies for consumers should still apply, however, location, company type, and behavioral characteristics are the most important.

Market segmentation is a useful tool as long as the segmented markets are truly measurable for size, purchasing potential, accessible through some sort of sales method, substantial enough to make it worthwhile, and actionable to be able to develop effective programs to attract and serve the segment.

Targeting your market is the next step after you have grouped your potential markets into segments. There are three potential strategies to use:

1. *Undifferentiated marketing*, which basically means your company ignores the segment differences and instead decides to develop one marketing program that would be attractive to the broadest number of buyers. The upside to this strategy is that it saves time and money as you would not need to modify the product for different markets, and need only one promotional plan and one set of promotional materials. The downside to this strategy is that it looks to attract the largest segments and ignores the smaller segments, which also attracts more competitors and thus will need more financial resources in order to compete. You also leave yourself open for niche competitors who will target the smaller markets you are ignoring.

2. *Differentiated marketing,* which means you will focus on your target market segments and develop a marketing plan for each. The upside is, as long as the costs of differentiation results in higher sales and higher profits, it is well worth it. The downside is more time and costs are needed. You would need

to modify the product for certain segments, need more than one promotional plan, and need more than one set of promotional materials.

3. *Concentrated marketing,* which means a company with limited resources focuses on getting a large share of just one or two market segments. This is a good strategy for niche players to use because they are focusing on just one or two segments, which are normally ignored by the larger competitor.

Once your company has determined its target markets, research needs to be done to find out facts, such as projected sales growth rates, estimated profit margins, and comparing the strategies from your competitors. All of this information is needed in order to develop a strong marketing plan.

You need to know the market size such as what percentage of the market is already penetrated, and the percentage already taken by your competitors. Also, there might even be a possibility for a new product release based on your research. A good source for researching other businesses and estimating the targeted market size is through the IRS, Dun & Bradstreet, and the Census bureau.

The next step would be to try and measure the current market demand for the product by means of *total market demand, area market demand*, and *actual sales and market shares.* There are also techniques to use to forecast future demand such as surveys of buyer's intentions, sales force opinions, and leading indicators.

The last step would be to determine your company's strengths and weaknesses within the targeted market segment and customer base. You need to make sure you can truly market the product effectively and provide the needed support. There will be more on this subject in the 5 C's and Marketing Strategy Basics later in this lesson.

The Marketing Mix or "The 4 P's of Marketing"

The term "Marketing Mix" refers to a combination of many elements that a company uses to market its product, as there is much more to marketing than just advertising. It essentially looks at everything your company can do to ensure its success in marketing the product. The marketing mix is designated by the common phrase penned by Jerome McCarthy as, "The 4 P's of Marketing." The 4 main "P's" are Product, Price, Place, and Promotion. They are the foundation to the marketing mix. However, in this day and age the marketing mix has extended to 3 more P's. They are People, Process, and Physical Evidence (including Packaging). Positioning, which is also sometimes known as one of the P's in the marketing mix, will also be discussed.

Anytime a decision is made to make a change with one of the "P's", it also makes an impact on decisions in other areas. For instance, a change in the "Price" of a product, such as lowering the price, could impact the "Place" or distribution area as it requires increased product shipments to retail stores. This is why it is extremely important for the marketing department to meet with other departments to discuss any possible ramifications, and to make sure everyone is on the same page.

Example – The foundation of the Marketing Mix – The 4 P's of Marketing

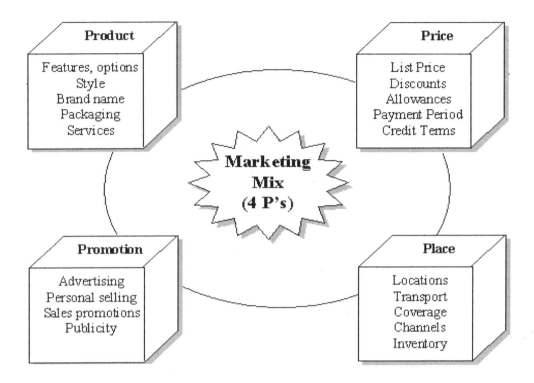

Product

Here is a detailed overview of the *product* segment within the marketing mix. The perspective from a customer-centric point of view is in parenthesis:

Product (Customer Value). This is what the company actually sells, or a service it provides. It may even be ideas or intellectual property like images, patents or copyrights. The first step is the design of the product.

Before a new product is developed, it needs to go through a product-development process. It starts off with the idea itself, then the concept, followed by a prototype, which is then product tested, market tested, and finally launched. Research and Development or R&D, sometimes also considered hardware and software engineering, would be involved with the technical aspects of developing and building the product. R&D will either develop new products, or improve existing products.

Once the product has been "created" by the engineering and/or R&D team, marketing would then determine how to get it out to the marketplace.

Some factors to consider is whether the product is a non-durable good that is usually consumed quickly, durable good that can be used many times, or a customer benefiting non-tangible service. There are also decisions to be made on whether it is a consumer or industrial good. A *consumer* good can be, a convenience good when the customer does little comparing, a shopping good when the customer will most likely compare, or a unique specialty good. An *industrial* good can be materials and parts for products to be produced, capital items like equipment, supplies and services.

Decisions also need to be made regarding a perfectly fitting brand name, functionality, styling, add on's, apps, privileges, information, quality, safety, packaging, warranty, accessories, repairs, service, and support. In most companies, marketing and sales play a major role with any decisions regarding the company's products. The product should fulfill a customers needs, be easy to use, the quality matches the price, is safe to use, and whether it is a good fit with the rest of the company's business. These can be tangible items like a physical product, or intangible items like services offered.

Customers need to be convinced, and have a perception, of the value they are receiving with the product. This is usually measured by how much benefit they feel they are getting for their money. Marketing starts off by identifying the benefits of the product, which are then pitched through features such as a convenient size, special technology, or how the product solves problems. The goal is to always try to find something that adds value.

These ideas and/or improvements are carefully determined not only with marketing, but with engineering, R&D, sales and senior management. It is very important to determine whether the feature truly benefits the customer. For example, a *feature* such as a car engine with 350 horsepower would not *benefit* your customer base that is primarily looking for an economic vehicle. A feature that does not deliver a benefit is useless from a marketing point of view. You must always think in terms of the customer.

If your company is a *manufacturer* of the product, you need to know:

- How is it going to be produced?
- What materials and labor are needed?
- What R&D has been conducted and what is expected in the future?
- Is there a good Q/A or Quality Assurance test plan ?

If your company is providing a *service*, you need to know:

- What services do you offer?
- How do they work?
- What kind of skilled labor is needed?
- What materials and equipment is needed?
- What are the steps involved with providing this service?

When it comes down to it, marketing needs to know everything there is to know about the company's products and/or services, and find all the benefits to be able to best market it.

Example – Product release roadmap

Sample Corp

Sample Corp Product Roadmap

	Q1 2009	Q2 2009	Q3 2009	Q4 2009	Q1 2010	Q2 2010
Project 1				10/24		
P2	4/24					
P3	4/24					
P4	Launched 1/3					
P5	4/24					
P6				Future Idea 2		
P7				Future Idea 3		

Today   Rocket location is estimated launch date.

Price

Here is a detailed overview of the *price* segment within the marketing mix. The perspective from a customer-centric point of view is in parenthesis:

Price (Cost). What the customers pay for the product or service. When determining a product's price as it relates to the target market, and how to position that product in the market (positioning will be discussed later in this lesson), a company must consider how it must price the product in order to keep the business afloat. Pricing mistakes can kill a good product. First off, you need to determine the price in relation to the prices of similar products that either your company or your competition sells. This is called the *price point*. You then determine the point where you will make money on the product. Here are some basic pricing strategies:

- *Premium Pricing,* which sets a high price because the product is unique.

- *Penetration Pricing,* which sets the price low to discourage competitors and capture a larger market segment. Once the market share goal is achieved, pricing will be increased.

- *Economy Pricing,* which is used to sell no-frills products at a no-frills price. Manufacturer and marketing costs are kept to a minimum in order to make a profit.

- *Skim Pricing,* which sets the price high to capture short-term profit until competitors enter the market or demand drops.

- *Competitive Pricing,* which is selling your product at the lowest price of all your competitors. This strategy is used mostly when dealing with commodities and in retail where high volume is key.

- *Cost-Plus Pricing,* which takes the company's cost to sell or make the product, and then adds on the profit in order to pay its bills, make payroll, etc. For example, if a manufacturer's cost to make the product is $60, and they need to make a gross margin (profit) of 40%, they would have to sell it for $100 (this was determined by 100 – 60 = 40 and 40 ÷ 100 = 40%). The formula used to determine the gross margin of the product is by subtracting your costs from the consumer cost. This type of strategy is used mostly with labor-intensive services and manufacturing businesses. It is straightforward and ensures that you will make money if you are able to sell the product. This could also be known as *Keystone pricing*.

- *Discriminatory pricing,* which is used for customers who will pay different prices for the same product or service, such as charging less for a child at an amusement park.

- *Value Pricing,* which bases the price on the value delivered to the customer. An example would be a high tech product with very high appeal in which a customer is willing to pay a high price. In time, however, the price will inevitably fall. Another example of value pricing would be a fine dining restaurant in which you are paying more for the atmosphere, or because it is trendy. In fact, high prices can automatically create the perception of value. This phenomenon is called the Veblen Effect and can also be considered as *Psychological Pricing*. This type of pricing goes against normal *price theory* in which the lower the price, the more you will sell.

- *Promotional Pricing,* which is a low price for just a temporary period. The hope is for the consumer to like the product so much that they will pay the inevitable higher price.

- *Geographic Price,* which charges different prices for different regions.

- *Pricing Leader,* which determines whether you will be a price leader or follower.

- *Fixed Pricing,* which is non-negotiable between buyer and seller.

- *Variable Pricing,* which is negotiated between buyer and seller.

- *Price Lining,* which sets just a few prices for all of its product line.

- *Customary Pricing,* which has a set price at a standard level.

- *Prestige Pricing,* which equates price with quality and status.

- *Optimal Product Pricing,* which is selling options or accessories along with the main product.

- *Captive Product Pricing,* which sells the main product for a low price knowing that the consumer will have to continually buy supplies in order to use the product. An example would be printer ink set at a high price with a high margin.

- *By-Product Pricing,* which is used to sell waste or by-products from the manufacturer of its core products. An example would be an oil by-product used to make plastics.

It is a good idea to always consider all possible pricing strategies. Pricing is dynamic because as products, competitors and customers change, so must the price. Other economic factors like recessions, booms, inflation, and interest rates also come into play.

It is important to determine a pricing strategy. You need to be able to make decisions to determine, for example, if you are looking for a profit or just a "Return On Investment" (ROI)? You need to be able to answer questions like these. For example, if a product costs more to make than you are selling it for, you might think there is no sense in making it. However, you might want to attract customers to possibly buy other products you offer by selling this particular product. It might be worth selling, even if you do not make any profit. This is called a *loss leader*.

Decisions need to be made regarding suggested retail price, volume discounts, wholesale pricing, cash and early payment discounts, seasonal pricing, and bundling. The pricing structure can say a lot about the product. If priced too high, it can drive customers away, while a price that is too low, may leave potential customers wondering what is wrong with the product. The value of the product must justify the price. This is why it is so important to clearly let the customers know what they are going to get. For example, if your company provides 24/7 customer support, advertise that fact as it is a service that clearly adds value. A low price shouldn't be the only competitive edge. There will always be competition that will sooner or later beat that price.

While the price may motivate customers to buy, it is also just as important to state the features and value that are associated with the product that separates your product from the rest. It is also important to know that Internet buyers are more price-savvy than traditional consumers because they can easily shop around for competitive pricing and features. The bottom line, pricing needs to be competitive, yet still allows your company to turn a profit. One last thing to keep in mind, there are laws that regulate pricing, such as the Clayton Act, regarding monopoly issues that might need further investigation.

Place (Distribution)

Here is a detailed overview of the *place* or distribution segment within the marketing mix. The perspective from a customer-centric point of view is in parenthesis:

Place/Distribution (Convenience). There are many "Places" you can decide upon to distribute and sell your product. These places are known as distribution channels. After you have determined what markets you are going to reach, a distribution strategy is needed to determine what your are selling, who are the prospects, where are they, how to reach them, knowing how the distribution channel works, the costs through each channel, and how many channels you should use. Examples of different distribution channels are:

- *Directly to consumers*. This would be considered a zero-level channel since it is going from your company direct to the individual with nothing in-between.

- *Directly to retailers* (stores that sell direct to individuals). This would be considered a one-level channel as it goes to a store first, and then to the individual.

- *Directly to resellers* (outside company that sells your product). This is also considered a one-level channel.

- *To wholesalers* (the middleman) who in turn sell to resellers or retailers. This would be considered a two-level channel.

It will need to be determined how many and what types of intermediaries or third party channels you want to have.

You'll also need to decide on the terms on how and who is going to stock your product. It can be through an *intensive distribution* method in which you stock your product in as many places as possible, an *exclusive distribution* method in which limited dealers will be granted the rights to distribute your product, or *selective distribution* in which you choose only some of the available outlets in an area to distribute your product. These channels will need to be motivated to sell your product if it or your company is unknown. If your product or company is well known, the channel members will most likely be knocking on your company's door...

There are channel regulations your company should be aware of such as the Sherman Antitrust Act and the Federal Trade Commissions Act. These laws are put in place to protect free trade and competition.

Manufacturers need to constantly evaluate its channel members through sales quotas, inventory levels, RMA's, and ongoing training.

Here are some other ways to get your product out to the marketplace:

- Through the company's internal and external sales force.

- Telemarketing by means of selling over the telephone.

- Purchasing online. Selling over the Internet has had a tremendous impact on traditional marketing techniques. Things to consider are web site design, Search Engine Optimization (SEO), newsgroups, getting linked up, and many other ideas that are a course in itself.

- Delivery and manufacture-on-demand.

- Directly selling through mail or magazines in which customers either mail in or call to place their order.

- Agents who do not work for the company, but make commissions when they sell the product.

- Internationally by means of exporting.

- Joint marketing agreements in which your company supplies your product to a larger company to sell.

Once you have your distribution channels set up, you need to carefully plan, implement, and control the actual physical flow to get your products into that channel. You will need to determine logistical costs, planning, and methods of transportation, inventory management, warehousing, sturdy packaging for shipment, material handling, and order processing. See lesson 9 for more information regarding inventory management and supply chain.

The basic objective for your physical distribution operations is to:

- Get the right products, to the right place, at the right time, in good condition, for the least cost.

- Have a streamlined order processing method from the time the order is placed, to the time it is ready to ship.

- Have your warehouse in the most logical, yet least expensive, location to deliver and receive the products on time and without having to constantly maneuver goods due to lack of space.

We've discussed how to get the product out to the market, but we also need to consider how a customer can return the product back to your company. This is known as Return Merchandise Authorization (RMA). You should have a well-known and clear-cut return policy indicating time limits and any other conditions well in advance. If a customer returns a product with little to no hassle, they are more likely to come back for more.

Promotion

Here is a detailed overview of the *promotion* segment within the marketing mix. The perspective from a customer-centric point of view is in parenthesis:

Promotion (Communication). This is the essence of marketing. You first need to establish a brand such as Ford or Coke, then product name such as Mustang or Diet, along with a logo. Any type of identifier that can separate your product from the rest is also beneficial, such as the unique shape of an Orangina bottle. You also need to know whom you are targeting, which is known as demographics as previously discussed.

Once you have your brand and demographics in order, you need to choose the way you want to present the product. You should determine facts like whether it should be demonstrated, dramatized, explained, or displayed. Ways to help make sure you have fully developed the content of the message, also known as the "ad copy," are through various guidelines like AIDA and USP.

AIDA is an acronym for:

- Get **A**ttention by using humor, color, models, etc.
- Hold **I**nterest with a question or statement that makes you think about the product.
- Arouse **D**esire that makes you want the product.
- Obtain **A**ction that tells you what you need to do to get the product.

USP is an acronym for **U**nique **S**elling **P**roposition. The message focuses on the products uniqueness, which is the motivational reason for people to buy it. This is usually communicated through a memorable tag line that says it all about the product. An example would be, "Milk, it does a body good." Whether this is actually true or not, the message makes you think one important and easy to remember thing about milk, if you drink it you'll be healthy.

The *promotional* mix is made up of four main tools, Advertising, Personal selling, Sales promotion, and Publicity.

1. **Advertising** – This is the most common form of promotion. The three most common types of advertising messages are:

    - *Creative messages*, which uses humor, seduction, or desire to try to attract the customer based on the image, rather than the quality. This type of image advertising creates a mood or feeling around the product rather than focusing on the features or benefits. An example of this type of message is a seductive jean commercial that says little about the actual quality of the product.

    - *Statement messages,* which focuses more on a "quick and to the point" message around the features and benefits of the product. An example of this type of message is a cold medicine that lets you know that once taken, you will sleep easier.

    - *Creative and Statement messages,* which looks for the perfect combination of the two. It clearly lets you know the features and benefits, and at the same time uses a funny or desirable image that is instantly recognizable. This is the optimal type of message, but it is hard to find the perfect combination to get the point across. A successful example of this type of message is the old Verizon commercial with the phrase, "Can you hear me now? Good." You know you are going to get a phone that can make a call anywhere due to the image of person going around the country confirming that fact.

    Once the content of the message has been established, it's time to consider which media you will use to get your message out and create an *awareness* of your product. This lets people know your product exists, and helps when making a choice on which product to buy based on seeing or recalling your ad.

    Advertising methods most commonly used are through magazines, newspapers, TV, radio, direct mail, trade shows, yellow pages, e-mail blast, billboards, posters, and over the Internet. It is also a great idea to list testimonials, customer statements, and case studies about the value of the product on your company's web site.

Advertising through *media buys* can be costly and needs to be carefully budgeted. One way to set up a budget is to estimate the expected sales. For example, if the expected sales are $100,000, you can budget a figure like 5% towards the ad campaign, or $5,000. You can also use the industry average towards advertising costs.

Here is an example of a common way for a retailer or service based company to budget for advertising:

Projected gross sales, times 12% (common percentage), minus the cost of occupancy (rent), equals the advertising budget. For example, it the gross sales is projected to be $100,000, and the cost of occupancy is $5,000, then the advertising budget should not go over $7000.

$$100,000 * .12 - 5,000 = 7,000$$

A couple of ways to measure the amount of people who might view your advertisement is through *Reach, Frequency & Impact*. *Reach* calculates the number of people who were potentially exposed to the ad, *Frequency* measures the number of times people see or hear the advertisement, and *Impact* determines whether the ad is remembered and communicated as intended, which is usually seen in a higher increase in sales.

2. **Personal Selling** – This involves face-to-face communication. Although it can be expensive if the salesperson is salary-based rather than commission based, it is highly effective as people are more willing to buy your product, and it also creates long lasting relationships. There will be more information about the sales force later in this lesson.

3. **Sales Promotion** - Some common promotional tools used are coupons, discounts, incentives, rebates, contests, and sponsoring special events. These tools help getting people to buy the company's product. You can also use *premiums* such as coffee mugs, T-shirts, and tote bags. Giving out these free premiums gets the company's name out to your current or potential customers. Free samples such as cereals or snack foods are also effective for consumer-based products. Demonstrations like test drives or playing computer games are also a very effective way to promote the product.

Sales promotions to businesses and industries such as offering quantity discounts, free merchandise or buy-back allowances, are effective and build trusting and workable relationships.

4. **Public Relations (PR)** – This is one of the best and most effective ways to promote your product. Contacting magazine editors, local TV stations, newspaper journalists, or any other type of communications to set up interviews or set up public speaking events with some of the company's experts is a great way to promote the company and its products. These experts are the spokespeople for the company and they can help create public interest within their industry. Winning awards, creative articles, and

press releases about a new product offering, also helps get the word out. A positive story about your company and its products can be more effective than paid advertising. This is because it builds credibility, and people tend to take this information as fact.

People, Process, and Physical Evidence (Packaging)

Here is a detailed overview of the People, Process and Physical Evidence (Packaging) of the marketing mix. By adding these three aspects to the marketing mix, you get what is known as the *"7 P's of Marketing."*

People. An extremely important part of any company is having the right people to support the company's products and/or service. Excellent customer service personnel who can provide support with clearly known expectations, such as hours of operation and average response time, is key to maintaining a high level of customer satisfaction. Customer service skills were discussed in lesson 9. Lessons 1 through 4 cover everything from how to lead the people, to hiring, retaining, training, and building teamwork. Knowledgeable staff adds much value to the product offering.

Process. Solid procedures and policies that are in place, which pertains to the company's products and/or service, is an extremely valuable element to the marketing strategy. Customers want to understand more than just your product; they also want to focus on the shape and form your business will take.

Physical Evidence/Packaging. This refers to the way your product, service, and everything about your company, appears from the outside. Decisions need to be made about the size, shape, color, material, UPC bar code, and label of the packaging. This should be customer tested and updated when needed. It should fall in line with your other product offerings as well. Packaging involves the visual layout, practical setup, and when needed for products, clear and precise installation instructions.

Product liability insurance is needed in case anyone suffers any harm from your product. Engineering tests are also needed to make sure the package can stand up to abuses. There may also be regulatory issues to consider.

Visual packaging of a tangible product can make or break a purchase. Small improvements in the packaging or external appearance of your product or service can lead to completely different reactions from your customers.

It is also important in selling and marketing services and intangible products that you *can't* see, but that you can provide the support needed to the customer who *can* see and feel the physical evidence.

Physical Evidence can also refer to the people within your company and how they dress and act. It can refer to how your office is set up, the professionalism of your staff, nice brochures, how you interact with your customer base, and every single visual element about your company.

Positioning the Product

Positioning is the way a consumer sees your product as it compares to other similar products on the market. Positioning can also be considered one of the P's in the marketing mix. Products can be positioned by its features, benefits, class, special occasions, holidays, or against a competitor. Even positioning your product against another product class as an alternative, such as margarine against butter, can be successful. Re-positioning your product against a competitor by just claiming their product is not good can also work. Political campaigns are a great example of re-positioning, even if not product related, of how negative attacks against their opponent can be more effective than a positive statement about their own candidacy.

The goal is to position the product in the customers mind to create a certain perception, impression, and feeling that will end up offering the greatest sales potential and hopefully surpass your competitors. A simple message that creates a great first impression is key. You want to try to be the first to claim a unique position in the customers mind. Even if your product might is not the first of its kind, you should still try to create a uniqueness and statement about your product that gets into the consumers psyche.

Two examples of claimed unique positions that's most likely already engraved in your mind is that; *Geritol* goes with age, and *Nyquil* goes with nighttime cold medicine. If you know your product cannot be the number one brand, find a way to relate to it that still says your product is viable. A good example of this is how Avis Rent-a-Car, knowing that their competition Hertz is number one, advertised the fact that the reason to go with Avis is, "We try harder." This ended up positively capturing the minds of many consumers.

You need to know your positioning message and find your own place. The message should be just a few words like Avis's, "We try harder." It should be easy to identify, understand, and remember the position you are trying to claim. The message should appeal to the customer's emotions, not by using logic. Logic is cold and boring, whereas emotion gives hope and excitement. People are more willing to spend their money on inspiration, rather than on fact.

Market Opportunities

Marketers analyze the market opportunities for the company's products and/or services towards the target markets. A good planning tool for analyzing market opportunities is Ansoff's product/expansion grid. This tool helps identify new *market opportunities* by considering four possible directions:

1. **Market Penetration**, which is used to find new ways to increase sales with the current product without having to change it. This tactic is to convince users of similar products made by another company to switch to its product, such as how Pepsi tries to convince drinkers of Coca-Cola to switch. Other tactics are by cutting prices or improving advertising to make the product enticing, thus encouraging new and current customers to buy more of the product.

2. **Market Development**, which is used to find new market segments for the current product. Ways to accomplish this would be to expand distribution channels, sell in new locations, or find new users. An example would be to look for new demographic markets to try and attract working moms or senior citizens to buy a product they currently do not use.

3. **Product Development**, which is used to grow the business by improving existing products or developing new ones into market segments in which you are already successful. Developing new features, improved technology, and improved quality are just a few development ideas.

4. **Diversification**, which is used to grow the business by starting up an entirely new product line outside the present business. One factor to consider when thinking about diversifying the company would be the strengths and weaknesses of the competition. The diversification strategies are of three types:

   - *Concentric Diversification Strategy*: Develop new products with the earlier technology for new segments.
   - *Conglomerate Diversification Strategy*: Develop new products for new markets.
   - *Horizontal Diversification Strategy*: Develop new products with new technology for old customers.

Before taking on new market opportunities, it is important to be sure your company has the financial capital to fund the costs. If not, you're putting your company at risk. If so, does your company have the necessary production facilities and the expertise to successfully produce and market the product and/or service? If so, then you need to look at the distribution capacity to get the new product into the marketplace. If this is not likely, then it might be a better idea to pass on the opportunity.

If an opportunity were considered viable, determining the market segment you want to target would be the next step.

The 5 C's and Strategic Marketing Basics

Once you know the marketing mix, goals, and targets of your marketing effort, the next step is to develop the marketing strategy. A good guideline to make the right decisions, while constructing a marketing plan and strategy, are the 5 C's:

1. **Customer** – Determine what needs from which clients you're trying to satisfy. A few areas to research would be the market segments, benefits the customer wants, if the value of the benefits outweigh the costs, frequency of purchases, quantity of purchases, retail channel, and needs based on trends over time.

2. **Company** – Determine if your company can meet those customer needs. For example, does your company have the right product line and/or technical expertise? A good tool to help determine your company's strengths and weaknesses is "SWOT" analysis. This stands for *Strengths* such as innovative products, expertise, great processes and procedures, *Weaknesses* such as the lack of knowledgeable technical support or poor product quality, *Opportunities* such as a new international market or a market led by a weak competitor, and *Threats* such as a new competitor or price war. This is a very good tool to analyze the internal strengths and weaknesses, and the external opportunities and threats.

SWOT diagram

Internal

Strengths	Weaknesses
Opportunities	Threats

External

3. **Competition** – Determine who competes with your company in meeting the customer's needs. Is it an active competitor or a potential threat? What are their products exactly? What are their strengths and weaknesses?

4. **Collaborators** – Determine if there is any outside source that can help the company such as distributors, suppliers, etc.

5. **Context** – Determine if there are any limitations due to *Political* issues such as legal problems, trade regulations, taxation, and labor laws, *Economic* concerns such as growth rate, labor costs, and business cycle stage, *Social* impacts such as demographics, education, and culture, and *Technological* developments such as the impact on cost structures. This is also known as "PEST" analysis. These forces can be dramatic and difficult to predict.

Strategic marketing decisions are mostly based on price and quality. A product can be of exceptional quality at a high price like a Rolls Royce, or of a lower quality but lower price like a Hyundai. Economically, it is not expected that the price of a Rolls Royce will be the same as that of a Hyundai.

A strategic decision companies face is to choose whether they will compete on price or quality. Marketing would then focus its efforts on the results of that decision. For example, if the company were a thrifty clothing store, the message would focus on the low price for its everyday goods. If the company were a Beverly Hills clothing store, the message would focus on the elite quality and design with the price being of little concern.

Companies also compete on service such as post-sales support and warranties. They can also compete based on the novelty, design, prestige, ease of use, and technical sophistication of the product. Product differentiation, like improved performance, improved appearance, and improved image, is a good way to make a product different from others like it. Overall, the essential goal of a marketing strategy is to have a competitive advantage and to get that word out to the marketplace.

A market-driven company looks for and listens to customers to learn why and how customers use their products. They look at trends in the marketplace in technology, pricing, and packaging, not to mention watching what their competitors are doing.

Marketers also try to understand who will likely influence the decision-making process for their target market. They will not only try to design their promotions around the buyer, but also all those who may also be involved. For example, the father will make the decision on which vacation package he will buy, however, he will also be influenced on other factors such as his wife and children. Here are the 5 decision-making steps:

1. The *initiator*, who might be the child who wants to go to Disneyland.
2. The *influencer*, who might be a travel agent.
3. The *decider*, who might be the parent's.
4. The *buyer*, who might be the father who used his credit card.
5. The *user*, who reaps the benefits, which in this case was the child who was the initiator.

The buying process consists of:

- *Problem recognition,* which could be a simple need, to a complex want.
- *Information search,* which is how they will find the need or want.
- *Evaluation of alternatives,* which is when they compare with other products.
- *Purchase decision*, which is made after all alternatives have been evaluated.
- *Post-purchase behavior,* which is whether they were satisfied, or have a case of buyer's remorse.

Whenever a new product is released, one way to look at how the new product will be adopted by buyers is the "Product Adoption Curve." It states the there will be various categories of buyers in a predictable order. Most buyers wait to buy something new until the more innovative buyers adopt the product first.

Example – Product Adoption Curve, aka Technology Adoption Curve

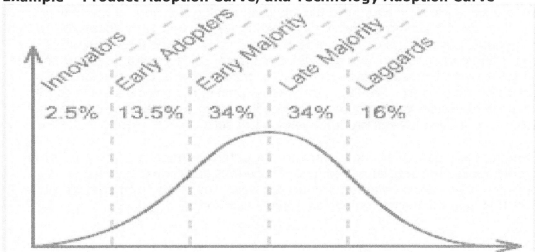

As you can see from this graph, 2.5% of the buyers of a new product will be the innovators. The next 13.5% will be the early adopters of the product, 34% will be the early majority, and 34% will be the late majority, followed lastly by the 16% who are the laggards. Marketing will seek out the innovators and try to persuade them to try something new and unproven. Early adopters will also need to be persuaded, however, they can look at success stories from the innovators. Marketing needs to get to the early majority quickly as they will face many competitors if the product is successful. For the late majority, marketing will try things like discounts and service plans. By the time the company is selling to the laggards, the price will be lower so the focus will be on ways to reduce manufacturing costs to get as much profit out of the product as possible while it is still viable.

A way to measure the products life cycle is through phases of introduction, growth, maturity, and then decline. Basically, products are developed, continue to grow until they have reached a period of maturity, and then inevitably start to decline. Usually the phases are shown on a curve that plots sales over time:

Example – Product Life Cycle Curve

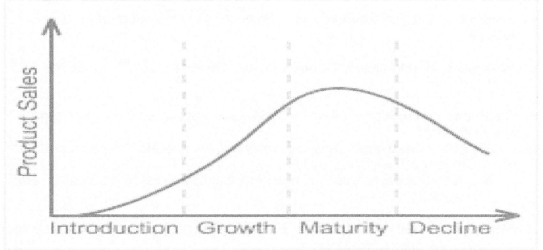

Each phase presents a different marketing and sales challenge. In the *introduction* phase, the sales are slow and the challenge is spreading the word of the new product and finding the first customers, which are the innovators and early adopters. In the *growth* phase, the sales rise, however, the challenge is to beat the competitors getting to the early adopters. In the *maturity* phase, sales growth levels off and the challenge is controlling sales costs, fighting for market share, and developing variations of the product. Finally, in the *decline* phase, the sales decrease so the challenge is to decide what to do with the product, such as whether it can be revitalized, or if even it's still profitable enough to sell.

The length of any particular phase can vary for different products. The product life cycle only applies to successful products. Those that don't make it past the introduction phase are considered product failures. There is also the chance that a product that is in the decline stage can make a comeback.

Creating a Marketing Plan

By utilizing the subjects taught so far in this lesson, you can now create a marketing plan that should be simple and clear with a focused strategy. An example of a marketing plan would be structured something like this:

1. **Executive Overview**   *(summarizes the marketing plan including a brief overview of steps 2 through 9).*

2. **Market Review**
   a. Trends overview   *(How big is the potential market? Is it growing? Competitors?)*
   b. Market segments *(see Market Segments and Target Market section of this lesson)*
   c. Target market   *(see Market Segments and Target Market section of this lesson)*

3. **Competitive Review**   *(those who offer a similar product with similar attributes)*

4. **Product or Service Review**   *(see Products and Prices section in this lesson)*

5. **Strengths, Weaknesses, Opportunities, Threats**   *(SWOT – see the 5'Cs in this lesson)*

6. **Goals and Objectives**   *(describe where you want to be both short-term and long-term)*
   a. Sales objectives   *(measurable in dollars, specific timetable, and expected profit)*
   b. Marketing objectives   *(i.e. increase existing customers' buying rate by 25%)*

7. **Strategies**   *(see the associated "P's" segments throughout this lesson along with strategic marketing decisions)*

        a. Product
        b. Pricing
        c. Place/Distribution
        d. Promotion
        e. People
        f. Process
        g. Physical Evidence/Packaging
        h. Positioning

8. **Action Plan and Implementation** *(such as how are you going to achieve the goals? What is the timeframe or marketing calendar? What are the projected costs? Who is doing what?)*

9. **Evaluation** *(How will it all be tracked and measured?)*

10. **Conclusion** *(Wrap it all up. Try to make the overall marketing plan as short and to the point as possible)*

Besides the marketing plan, it is also a good idea, for quick discussion, to have a separate *creative plan* that only focuses on the content of your marketing materials, which would be the purpose, how the purpose will be achieved, and the tone of the advertising, and a *media plan* that only focuses on the type of media that will be used along with the media calendar.

Marketing vs. Sales

Basically, think of marketing as selling the idea of a product and/or service to everyone, whereas sales sells the product and/or service one-on-one. Marketing generates the interest, sales brings in the money. Marketing does everything they can to reach and persuade prospects. The sales process does everything they can to close the sale and get a signed agreement or contract.

Selling the idea, which is marketing's responsibility, can be through such media as an advertising campaign, an e-mail blast, or through the company's web site. Selling to the customer, which is sales responsibility, can be through such ways as inside sales making phone calls, outside sales setting up appointments to meet with the customer face-to-face, or being approached by a consumer who is interested in the company's product and/or service.

The job of sales is one of the toughest and most important positions in the company. They are the ones who have to get the customer to give up their money. Marketing, which is usually located at the company's headquarters, tends to think strategically by identifying groups who might need the company's product. Sales, which mostly resides in the field, tends to think tactically by going to the individuals within those groups to try to meet those needs with the company's product. Strategies are best explained as the direction the marketing effort takes over some period of time, while tactics are actionable steps or decisions made in order to follow the strategies established. Performing strategic and tactical planning activities before taking action is considered critical for long-term success. Basically, in most cases marketing exists to support the salespeople.

Marketing approaches their work in a think tank environment constantly looking for ways and ideas to promote and differentiate the product or service. Sales are in the real world and are constantly looking for ways and ideas to try and persuade the reluctant buyer. This is why there is often tension between sales and marketing. Marketing tends to think of salespeople as mere tools to execute their creative plans, whereas sales tends to view the marketing staff as unrealistic who would be hopeless at actually making a sale.

The way to find harmony within the two departments is making sure they constantly work together, truly understand each other, and are always making decisions together. It is a good idea for each department to walk in each other's shoes for a while to observe the successes and difficulties each department faces.

Much of what determines the relationship between marketing and sales depends on the product or service. If an individual customer is buying something for themselves with their own money, it is considered *consumers sales*. Examples of consumer-packaged goods would be cereal or toothpaste. A lot of advertising through marketing is needed to get people interested in the product. If the individual is buying something for their organization with the company's money, it is considered *commercial sales*. Commercial sales are also known as corporate, industrial or business-to-business sales. Sales has to do more work to get the *customer* to purchase the goods.

As you can see, how they work together depends on the type of product or service that is offered by the company. The important thing is that they always work together.

Sales Types, Process, Tactics and Growth

Once marketing has strategically identified the markets, sales tactically tries to win the customers. Marketing gets the word out, and sales helps the customers find what they want.

The different possible sales types are:

- *Order Takers,* which the customer asks for something and their order is then taken.

- *Active Selling,* which involves a sales-person approach to the customer such as a car lot. The sales-person needs to be more aggressive, which usually leads to the customer being resistant. Active selling involves overcoming sales resistance.

- Inside Sales, which is done mainly by sales people, such as telemarketers, making outgoing calls to customers.

- Outside Sales, which is going to the customers premise after an appointment has been made.

The sales process and tactics starts with two simple goals; selling to current customers, and finding new ones. Marketing has done all of the strategy to find the targeted market segment; it is now time for sales to tactically find ways to sell to the targeted marketplace. In retail, the sales challenge is lower since the customer comes to the store. In many businesses, however, the sales people must look for customers who might be interested in the product. This is called, "Prospecting." A sales person will normally make a telephone call to a targeted individual, or prospect, who they do not know, to make a sale or make appointments for a future visit. This method is called *cold calling*. A *sales lead* is the name of a person who has been identified as a prospect. The term "sales call" can refer to a phone call or a personal visit.

The process of determining whether a sales lead has the potential to become a prospect is known as "qualifying" the lead. If a prospect has been qualified, the sales person's next task is to prepare for an eventual sales call. The sales person will then build a rapport with the prospect by gaining background information and then assessing the prospects needs. Once the need has been established, the sales person will present a solution. For example, the customer is not sure what kind of phone system to get, so the sales person asks questions about what size and features are needed (assessing the needs), and then determines the perfect fit (presents the solution). The sales person might then need to do some persuading to close the sale. A trick of the trade is to continually ask questions to keep the customer involved while moving toward the close. The *hard sell* is when the sales person aggressively starts to push the product to the reluctant buyer, even to the point of using intimidation tactics. The overall goal, however, is not just to make the sale, but to have a satisfied customer.

Sales growth is needed in order for the company to grow. This means the dollar volume of sales must increase in order to always be higher in the next year. In order to succeed in sales growth, goals should be concrete and measurable (in terms of dollars and units), set at a level that is challenging but not impossible to reach, set on a specific timetable for measuring success, and linked to projected profits. Here are 5 ways for sales to try and achieve those goals:

1. *Increase the price of the product or service.* This is the simplest way and might even be justified in order to increase the dollar volume. However, customers do not like to pay a higher price. This is called, "Price resistance." When customers see higher prices, they look elsewhere or constantly try to bargain. If there are few competitors, however, there is a chance that the price increase will work.

2. *Sell other products to existing customers.* This strategy can be used if the company has other products that work in harmony with existing products currently being sold. This is called, "Cross-selling." A good example of this is when you order a burger, the order taker asks, "Would you like fries with that?"

3. *Sell new products to existing customers.* Companies need to always develop new products to keep the existing customers satisfied. If they don't, competitors will find ways to steal the customer base with better, and maybe even less expensive alternatives. The key is to always improve on current products, and develop new ones to meet the customer's needs.

4. *Sell existing products to new customers.* A company should never be complacent with their existing customer base. They should always look for

new prospects. The search for new customers should never stop. Existing customers can leave for reasons such as going to a competitor, not satisfied with customer support, changing their business model, or even going out of business.

5. *Sell new products to new customers.* When sales of existing products are decreasing, due to market maturity or saturation (which basically means everyone who wants and can afford the product, already has one), it is time to come up with new products for new customers. It's important, however, to make sure to come up with a product that is close to the main business outline. For example, Nike started off with sport shoes and then started selling sports related products like active wear and golf clubs.

The Sales Force – Size, Organizing, Training, Motivating & Compensating

The sales force needs to be properly organized, motivated and compensated in order to have the right size to do the workload, alignment to cover all needs, and keeping them happy and selling. In most companies, the sales force is the most critical part of the business. At the end of the day, they are the ones who get the customer to give up their money for the company's product or service. They are the ones who are face-to-face with the customer earning the money that pays your wages. The sales force needs to be supported by the whole company, even if they do put you in an uncompromising position with a customer.

The size of the sales force greatly depends on the way the department is organized. In its simplest terms, you can keep on hiring until the last sales person does not produce more in sales than they earn. However, there is more to consider than just that simple philosophy.

Sales management can organize the sales force either by *geographical* divisions, who are fully responsible for their region, *product specialists,* who will only work with customers on the specialized products they know, or *VIP customers,* who need extra special attention because the sales person "understands their business." You can hire less sales people by organizing the sales force geographically, but they might not be as knowledgeable about all of the products offered. You can hire product specialists who will be able to be experts on all products, but more staff will be needed. It is up to sales management on how best to organize their sales force. The main goal is to have a sales force that can give the attention needed to each possible prospect and customer. Regular sales calls, or "coverage," need to be made in order to keep the customer from feeling neglected.

Good sales training is imperative. In many cases, a sales person is given some brochures, taken on a sales call, and then expected to be an expert. This is not the best scenario. Sales volume will increase when a sales person has excellent knowledge of the product and how their company functions. It also greatly helps customer service in that they do not have to explain how "something that was promised by sales can't be delivered." First-rate sales people can answer virtually every question about the product they sell. They will also know how the product stands up to the competition. Product knowledge is essential, especially if the sales person is a product specialist. It is sometimes harder for a sales person who is geographically based because they have to be a "jack of all trades."

The best way to motivate the sales force is through compensation. Sales are usually paid in the following three ways:

1. *Straight Commission*, which means they get a certain percentage of each sale they make. They do not get any salary; they are only paid on a commission basis. This is motivating when sales are good, but depressing and very un-motivating when sales are bad.

2. *Straight Salary,* which means they only get paid salary with no commission based on a percentage of sales. This is the easiest to administrate, but is not very motivating.

3. *Salary Plus Commission*, which means they get both a base salary and a commission based on a percentage of sales.   This is the best for motivating, but hard to administrate.

Other ways to motivate are through sales quotas in which the sales person has to hit a certain level of sales made, and income generated. Sales quotas work well because higher commissions and bonuses are tied to quotas. The other motivating factor of hitting a sales quota is justification for the sales person to keep their job. If they continually miss the mark, they will most likely be let go.

Presidential awards, company retreats, sales events, and monetary or vacation grand prizes are also good motivational tools for the sales force. At the end of the day, however, it really is mostly about the money. A promotion to sales management might be motivating, however, most sales people do not make good managers. They like to depend on themselves, not others.

Customer Relationship Management or CRM

CRM stands for Customer Relationship Management. It is a process or methodology used to learn more about customers' needs and behaviors in order to develop stronger relationships with them. The more useful way to think about CRM is as a process that will help bring together lots of pieces of information about customers, sales, marketing effectiveness, responsiveness and market trends. A CRM that is widely known and used is Salesforce.com.

CRM helps businesses use technology and human resources to gain insight into the behavior of customers, and the value of those customers. It can help provide better customer service, increase customer revenues, discover new customers, cross sell/up sell products more effectively, help sales staff close deals faster, make call centers more efficient, and simplify marketing and sales processes.

The types of data CRM projects collect are responses to campaigns, shipping and fulfillment dates, sales and purchase data, account information, web registration data, service and support records, demographic data, and web sales data.

Within a CRM there is software that has the following possibilities:

- *Contact management,* which stores, tracks and manages contacts and leads of an enterprise.

- *Lead management,* which enables an organization to manage, track and forecast sales leads. It also helps understand and improve conversion rates.

- *Self Service eCRM,* which enables web based customer interaction, automation of e-mail, call logs, web site analytics, and campaign management.

- *Survey management,* which automates an enterprises' electronic surveys, polls, and questionnaires that helps understand customer preferences.

- *Customer Service,* which has call center, help desk, and support tracking capabilities.

- *Contract management*, which enables an enterprise to create, track and manage partnerships, contracts, and agreements.

Quick Lesson Summary

- A Market is a group of customers or potential customers. The market starts with the total population, then *Potential* markets that have an interest, then *Available* markets that have the money, then *Target* markets that are the customers the company has determined to serve (the served market), then finally the *Penetrated* markets who have already bought your products and/or services.

- The Marketing Department's key responsibilities is to determine the needs, which represent items such as food, housing, and clothing, and wants which represent cultural based items such as makeup or vacations.

- Marketing needs to know how their decisions could lead to problems for other departments within the company. *Microenvironment* deals with internal factors that can influence the company directly. *Macroenvironment* deals with the external factors outside of the company's direct control.

- Market Research helps companies understand and analyze their customers. Market research mostly focuses on the following four types of information: *Demographic characteristics*, which would include the age, race, sex, education, marital status, housing, income, and number of children. *Buying behaviors,* which studies how customers buy products such as in a retail store or online. *Lifestyle or psychographics* that researches the type of hobbies, sports, and even personality traits and sexual orientation. And *Customer Satisfaction,* which surveys on the perceived value of the overall product, and whether they are likely to purchase more product in the future.

- There are basically two types of market research; *primary market research,* which involves surveys, observations and experimental approaches, and *secondary market research*, which involves checking articles in newspapers, magazines, and books.

- Four strategies marketers use as a competitive edge is to best determine if they are *Market leaders* who are looking to dominate the industry, *Market Challengers* who are looking to challenge the market leaders, *Market Followers* who are happy to stay at their current position, and *Market Nichers* who are looking at just a few specialized target markets.

- Market Segments are parts of a market that are different from one another. Six common segmentation strategies are Geographic, Demographic, Psychographic, Behavioristic, Product, and Sales channel.

- The 4 P's of the Marketing Mix refers to the Product, Price, Place, and Promotion. They are the foundation to the marketing mix. There is also the 7 P's, which include People, Process, and Physical Evidence (including Packaging). Positioning, which is also sometimes known as one of the P's, can be part of the marketing mix as well.

- A strategic decision companies face is to choose whether they will compete on price or quality. Marketing would then focus its efforts on the results of that decision. Companies also compete on service such as post-sales support and warranties.

- Whenever a new product is released, 2.5% of the buyers will be the innovators, 13.5% will be the early adopters, 34% will be the early majority, 34% will be the late majority, and 16% will be the laggards. This tends to follow the product life-cycle curve in which in the *introduction* phase, the sales are slow and the challenge is finding the innovators and early adopters. In the *growth* phase, the sales rise and the challenge is to beat the competitors getting to the early adopters. In the *maturity* phase, sales growth levels off and in the *decline* phase, the sales decrease. These last two phases hold the late majority and laggards.

- The difference between marketing and sales is basically; marketing sells the idea of a product and/or service to everyone, whereas sales sells the product and/or service one-on-one.

- The different possible sales types are Order Takers, Active Selling, Inside Sales, and Outside Sales. The sales force needs to be properly organized, motivated and compensated in order to have the right size to do the workload, alignment to cover all needs, and keeping them happy and selling. A common system used by marketing and sales to learn more about customers' needs and behaviors, is CRM or Customer Relationship Management.

COURSE CONCLUSION

A wealth of information...

The information and knowledge you have just learned and obtained in this "Management and Leadership Training Course" will significantly help launch or enhance your managerial career. You should now be able to recognize and handle the typical managerial scenarios and situations that come your way.

By utilizing the skills taught in this course, you should now have the assurance and confidence to lead your team to success, share your vision and goals, be secure in your leadership capabilities, use a proven model to improve, plan and structure your department for optimal success, create and build a strong team, inspire teamwork, motivate and reward the individual, know how to appraise job performance, deal with different personalities, hire the right people, know the right questions to ask when hiring, retain the best people, deal with conflict, handle difficult and problematic employees, deal with violent situations, address attendance issues, address job performance related issues, know how and when to fire someone, confidently be able to delegate, know how to multitask and prioritize efficiently, manage your time effectively, make the right decisions and solve difficult problems, communicate professionally both verbally and in written format, hold effective meetings, give powerful presentations, get the department to embrace change, and handle the other day-to-day idiosyncrasies that are all part of managing a department.

You have also been taught the basics in business. You should now be able to understand the different business types, business ethics, basic economics, the basics of finance and accounting, know the importance of financial statements, know how to examine a balance sheet and income statement, know the important ratios used in financial analysis, understand the budget process, know the operating functions within a business, know the basic tools used to manage a project, understand the importance of quality management, know how goods are tracked within inventory management, know the functional importance within customer service and technical support, know the responsibilities of IS/IT and HR, know what constitutes a market and marketing, understand the importance of marketing research, know the market segments and target market strategies, know what makes up the marketing mix, understand the product adoption curve and product life cycle, know how to create a marketing plan, know the difference between marketing and sales, understand sales tactics and growth, understand the importance of how a sales force is organized, and have a basic understanding of the many other related functions that make up a business.

Remember to always incorporate confidence into your newly learned business, management and leadership skills. Be the leader that inspires people to want to follow you and share in your vision of success. Be the manager that plans, motivates and directs people to obtain the goals surrounding that vision. Do this, and you will be known as a great manager and a strong leader...

INDEX

About the Author

William L Evans has been in the field of Telecommunications, Customer Operations and Customer Care Management for over 15 years. His long career with major corporations has given him years of "real life" managerial skills. He enjoys sharing his obtained knowledge through his many "How to..." process and procedural books. His success as an author has been greatly attributed to his skill of combining a practical managerial approach with the basics of business management theory.

William knows how to deal with all levels of employees, as he has been in the trenches providing front line support all the way to Executive VP. Because of this, he is able to relate to everyone through his writing skills from the first time supervisor to the seasoned executive.

William's knowledge of computer technology and advanced telecommunications has also led him to the development of an online management training business certification course at www.masterclassmanagement.com, which is solely based on the book "Management Skills & Leadership Development – How to be a Great Manager & Strong Leader in 10 Lessons."

Made in the USA
Las Vegas, NV
11 December 2024

13890066R00168